Fifty GRAND MOVIES of the 1960S and 1970S

Fifty GRAND MOVIES

of the
1960s
and
1970s

Including interviews with their stars,
directors, and screenwriters

by
David Zinman

Crown Publishers, Inc.
New York

Photo Credits: Allied Artists, Warner Bros.-Seven Arts, United Artists, Paramount, 20th Century-Fox, Columbia Pictures, Universal Pictures, United Film Distribution Co., Midwest Film, Metro-Goldwyn-Mayer, Screen Gems.

Published by Crown Publishers, Inc., 225 Park Avenue South, New York, New York 10003 and represented in Canada by the Canadian MANDA Group

CROWN is a trademark of Crown Publishers, Inc.

Manufactured in the United States of America

Library of Congress Cataloging-in-Publication Data
Zinman, David (David H.)
Fifty grand movies of the 1960s and 1970s, including interviews with their stars, directors, and screenwriters.
1. Moving-pictures—United States. I. Title.
II. Title: 50 grand movies of the 1960s and 1970s.
PN1993.5.U6Z47 1986   791.43′75   86-4212

ISBN 0-517-56256-1

Designed by Lauren Dong

10 9 8 7 6 5 4 3 2 1

First Edition

To my beloved Caroline, Daniel, and Elizabeth,
who, with your mother,
are the stuff my dreams are made of.

Contents

Acknowledgments

I am indebted to the staff of the Billy Rose Theater Collection of the New York Public Library at Lincoln Center in New York City, where I did most of my research.

I owe special thanks to John Cocchi of Brooklyn, who checked my material for accuracy and helped identify character actors in the stills, although I take full responsibility for any errors.

For lending me hard-to-find stills, I am grateful to Thomas L. Fielding, James C. Tillman, and William Jeff Jones, all of Silver Springs, Maryland; Poster City of Orangeburg, New York; and Cocchi.

For giving me the chance to interview them, I am grateful to directors Robert Altman, Frank Perry, John Frankenheimer, George Romero, Joan Micklin Silver, Stuart Rosenberg, Bob Rafelson, and Herk Harvey. (Paul Mazursky was interviewed by guest writer Stan Isaacs.)

For other interviews, I thank the following stars: Kirk Douglas, Janet Blair, Charlton Heston, Keir Dullea, Carol Kane, Olga Bellin, and Candace Hilligoss. And thanks, too, to screenwriters William Goldman, Horton Foote, and James Dickey. For his support and perceptive suggestions, I am thankful to Brandt Aymar, my editor at Crown.

The book includes three chapters by guest writers. For two of them, I am grateful to colleagues at *Newsday*, the Long Island newspaper where I work. Stan Isaacs, sports columnist, wrote the engaging piece on *Harry and Tonto*. David Behrens, features writer, did the probing study of *Don't Look Now*. For the third chapter, I owe a debt of gratitude to Sara Zinman, the lovely, blue-eyed South Carolina belle whom I married in 1956. She did the splendid chapter on *The Leopard*, one of her all-time favorite movies. If that be nepotism, I have made the most of it.

Introduction

I write not as a scholarly and sometimes jaundiced critic for a narrow circle of film aficionados, but as an enchanted and often captivated moviegoer for a wide group of kindred souls.

I see myself as a guy in the tenth row trying to convey to other members of the popcorn brigade why the fifty movies selected from the 1960s and 1970s fascinate today as they did in another era.

To add dimension to the book, I have interviewed many of the directors, actors, and screenwriters whose films are presented. They include Robert Altman, Bob Rafelson, Joan Micklin Silver, Kirk Douglas, Charlton Heston, Janet Leigh, Horton Foote, and James Dickey, among others.

Who am I to talk to these celebrated people and compile such a work? I reply as I did in 1970 when I wrote my first movie book, *50 Classic Motion Pictures.*

I make no pretense about being a movie scholar, historian, pedant, expert, or buff. Even a buff implies discrimination. I am purely and simply a movie bum, a film addict.

In the 1960s, I was so thoroughly hooked I routinely set my alarm clock for 3:00 A.M. whenever *The Maltese Falcon* showed up at that hour on a TV late late show. Today, with a videocassette recorder in the living room, I can sleep more regular hours (and, I am told, have filled out some of the dark hollow spaces around my eye sockets).

Nevertheless, I stand proudly as a retread from the Saturday-afternoon-at-the-Bijou gang. My philosophy, then as now, is that motion pictures were made for the general public, and so I think it is fitting for a book on film to be written with them in mind.

So this is an ode to the movies of the 1960s and 1970s, written not with the careful and sometimes acerbic words of a pundit but with the nostalgic and sometimes adoring pen of someone who seeks to recapture the glitter and fantasy of that make-believe world in darkness. And, of course, the dreams.

Readers will find a wide variety of selections. They range from such universal favorites as *Annie Hall, Nashville,* and *2001: A Space Odyssey* to pictures that seldom appear on any list—such as *Lonely Are the Brave, Carnival of Souls,* and *Don't Look Now.*

Some of the movies reflect events of the times. *Apocalypse Now* and *The Deer Hunter* tell about the Vietnam War and its aftermath. *Easy Rider* shows us the counterculture world. *The French Connection* takes us on the heroin trail. *The Battle of Algiers* documents the surge of third-world countries toward independence. And *The Manchurian Candidate* presages the assassinations of the 1960s.

Also included are pictures from the independent film movement that began in the 1960s, like *David and Lisa, Hester Street,* and *Night of the Living Dead.*

In picking my fifty pictures, I made two stipulations. First, they had to be made in the 1960s and 1970s—the decades I was writing about. Second, they had to be movies that were distinctive in some special way and held up on rescreenings. This makes my list a personal one. But in the end, every list has to be a personal statement. Naturally, there will be disagreement. This is a reader's privilege. And didn't the feller say, "If we all thought alike, we'd be married to the same person"?

My choice for the best ten movies of the 1960s and 1970s:

1. *Annie Hall*
2. *Dr. Strangelove: Or, How I Learned to Stop Worrying and Love the Bomb*
3. *Nashville*
4. *2001: A Space Odyssey*
5. *The Godfather*
6. *Deliverance*
7. *Psycho*
8. *Five Easy Pieces*
9. *The Deer Hunter*
10. *Hester Street*

We are such stuff as dreams are made on,
And our little life is rounded with a sleep.
Shakespeare, *The Tempest*

WARD BOND: It's heavy. What is it?
HUMPHREY BOGART: The stuff that dreams are made of.
Final sequence from *The Maltese Falcon*

Annie Hall ☀

(1977)

Directed by Woody Allen. ☀ Based on a script by Allen ☀ and Marshall Brickman. ☀ Photography, Gordon Willis. Editor, Ralph Rosenblum. Art direction, Mel Bourne. Songs: "Seems Like Old Times" (Carmen Lombardo, John Jacob Loeb); "It Had to Be You" (Isham Jones, Gus Kahn). Produced by Charles H. Joffe for Jack Rollins–Charles H. Joffe Productions/United Artists. Executive Producer, Robert Greenhut. 94 minutes.

Alvy Singer	WOODY ALLEN
Annie Hall	DIANE KEATON ☀
Rob	TONY ROBERTS
Allison	CAROL KANE
Tony Lacey	PAUL SIMON
Mom Hall	COLLEEN DEWHURST
Pam	SHELLEY DUVALL
Robin	JANET MARGOLIN
Duane Hall	CHRISTOPHER WALKEN
Dad Hall	DONALD SYMINGTON
Grammy Hall	HELEN LUDLAM
Marshall McLuhan	MARSHALL McLUHAN
Alvy, age 9	JONATHAN MUNK
Alvy's dad	MORDECAI LAWNER
Alvy's mom	JOAN NEWMAN

☀ Academy Award winner

Woody Allen is standing in a movie line in front of a long-winded boor who is pontificating about Fellini and Marshall McLuhan.

The man's voice ripples forth like an ocean wave, and Allen is inundated, drowning in this dreary diatribe. But he cannot give up his spot. So he stays there wincing, complaining softly while the pseudo-intellectual drones on.

"We saw a Fellini film Tuesday ... not one of his best... lacked a cohesive structure... I always felt he was essentially a technical filmmaker.... McLuhan deals with it [TV] in terms of it being a high-intensity, you understand, a hot medium..."

How many times has this happened to us—suffering a pompous egotist at a party, a dinner, on a plane. We sit there a captive, listening helplessly while the pretender expostulates. Ah, but Woody Allen has a way of bringing things to a thumping halt. In this sequence from *Annie Hall*, Allen summons up the courage to turn around and face his tormentor.

"You don't know anything about McLuhan's work," Allen says.

"Really?" the man responds indignantly, "I happen to teach a class at Columbia University called 'TV, Media and Culture.'"

Suddenly, Allen ducks behind a lobby placard and pulls out McLuhan himself. "I heard what you were saying," McLuhan says, confronting the long-winded one. "You know nothing of my work.... How you ever got to teach a course in anything is totally amazing."

The monologist is speechless, unable to respond to this ultimate put-down. "Boy," Allen says, "if life were only like this."

Woody Allen. He is an original filmmaking talent. He may be awkward and clumsy and somewhat intense, but since the 1960s, no other comedian has so tickled the funnybone of the nation.

The reason is a little puzzling. At first glance, one would think Middle America would have difficulty relating to Allen's ethnic background and exotic personality. His roots are urban Jewish and he is a confirmed neurotic. Allen is the consummate worrier who magnifies petty fears into major personal problems until life becomes one ordeal after another.

But audiences invariably identify with the underdog. And since

The two young lovers (Woody Allen and Diane Keaton) stroll through the streets of New York.

Allen uses himself as the source of his material, his foibles are a touchstone for us all.

Allen thinks the explanation for his success might be more complex. "I don't know if there is a little of me in everybody," he told *Newsday* writer Al Cohn. "Or there's no me in everybody. And that's why they laugh. Or they laugh because I'm going through the suffering they would go through. Or they empathize. . . . It's really impossible to tell or isolate any of those things. . . . It may be beyond all those things."

Whether Allen perceives the reason for his audience's kinship, it is certainly there. By baring his gloomy soul, he strikes a responsive chord with everyone struggling to fend off the pressures of modern life. Like Allen, we, at one time or another, are troubled by guilt, contemptuous of the Establishment, insecure, afraid of failure, wary about our sexual inadequacy. "I'm one of the few men who suffer from penis envy," says Allen.

Born Alan Stuart Konigsberg in Flatbush, Allen was at odds with the Establishment from the start. He was a problem student at Midwood High School and at New York University. The problem was his uncontrollable wit. "I was in trouble at school because of my inability to suppress thrusts. I would go to the movies and yell out hilarious things at the screen. It would kill me at school. . . ."

But he had a flair for writing, too. At sixteen, he was sending jokes to Earl Wilson and Walter Winchell. (Later, he would write short humor pieces for *The New Yorker*.)[1]

At twenty-one, a college dropout, he had already married[2] and was undergoing psychoanalysis— a therapy that has carried over into his middle years.

His career goal was then unclear. He regarded himself as a likable but self-deprecating schnook. He looked the part. A worried stare haunted his short (five feet

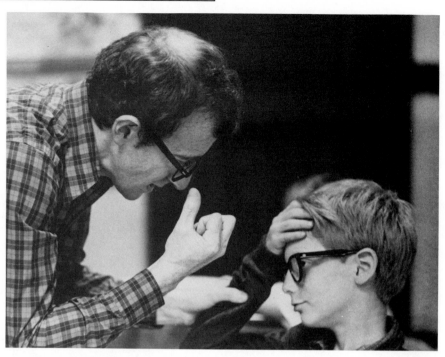

Recalling childhood memories, Alvy (Allen) encounters himself as a nine-year-old (Jonathan Munk).

five), slight (115 pounds) frame. He had thick glasses, a prominent nose, stringy reddish hair. He also had a rapier wit and a creative mind, and he was soon making good money as a television comedy writer for Sid Caesar, Art Carney, and others.

At twenty-five, he gave up his lucrative TV writing career to begin working as a $35-a-week nightclub comedian. It was a late start for a stand-up comic. But in his tough proving ground, he honed what was to be the Woody Allen personality—the Jewish half-pint, threatened and insecure, but able to toss off brilliant one-liners and zingers like so much confetti.

One night at the Blue Angel, producer Charles Feldman saw his act and was impressed enough to give Allen a chance to write and

star in a movie. The result was *What's New Pussycat?* (1965). It grossed $17 million and set the direction of his movie career.

Nevertheless, Allen was not pleased with the results. "I hated making it," Allen said. "It was the reason I became a director. I knew if I had to write a script and let other people make it that I would never want to do it."

Still, four years and several credits later (including two Broadway plays and some TV network specials), he was able to write and direct his next movie—*Take the Money and Run* (1969). That gave him control over his material and led to a series of fast-moving but uneven comedies Allen refers to as "cartoons." They include *Bananas* (1971), *Play It Again, Sam* (1972), *Everything You Always Wanted to Know About Sex But*

---

[1]Allen's own comic idols include Groucho and Harpo Marx, W. C. Fields, S. J. Perelman, and Robert Benchley. But he is not a big fan of Buster Keaton, Harold Lloyd, or James Thurber.

[2]He was married at nineteen. His second wife was Louise Lasser, TV's Mary Hartman.

After a round of tennis, Annie (Keaton) looks like a modern-day Charlie Chaplin in her man's hat, polka-dot tie, and baggy pants.

Were Afraid to Ask (1972), *Sleeper* (1973), and *Love and Death* (1975).

"I was struggling to develop a sense of cinema, a better feeling for technique," Allen said. "But even though those films tried for some satirical content, they were still cartoons."

Maturity finally came in 1977 when he did *Annie Hall*, a film that combines the best of his special humor with a bittersweet romance.[3]

In fact, the first cut was a very different picture. "Far from being the story of a love affair," said Ralph Rosenblum, the film editor, "... it was the surrealistic and abstract adventures of a neurotic Jew."

The original version had some of Allen's funniest material. But Rosenblum felt it didn't hang together. It was a "chaotic collection of bits and pieces that seemed to defy continuity." Equally important, it obscured the real core of the movie—the relationship between Alvy and Annie. After months of editing, which Rosenblum said he did with Allen, the concept of the film changed and the movie fell into place.

In a way, *Annie Hall* is a 1970s *Pygmalion*. It is a movie about a neurotic New York City comedian and the aspiring singer he meets, helps develop, falls in love with, then loses to her newly acquired independence and life-style.

The picture is partly autobiographical. Like Keaton, Annie Hall is a girl from the Midwest who comes to the city for a show-business career. In real life, Allen and Keaton (whose nickname is Annie and whose real name is Diane Hall) shared an apartment, as did Alvy Singer and Annie Hall. Keaton did not desert Allen for the greener pastures of Cali-

fornia. But they did stop living together.

"Annie and I broke up," Alvy Singer says in a monologue at the outset. "And I still can't get my mind around that. . . . Where did the screw-up come?"

The film evolves into a narration that is more a series of vignettes than a conventional storyline. The camera shifts to Alvy's childhood in Brooklyn, where he lived in a house underneath a Coney Island roller coaster. We see him in school. Then, suddenly, he is grown and meeting Annie Hall, a flaky, reed-thin girl with an infectious laugh and waifish smile.

We see sparks of their volatile relationship, and the camera drifts back in time to their first encounter at a tennis court. They are leaving after playing a doubles match. She looks like a female Charlie Chaplin, dressed outlandishly in baggy pants, man's hat, polka-dot tie, shirt, and vest.

"Bye," Annie says.

"You play very well," says Alvy.

"So do you. Oh, God, what a dumb thing to say. You say, 'You play well.' So right away I had to say, 'You play well.' La-de-dah. La-de-dah. La-la."

In the end, they go off in Annie's car. She drives (wildly) to her apartment, where they open a bottle of wine.

"Well, you are what Grammy Hall calls a 'real Jew,'" she tells him.

"Thank you," he says, trying to accept this bizarre observation graciously.

They make a date for Saturday night, when Annie is auditioning at a small club. To the cacophony of scraping chairs, clicking glasses, and a ringing telephone, she sings "It Had to Be You." Outside the club, she pours out her deep embarrassment and disappointment.

Alvy won't let her despair. "You have a wonderful voice," he tells her. And they kiss.

A few weeks later, Annie moves in with Alvy. At his suggestion,

---

[3]Allen's original title for the movie was *Anhedonia*, meaning incapable of experiencing pleasure. No one else liked it. But Allen fought efforts to change it until he saw blank looks on the faces of screening audiences. Then the title became *Anxiety, Annie and Alvy*, and finally *Annie Hall*.

Alvy takes best friend Rob (Tony Roberts) and Annie to the Brooklyn schoolyard where he grew up.

she starts taking adult education courses to improve herself. Then, when he goes on the college circuit to play some comic dates, she joins him. The trip gives them a chance to meet her all-American family. At dinner, he imagines himself as he thinks her Waspy grandmother sees him—a bearded Hasidic Jew wearing a hat, side curls, and black frock coat.

Back in New York, he and Annie renew their emotional ups and downs. They battle because Alvy thinks she has let her adult education professor become too familiar. Like Alvy, Annie starts psychoanalysis. It doesn't prevent them from breaking up. But their estrangement is a brief one, and they are soon back together. What Alvy doesn't realize—but will

soon learn—is that Annie has matured and become an independent person in her own right.

On a sentimental journey with Annie and Rob (Tony Roberts), Alvy's best friend, they wander through Alvy's old neighborhood. "I was a great athlete," he tells them. "I was all-schoolyard."

Then Annie gets another night-club date. In a measured, smoldering voice, she sings, "Seems Like Old Times." A major recording producer, Tony Lacey (Paul Simon), is impressed by her performance and asks her to record. When he invites her to a party, Alvy, seething with jealousy, makes her beg off and go to a movie with him instead.

Now her analysis sessions get more intense. So do his.

The scene shifts to California,

where Alvy has gone for a TV appearance. Annie is with him, and she admires the clean Beverly Hills landscape. "That's because they don't throw their garbage away," Alvy says. "They make it into television shows."

They visit Lacey's sumptuous home—complete with pool, tennis courts, sauna, and screening room—and he invites Annie to stay and cut a record. She turns him down again.

But flying back to New York, she runs over the trip in her mind and decides she isn't so happy to be leaving. "That was fun," she thinks. "I don't think California is bad at all. It's a drag coming home."

She turns to Alvy. "Let's face it," she tells him. "I don't think our relationship is working."

Alvy and Annie spend a weekend at a beach resort to try to solidify their relationship.

To her surprise, he agrees. "A relationship is like a shark. It has to constantly move forward to be working. I think what we've got on our hands is a dead shark."

With Annie gone, Alvy tries dating other women. His jokes fall flat. Things just aren't the same. He sulks, talks to himself, shares his misery with people on the street. Finally, he flies to California and asks her to marry him.

Annie says she appreciates Alvy's support. "I was able to sing and get more in touch with my feelings," she tells him. But she has discovered a new life now. "We're friends," she says. "I want to remain friends."

"So what are you saying? You're not coming back to me?"

That's just what she is saying. Alvy returns to New York alone.

He writes a play about the affair, giving it a happy ending. But life is not like art. Some time later, he runs into Annie at a revival movie house. They share lunch and a few laughs. And that's it.

And so as the screen flashes back highlights of their topsy-turvy affair, Alvy sums it all up as Annie's voice sings in the background.

"I realized what a terrific person she was. And how much fun it was just knowing her. And I thought of that old joke. You know, this guy goes to a psychiatrist. He says, 'Doc, my brother's crazy. He thinks he's a chicken.'

"The doctor says, 'Well, why don't you turn him in?'

"The guy says, 'I would. But I need the eggs.'

"That's pretty much how I feel about relationships. They're totally irrational and crazy and absurd. But I guess we keep going through it because most of us need the eggs."[4]

---

[4]The ending—the images of Keaton and Allen flashing on the screen while Keaton sings her nightclub number "Seems Like Old Times"—is a poignant moment. "The whole film could have gone into the toilet if there hadn't been that last beat on it," said Marshall Brickman, who wrote the screenplay with Allen. "I think every writer of comedy wants to send them out with something like that, to keep them laughing, extremely hysterical, for an hour and twenty-eight minutes, and then for the last two minutes turn it around and let them walk away with something they can chew on."

The Apartment ☠
(1960)

Produced and directed by Billy Wilder ☠. Screenplay, Wilder ☠ and I.A.L. Diamond. ☠ Art director, Alexander Trauner. ☠ Cinematography, Joseph LaShelle. Editor, Daniel Mandell. ☠ Set director, Edward G. Boyle. ☠ Music, Adolph Deutsch. Songs: "Lonely Room" (theme from *The Apartment*) by Deutsch; "Jealous Lover" by Charles Williams. A Mirisch Company Production. B/W. 125 minutes.

C. C. "Bud" Baxter	JACK LEMMON
Fran Kubelik	SHIRLEY MacLAINE
Jeff Sheldrake	FRED MacMURRAY
Joe Dobisch	RAY WALSTON
Al Kirkeby	DAVID LEWIS
Dr. Dreyfuss	JACK KRUSCHEN
Sylvia	JOAN SHAWLEE
Miss Olsen	EDIE ADAMS
Margie MacDougall	HOPE HOLIDAY
Karl Matuschka	JOHNNY SEVEN
Mrs. Dreyfuss	NAOMI STEVENS
Mrs. Lieberman	FRANCES WEINTRAUB LAX
Blonde	JOYCE JAMESON
Mr. Vanderhof	WILLARD WATERMAN
Mr. Eichelberger	DAVID WHITE

☠ Academy Award winner

Billy Wilder got the idea for *The Apartment* while watching *Brief Encounter* (1946), the classic British film starring Trevor Howard and Celia Johnson.

It told of the short-lived affair of two mature married people. As I.A.L. Diamond, Wilder's screenwriter, remembers it, Wilder got to thinking what it was like for the fellow who owned the apartment where the lovers met. How did he react when he came home to find the bed rumpled, ashtrays full, dirty glasses everywhere? But neither Wilder nor Diamond worked out a story, and several years went by.

"Then something happened in this town," said Diamond. "A producer caught his wife with an agent and shot him. It turned out that the agent was using the apartment of a subordinate in the same agency. Suddenly, that gave us the plot."

The Apartment, the Oscar-winning movie they wrote, is a comedy. Yet it has serious undertones, too. Stripped of its humor and its appealing characters, the film becomes a tale of ambition and adultery running rampant in the corporate world.

In the end, the hero, Jack Lemmon, tries to make amends by quitting and telling off his philandering boss. But his motive is not entirely pure. His girl has become the target of his boss's roving eye. In a sense, he is stirred to action as much out of self-interest as principle.

Yet, none of the darker sides of the movie come through. If the picture had been made in France, audiences of the 1960s would have been talking about its daring story. If it had been shot in Italy, moviegoers would have seen the depravity and degradation of the corporate structure. But through the prism of Wilder's eyes, *The Apartment* becomes a totally different experience.

All the seedy features are there, only they are there on a muted level, sublimated to the poignant tale of two innocents finding their way to happiness in the amoral world of big business. We are won over to a more decent side of the plot by the wholesomeness of the characters played by Lemmon and Shirley MacLaine. After the film ends, moviegoers, instead of clucking about the decline of

Jack Lemmon is Bud Baxter, a clerk in an insurance firm, and Shirley MacLaine plays Fran Kubelik, an elevator operator he takes a shine to.

Baxter's bachelor pad has made him the envy of married executives in his company. Vying for use of his apartment are (*from left*) Ray Walston, David White, Willard Waterman, and David Lewis.

Baxter shows some unique culinary improvisation as he dishes up spaghetti with a tennis racket.

Jeff Sheldrake (MacMurray), a fast-talking corporate executive, who has an affair with Fran.

American morality, emerge from the theater teary-eyed, moved by the simple tale of virtue coming out ahead.

In fact, there are no real villains in this picture except Fred Mac-Murray. And he seems miscast. At any rate, he gets a double come-uppance. One from his wife, who leaves him when she learns about his cheating heart. And again from MacLaine when she discovers Lemmon has had the guts to walk away from his job rather than continue providing a setting for his boss's sordid affairs.

Some were puzzled by the plot. In part, that had to do with the timing of its release. *The Apartment* came out in 1960, at the end of the sterile Eisenhower years and well before the liberated era of the later 1960s and 1970s. Stanley Kauffman thought the use of a lower-echelon employee's apartment as a love nest for his bosses was a "tasteless gimmick." Dwight MacDonald found the picture "immoral," "dishonest," and "without style or taste."

But they were in a minority. Bosley Crowther, the *New York Times* critic, was one of many reviewers who enjoyed Wilder's satire. The important thing to know about *The Apartment*, Crowther said, was that it followed a "sophisticated balance between cynicism and sentiment, between irony and pity, that has run through most of the best American comedies."

That delicate balance was evident from the picture's start when Lemmon, playing C. C. "Bud" Baxter, a clerk in a vast Manhattan insurance firm, finds himself in an awkward situation. Word has gotten out that bachelor Bud has a cozy apartment near the office.

When his married superiors learn about it, they each quietly campaign to use his digs for an evening rendezvous. Bud has mixed feelings. He is not in sympathy with the morals of his bosses. Nor does he welcome spending part of the evening on a park bench, huddling against the cold.

On the other hand, he is a cipher in a huge corporation. And he is realistic enough to know that the favors he is extending are more apt to increase his chance for advancement than his own mediocre bookkeeping talents.

Bud's list of flat-lenders enlarges until his apartment is busy every night of the week. At first, he takes it all in stride. He regards it as one of those bothersome things that go with advancement, like flattering Sheldrake (MacMurray), his boss.

But when Bud catches cold, he gets second thoughts. He realizes he is getting tired of replenishing liquor and cigarettes.

The carryings-on are also an embarrassment. His neighbor, a physician (Jack Kruschen), regards Bud as a twentieth-century Don Juan. "You must be an iron man," the doctor says. "From what I hear through the walls, you must have something going for you every night." One day the doc asks Bud to will his body to his medical school.

The last straw comes when Bud realizes his boss is playing around with Fran Kubelik (MacLaine), the girl to whom Bud has taken a shine. She is an elevator operator at his company.

Ironically, it is her fling with Sheldrake that brings Fran and Bud together. Sheldrake has been stringing out the affair by promising that he will divorce his wife and marry Fran. Of course, he has no such intentions. "You see a girl a couple of times a week, just for laughs, and right away, they think you're going to divorce your wife," Sheldrake tells Bud.

On Christmas Eve, Fran gives Sheldrake a present at Bud's apartment. In return, he gives her a $100 bill. That puts a damper on the evening. Fran gets even more depressed when Sheldrake has to cut the evening short to join his family triming their tree.

Left alone, she swallows half a bottle of sleeping pills. Fortunately, Bud comes home to discover her. With the help of his doctor neighbor, he saves her.

Dr. Dreyfuss (Jack Kruschen) and Baxter keep Kubelik walking after she overdoses on sleeping pills.

Then, as she stays with him for a few days to regain her strength, a bond develops.

But their romance is interrupted after Sheldrake's marriage crumbles. A disgruntled employee has told Sheldrake's wife about his extramarital affair. "I fired my secretary, my secretary got to my wife, and my wife fired me," he tells Bud.

Using his newfound freedom, the tough-skinned Sheldrake makes still another pitch for Fran. He calls in Bud, who has climbed one more notch up the corporate ladder, and asks again for the key to his apartment.

In the meantime, Bud's con-science has finally prevailed over his vaulting ambition. He has decided his job isn't worth sacrificing his personal integrity. He has a neat way of telling off Sheldrake. Instead of giving him the key to his apartment, he gives his boss the key to the executive washroom.

That evening, Sheldrake, out with Fran to celebrate the New Year at a restaurant, apologizes for having to rent a car and take her to Atlantic City. "It's all Bud's fault," he explains. "He walked out on me. Quit. Threw that key right in my face.... Said I couldn't bring anybody to the apartment. Especially Miss Kubelik."

That's all Fran has to hear. The lights go out and everybody starts singing "Auld Lang Syne"—except Fran. When the lights go on and Sheldrake looks for her, she is gone. End of one love affair, beginning of another.

More than two decades later, in an era when sex has become more open and liberal, *The Apartment* still comes across as a funny, often touching, film.

Carnal Knowledge
(1971)

Produced and directed by Mike Nichols. Written by Jules Feiffer. Executive producer, Joseph E. Levine. Photography, Giuseppe Rotunno. Editor, Sam O'Steen. Art director, Robert Luthardt. Filmed in New York City and Vancouver, British Columbia. Avco Embassy. Rated R. 100 minutes.

Jonathan Fuerst	JACK NICHOLSON
Bobbie	ANN-MARGRET
Sandy	ART GARFUNKEL
Susan	CANDICE BERGEN
Louise	RITA MORENO
Cindy	CYNTHIA O'NEIL
Jennifer	CAROL KANE

"This one came so close to being what I wanted," says Jack Nicholson, playing the part of a skirt-chasing bachelor. "Good pair of tits on her. Not a great pair. Almost no ass at all. And that bothered me. Sensational legs. I would have settled for the legs if she had two more inches here and three more here. Anyhow, that took two years out of my life."

The dialogue comes from *Carnal Knowledge*, a trailblazing movie that explores the evolution of two middle-class males from the 1940s to 1970s as reflected by a single aspect of their lives: their sexual attitudes.

As it turns out, it is a static pattern. They never change because, like many of their generation, they are trapped in an adolescent fantasy.

They view women as one-dimensional, depersonalized objects, so much meat on the hook to be carved up into bosoms, behinds, and bodies—luscious wares created to provide pleasures of the flesh. For these men, love has no meaning beyond the act of fornication. Women offer a challenge to their ego, and when the conquest is made, their interest wanes. They go on to other women, other challenges.

This antimale theme—or antifemale, depending on your vantage point—emerged in a theater script by cartoonist Jules Feiffer. "The play illustrated, through the relationship between these two men and their encounters with various women, the way things have been for my generation," Feiffer said.

He sent the script to Nichols. Twenty-four hours later, Nichols called him and said it was a movie, not a play.

"It seemed to me," Nichols said, "it had to do with the expression in people's eyes. I wanted to be very close to them, especially to the men, when they did these monologues about how often they did or did not have sex. Because it seemed to me that the despair at being trapped in this macho role could best be expressed when you were right into those faces."

Feiffer, who had already written *Little Murders* (1971) as a movie, was an admirer of Nichols's work and eagerly accepted the suggestion. "If Mike had wanted to do this as a comic book, I would have," Feiffer said.

And so was launched one of the most innovative films of the 1970s. It was unique in that it was made in a series of vignettes tracing the two men's sexual experiences from their college days into their middle-age years. But instead of extolling the happily-ever-after, romantic side of love, as so many pictures have done, Feiffer chose to focus on the exploitation game some vacuous men play. The movie hit home because it was uncovering a truth. And it was on target.

If *Carnal Knowledge* was exploring new territory, it also drew criticism for this very reason.

Jack Nicholson as Jonathan and Art Garfunkel as Sandy, two college Don Juans whose relationship with women never matures beyond adolescent fantasy.

Left: Jonathan dating Susan (Candice Bergen), a challenge for him because she is his roommate's girl.

Below left: Sandy and Jonathan meet after college. Their sexual excursions have taken them in different directions. While Sandy places women on a pedestal, Jonathan pulls them down on a bed.

Critics attacked it because they said it was chauvinistic and obsessed with sex. True, much of the movie revolves around sex. But it is really the story of the relationship of two friends. The movie succeeds because it shows how their personalities never mature. Their lives are narrowed and diminished because they are unable to achieve a real sexual partnership.

If Sandy (Art Garfunkel) seeks spiritual fulfillment from his women, Jonathan (Nicholson) is searching for perfect sex. Jonathan flits from one affair to another as if they were restaurants. "I'd get married in a minute if I could find the right girl," he says. But he is only deluding himself.

Although it was Nicholson's sensitive acting that made the movie work, the picture was helped in no small measure by a surprisingly insightful performance by Ann-Margret. The musical comedy star was an offbeat casting choice. "She came into my office and was so scared and shy —what in Hollywood they call vulnerable—and I liked her very much," Nichols said. "Her own life has been like this girl she plays, surrounded always by

Lonely and depressed, an aging Jonathan finds he can overcome impotence only with a prostitute (Rita Moreno) who pretends to admire his masculine prowess.

horny guys who simply admire her as an object."

It was clear that the acting was exceptional from the outset, when we see Jonathan and Sandy as undergraduates at Amherst. Like many college kids, they are obsessed by thoughts of making out. At a mixer, they spot an attractive coed and Jonathan urges Sandy to go after her. She turns out to be Susan (Candice Bergen), a student at Smith College, and she dates Sandy after they get through some awkward moments.

Sandy's successful encounter only serves to spur on Jonathan. He decides he, too, must have Susan. Unbeknownst to his roommate, Jonathan begins taking Susan out and, in time, seduces her.

Eventually, Jonathan tells Sandy he has made it—but not with whom—putting Sandy down one leg in the game of one-upmanship. Predictably, Sandy resolves he must achieve what Jonathan has, and he coldly and calculatedly campaigns to seduce Susan too. One kiss becomes several and several kisses lead to lowered barriers. When at last Susan agrees to go to bed with Sandy, however reluctantly, she asks: "How can it be fun if you know I don't want it?" It turns out to be a joyless exercise, more a tribal ritual to be gotten through than a breathless act of passion.

A few years after graduation, Jonathan and Sandy meet at a skating rink in Central Park. Sandy has married Susan. Jonathan is still a bachelor.

As they chat, Jonathan notices a svelte skater clad in virginal white, spinning on the ice. The figure fascinates him, and her image will keep returning. She represents to him the perfectly formed female, the idealized woman that he must forever pursue.

Sandy, who has become a doctor, tells Jonathan about his marriage. He seems to be happy and fulfilled. Only when he comes to the end of his soliloquy do we re-alize just the opposite has happened.

"Susan and I do all the right things. We undress in front of each other. Spend fifteen minutes in foreplay. Do it in different rooms. . . . We're considerate of each other's feelings. . . . We try to be patient, gentle with each other. . . . Maybe it's not meant to be enjoyable with women you love."

Jonathan, mulling over his latest conquest, Bobbie (Ann-Margret), a stewardess.

It soon becomes evident that Sandy envies Jonathan's freewheeling life as a bachelor. A tax attorney, Jonathan has started going with a full-breasted stewardess named Bobbie (Ann-Margret). She is vibrant and attractive. But their relationship is doomed because any hint of matrimony has a chilling effect on Jonathan. Sometimes he runs into the shower and tries to wash away such disturbing thoughts.

In fact, Nicholson spends a good deal of the picture with water pouring down on his body —an idea Feiffer got while visiting *Playboy* magazine in Chicago.

"This guy who had just slept with a girl told me how upset the girl was when he got up after to take a shower," Feiffer said. "I mean, wow. She really didn't understand why. That's why Nicholson spends so much of this film in the shower."

Both Jonathan and Sandy do well financially. But as the years pass, they remain prisoners of their adolescent sexual mentality. To Jonathan, women are "ball busters." He says: "Women today are better hung than the men." Bobbie, depressed about her relationship with Jonathan, attempts suicide. Eventually, Jonathan marries her, but it soon ends in divorce, as does Sandy's marriage.

One day in the 1960s, Jonathan invites Sandy to his penthouse apartment. Sandy, dressed like a teenager in blue jeans, shows up with a nubile Village hippie (Carol Kane), young enough to be his daughter. Jonathan shows them his slide collection, pictures of the women—he calls them "girls"—in his life. He provides a running commentary that turns into a crude, bitter diatribe. This one was a "castrator." That one he "screwed."

Sandy and his date find it all distasteful and leave. Lonely and at loose ends, Jonathan goes to a prostitute (Rita Moreno). He is becoming impotent, and only she can restore his fading manhood by flattering him, telling him how macho he is.

She tells him, "It takes a true woman to understand that the purest form of love is to love a man who denies himself to her. A man who inspires worship because he has no need for any woman because he has himself. . . . You're getting hard and strong, virile, domineering, more irresistible. It's up. It's in the air."

Even as she is talking, Jonathan's thoughts are far away. He visualizes the skater, the frosty, perfectly formed figure, turning and spinning on the mirror-smooth ice.

The Man Who Loved Women

(1977)

Directed by François Truffaut. Screenplay by Truffaut, Michel Fermaud, and Suzanne Schiffman. Photography, Nestor Almendros. Editor, Martine Barraque-Curie. Music, Maurice Jaubert. Produced by Les Films du Carrossel and Les Productions Artistes Associés. In French with English titles. Cinema 5 release. 119 minutes.

Bertrand Morane	CHARLES DENNER
Geneviève Bigey	BRIGITTE FOSSEY
Delphine Grezel	NELLY BORGEAUD
Hélène	GENEVIÈVE FONTANEL
Martine Desdoits	NATHALIE BAYE
Bernadette	SABINE GLASER
Fabienne	VALÉRIE BONNIER
Denise	MARTINE CHASSAING
Nicole	ROSELYNE PUYO
Uta	ANNA PERRIER
Madame Duteil	MONIQUE DURY
Liliane	NELLA BARNIER
Juliette	FRÉDÉRIQUE JAMET
Christine Morane	M. J. MONTFAJON
Vera	LESLIE CARON
Urologist	JEAN DASTE
Publisher	ROGER LEENHARDT

"One funeral is just like another. And yet this one is special—not a single man. Only women. Nothing but women. Yes, definitely, I thought Bertrand would have enjoyed the sight of his own funeral."

These are the opening voice-over remarks in François Truffaut's *The Man Who Loved Women*, a film that many critics regarded as one of the French New Wave director's lesser works. They saw it more as a slight comedy than as one of his inspired cinematic ventures.

But, to me, the film is a provocative retelling of the Don Juan story, an engrossing and engaging picture that has a lot to say about what love is all about—or, more to the point, what it is not about.

The hero, Bertrand, played by Charles Denner, resembles Truffaut in at least two ways. Like Truffaut, he is an author. He begins writing his memoirs. (In fact, not one to miss out on any opportunity, he has a brief affair with the woman who edits his book.)

And, like Truffaut,[1] Bertrand's life-style is shaped by his childhood. Bertrand's mother neglected him for a series of lovers. In devoting his life to the pursuit of women, Bertrand seems to be seeking the love she denied him.

Truffaut, who has acknowledged that many of his themes are personal, said the movie was the fusion of two ideas. "I had wanted to do a story of a man who has no male friends," he said. "Another idea I had was to do the story of [the creation of] a book. The day I decided I could mix the two was when I found myself able to write the screenplay."

Truffaut is almost unique among directors. He started his career not as a craftsman learning his trade but as someone outside the

---

[1]Truffaut was a problem child, a school dropout at fourteen. In adulthood, he continued flouting the Establishment by rejecting Hollywood slickness. Instead of shooting in studios, he filmed on location, producing raw, grainy black-and-white pictures for authenticity and spontaneity. He also used natural street sounds, getting away from canned sound effects. Truffaut died in 1984 of cancer. He was fifty-two.

Bernadette (Sabine Glaser), accepts a dinner invitation from Bertrand (Charles Denner). "You have a way of putting it that's special," she says, "as if your life depended on it."

Geneviève (Brigitte Fossey), the editor who persuades her publishing house to buy Bertrand's novel. Fossey played the five-year-old lost girl in *Forbidden Games* (1951).

industry—as a critic. Fascinated by movies as a youngster, he began writing articles for *Cahiers du Cinéma*.

The magazine, one of the first to treat film as an art form, championed the movies of Howard Hawks, John Ford, Raoul Walsh, and Alfred Hitchcock. Truffaut revered Hitchcock and would later collaborate with him on a book about the British director's films. "He's the only director I've identified with completely," Truffaut said. "I like certain films of [Michael] Curtiz, [Billy] Wilder, [Otto] Preminger. But they moved through a wide range, whereas Hitchcock remained obsessively within one style of approach. His is an amazing unity."

Truffaut quickly decided on the type of movie that was most appealing to him. "From the beginning, I was not interested in seeing American 'costume pictures.' I did not like westerns, pirate films. I only wanted to see love stories and detective stories, and psychological thrillers."

And so it is no wonder that when he became a director, he concentrated on films dealing with inner motivation. At the same time, he was a gifted storyteller.

Bertrand, Truffaut's semiautobiographical hero, appears at first glance to be a one-dimensional character. He is basically a skirtchaser. But a closer look at him shows he is really a complex person.

A medium-size, hawk-faced man in his forties, Bertrand lives in Montpellier, where he works as an engineer in a lab testing wave and air dynamics on model ships and planes. After hours, he devotes his life to the pursuit of women. "If their hearts are free, their bodies are for the taking," says Bertrand. "And it seems to me I haven't the right to pass up the chance. . . . I look at everybody."

What attracts him first are their legs, especially if they are inside a fetching skirt that swings to the rhythm of their walk. Says Bertrand: "The legs of a woman are

like the stems of a compass that measures the terrestial globe in all directions—giving it balance and grace."

In fact, Bertrand is so fixed on the appendages of one young lady, who drives off after he sees her in a laundry, that he does not realize he has found, not her, but her cousin when he eventually tracks her down.

Other attractive women he encounters on his lifelong spree are:
● Delphine (Nelly Borgeaud), who likes to make love in dangerously public places—a department store, the garage of the apartment building where she and her husband live. As she tears off her clothes and pounces on Bertrand, she protests: "Goodness, the things you make me do."
● Hélène (Geneviève Fontanel), a woman of his own age who runs a lingerie shop. One of Bertrand's few failures, she rejects him at the outset because she is attracted only to younger men. That inspires Bertrand to write his memoirs.
● Vera (Leslie Caron), an old flame who runs into Bertrand in a hotel. She suggests they have dinner together. But Bertrand feels uneasy about rekindling glowing embers. "We're practically strangers. We'll have to accept it. . . . It's best."
● Geneviève (Brigitte Fossey), his editor. She persuades her publishing house to accept his book and later has an affair with Bertrand. But she tells him he has to learn to love himself before he can love others.
● Uta (Anna Perrier), a svelte blonde who comes to Bertrand's apartment to baby-sit. She finds only a doll in the supposed nursery. Where, she asks, is the child? "It's me," says Bertrand.

There is something unreal about his life of one-night stands. Bertrand is a joyless chaser, and his captured women are all so eager and willing that there is no conquest to be made.

Vera (**Leslie Caron**), a former sweetheart who bumps into Bertrand in a hotel. The embers still glow for her, but not for Bertrand.

In a French TV interview, Denner, the actor portraying Bertrand, says what prevents Bertrand from making lasting relationships is a fear of becoming dependent and getting hurt. By keeping his distance and limiting his engagements to one-night stands, he can control each situation and retain his freedom.

Bertrand blocks off romantic involvement because he has already been wounded. In flashbacks of his childhood, we see him as an unwanted, fatherless child. In voice-over Bertrand says: "Everything in [my mother's] behavior toward me as a little boy seemed to say: 'I'd have done better to break a leg than to give birth to this stupid child.'"

His mother's primary interest is her changing succession of lovers. One day, Bertrand finds her love letters. In living the life of a

Hélène (**Geneviève Fontanel**), an older woman who runs a lingerie shop. She surprises Bertrand by rejecting him. Her turndown prompts him to write his memoirs.

Bertrand looks over galleys of his novel with Geneviève and his publisher (Roger Leenhardt).

middle-aged Casanova and then setting it all down, Bertrand is unconsciously repeating the patterns of his mother's life.

At night, he is rarely alone. When he says goodbye to one woman, he is on the phone calling another. Some feel that there is a parallel in Truffaut's life and the many personal films he made. Says Annette Insdorf in her book, *François Truffaut* (Twayne, 1978): "He had admitted that the way he compensates for the feeling of disintegration at the end of shooting is by looking forward to a new project. The way that he guards against being too vulnerable to criticism when a film is released is by already having his next one in preparation.

"Perhaps, like his hero, he can only wave goodbye if he hears the phone that signifies new business.

Truffaut is as prolific as Bertrand is promiscuous, and as committed to (or even obsessed with) each project as Bertrand is to each woman."

One day, in pursuit of the perfect woman, Bertrand spots a beguiling pair of legs crossing the street. As he follows them, he fails to notice the oncoming traffic.[2]

He wakes up in a hospital, a critical intravenous tube stuck into his body. Then, alas, there is one final irresistible vision of loveliness—his nurse. Entranced by her legs, Bertrand falls out of bed as he reaches for her, unplugging himself from all life-sustaining machines, and he dies.

At the funeral, Geneviève, his editor, says she is the only woman there who knew everything about Bertrand. And yet his life puzzles her. "Why," she asks, "is it necessary to search through so many people looking for what our education tells us can be found in one person?"[3]

---

[2]The scene is reminiscent of a sequence in Truffaut's *Shoot the Piano Player* (1960), where a kidnapper explains his reckless mode of driving to one of his victims. The kidnapper says he does it to avenge the death of his father, an obsessive girl-watcher killed by an auto while chasing a short skirt across the street.

[3]The movie was remade by Blake Edwards in 1983. Burt Reynolds played a sculptor and Julie Andrews was his psychiatrist, who learns all about his affairs and has one with him as well. In terms of quality, there is little resemblance between this picture and the Truffaut film.

Life-Styles

EASY RIDER

FIVE EASY PIECES

THE GRADUATE

THE HUSTLER

THE LAST PICTURE SHOW

THE LEOPARD

LONELY ARE THE BRAVE

NASHVILLE

Easy Rider
(1969)

Directed by Dennis Hopper. Produced by Peter Fonda. Screenplay, Hopper, Fonda, and Terry Southern. Photography, Laszlo Kovacs. Art direction, Jerry Kay. Editor, Donn Cambern. "Ballad of Easy Rider" by Bob Dylan and Roger McGuinn, performed by McGuinn. Other songs by Hoyt Axton, Mars Bonfire, Gerry Goffin, Carole King, Jaime Robbie Robertson, Antonia Duren, Elliott Ingber, Larry Wagner, Jimi Hendrix, Jack Keller, David Axelrod, Mike Bloomfield. A Pandro/Raybert Production. Executive producer, Bert Schneider. Columbia. Filmed between California and Louisiana. Rated R. 94 minutes.

Wyatt (Captain America)	PETER FONDA
Billy	DENNIS HOPPER
George Hanson	JACK NICHOLSON
Karen	KAREN BLACK
Mary	TONI BASIL
Stranger on highway	LUKE ASKEW
Rancher	WARREN FINNERTY
Rancher's wife	TITA COLORADO
Lisa	LUANA ANDERS
Sarah	SABRINA SCHARF
Joanne	SANDY WYETH
Jack	ROBERT WALKER
Sheriff	KEITH GREEN
Cat man	HAYWARD ROBILLARD
Deputy	ARNOLD HESS, JR.

It was 1969, the year after the police-student clash at the Democratic National Convention in Chicago, a decade when the young waged pitched battles with authorities on campuses all over the country.

It was an era of social protest. Young people rebelled against the values of their parents, rejecting the traditional path of school, career, and marriage. Instead, they created their own counterculture —typified by long hair, casual clothes, communal living, activism, drugs, and rock music.

In the end, the young people failed to realize their goal of a new society. But their dream stirred a lot of people, and Easy Rider[1] was the movie that became the symbol of their ephemeral movement.

The picture focused on two free spirits on the open road. Audiences identified with them and then were shocked when they saw the hatred Middle America had for these restless mavericks.

The film had another distinction: its budget. Made for less than $400,000, the movie grossed more than ten times that amount —testimony to the fact that the under-thirty crowd buys 75 percent of movie tickets. In fact, because it was such a runaway hit, it forced studios to take another look at their big-bankroll films.

However, Easy Rider was more than a box-office smash. It was a brilliantly executed picture. It was a lyrical adventure, a picaresque west-to-east odyssey that melded beauty, comedy, violence, and surreal film technique with a disarmingly simple plot.

Insiders never expected much of it. They thought it was going to be just another cheapie motorcycle flick. They were mistaken. It mesmerized critics. "I couldn't shake what I'd seen even after I left the theater," critic Rex Reed wrote. Joseph Gelmis of Newsday, the Long Island daily, said he "hadn't been as emotionally devastated by a movie in years." Gelmis said he became so engrossed he cried aloud, "Oh, no, no," at the end.

The project began with a phone call. Hopper and Fonda had been working on a movie called The Trip (1967). When director Roger Corman showed no interest in filming an acid-trip scene, Hopper and Fonda went into the desert and shot it themselves (Hopper, in fact, had already been a professional photographer). The two found it to be a rewarding experience and decided to continue their filmmaking partnership.

Because both had acting commitments, nothing happened for a while. Then things started mov-

---

Peter Fonda, as Wyatt, on the open road on his high-handled chrome cycle.

[1] "[The name] is a Southern term for a whore's live-in boyfriend," says Fonda. "He's got his 'easy ride.' That's what happened to America, man. Liberty's a whore. And we're all taking an easy ride."

24

ing. Hopper recalled: "Peter called me from Canada and said: 'I've got a great idea for a movie. It's about two guys who score some cocaine and then take a trip from the Southwest to the Mardi Gras.' I said okay."

It took a little doing to get backing. They went to American International Pictures, which was then exploiting motorcycle and drug pictures. Hopper and Fonda had already done two motorcycle films for American, and both had made money. But nothing came of the *Easy Rider* deal—to the everlasting regret of Sam Arkoff, American's owner.

Hopper wanted to be the director. But he was virtually an unknown then. And he had a reputation for being difficult to work with on the set. So Arkoff, understandably, was unwilling to let Hopper do more than act. "I still thought we'd work it out," Arkoff said. "But before I knew it, Fonda and Hopper had made a deal elsewhere. The rest is movie history."

Hopper just wouldn't settle for half a loaf. "I wanted to become a director," he said.[2] "I felt the director-writer was the creative guy behind the film. . . . So we got the guys who produced *The Monkees* and who had made *Head* to put up three hundred and seventy thousand dollars. Everybody agreed to work for Equity pay scale."

Hopper and Fonda did the

Wyatt and road companion Billy (Dennis Hopper) share a moment.

screenplay along with Terry Southern, an established movie writer. However, Southern was really an afterthought to give the venture an aura of respectability.

"Southern was brought in as one of the writers so people wouldn't think it was just another Peter Fonda motorcycle flick," said Jack Nicholson. His funny, rounded performance as an easygoing, alcoholic Southern attorney earned him an Oscar nomination for best supporting actor and catapulted him to stardom.[3] "I don't think they would've gotten the money just for a picture directed by Dennis Hopper. I mean, if you know Dennis, you don't exactly just turn over some money to him and say, 'No problem,' you know what I mean?"

Hopper and Fonda shot the film in less than two months, including a week in New Orleans to make the Mardi Gras and graveyard sequences. The abbreviated shooting time was not unfamiliar to Hopper, who had become used to the quick production schedules of TV.

Easy Rider carried the social message that to be a young radical in America of the 1960s was to invite ridicule, repression,

violence, and even death. Billy (Hopper) and Wyatt (Fonda), two motorcycle-riding comrades, launch a cross-country jaunt underwritten by a cocaine sale they have pulled off.

Their newfound wealth does not always guarantee them a hearty welcome. On their first night, a motel owner slams his door in their face—turned off by their weird-looking, high-handled chrome cycles and their outcast appearances.

Billy sports a mustache, shoulder-length hair, a bush hat, and a fringed frontier-style jacket. Wyatt, whom Billy calls Captain America, is clad in a black leather jacket with an American flag on the back. He also wears a helmet with a stars-and-stripes design.

Later they are hassled by cops who arrest them for parading without a permit and by townsfolk who bait them in a local café. Says one good ole boy: "I thought at first that bunch over there, their mothers may have been frightened by a bunch of gorillas. But now I think they were caught."

But they are also befriended by a rancher (Warren Finnerty) who invites them to dinner with his family. He takes them to a desert

Camping out with George Hanson (Jack Nicholson), a Southern lawyer who joins Wyatt and Billy on their ride to New Orleans.

[2]For his efforts, Hopper won the 1969 Cannes Festival Award for the best movie by a new director.

[3]One of Nicholson's bizarre bits of movie business was to flap his arms like a bird and chirp "Nick-Nick" after the first drink of the day. Nicholson said he picked up the gesture, which was something akin to roaring "Vroom-vroom," from an old barfly. It became fashionable to imitate Nicholson at parties. But he himself was usually reluctant to repeat it on request.

Billy with Karen (Karen Black), a prostitute he meets at the Mardi Gras in New Orleans.

commune whose members plant their own crops.

The highlight of their journey comes when they meet George Hanson (Nicholson), an affable small-town lawyer who joins them on their trip to New Orleans. Despite years in Hollywood, Nicholson was having difficulty making it out of B movies. He had acted mostly in motorcycle, beach bikini, and horror pictures—"the kind of trash," said critic Reed, "that only a mother of a *Cahier* critic could sit through and love."

Nicholson's part, actually written for Rip Torn (who, it turned out, was unavailable), was originally conceived as that of a naive country-bumpkin type. ("Marijuana, Lord have mercy. Is that what this is?").

Nicholson saw the character from a different viewpoint. "My feeling was that the guy is an imprisoned cat. He's locked up in all this conditioning. . . . I wanted to show that he was really a worthwhile person who had instincts in all directions but was being aberrated by the environment. So by the end of it, he was really laying it all out—that freedom was really a very individual thing and that people are frightened of it."

Introduced to marijuana at a campfire in the woods, Hanson delivers a tongue-in-cheek monologue about Venusians who have migrated to Earth. "They've been coming here ever since 1946— when the scientists first started bouncing radar beams off the moon. And they have been livin' and workin' amongst us in vast quantities ever since. The government knows all about 'em. . . . [But they] have decided to repress this information because of the tremendous shock that it would cause to our antiquated systems. . . . So now, the Venusians are meeting with people in all walks of life—in an advisory capacity."

After rednecks taunt them at a greasy-spoon restaurant, Hanson explains why Billy and Wyatt have triggered such hostile feelings. "What you represent to them is freedom. . . . It's real hard to be free when you're bought and sold in the marketplace. Of course, don't ever tell anybody they're not free 'cause they're gonna get real busy killin' and maimin' to prove to you that they are. . . ."

Hanson's words prove prophetic. That night, a gang of men club and ax him to death in his sleeping bag.

Billy and Wyatt go on to a New Orleans whorehouse that Hanson had recommended. There, they celebrate Mardi Gras and go on an LSD trip in a cemetery with two young prostitutes. Then they are on the open road again, and Billy laughs triumphantly. "We've done it. We're rich, Wyatt. We did it, man." To which Wyatt answers cryptically, "We blew it."

Critics have debated his meaning. To me, Wyatt seems to be commenting on the futility of their nomadic life—a life that catches up much of the confused, aimless lives of the dissidents of their generation.

But Hopper said he really had in mind the fact that they have lost their innocence because their wealth is corrupt. It has come from a dope sale. "When Peter says, 'We blew it,' he's talking about easy money, that we should have used our energies to make it."

And then there is the final insult. Two hunters in a pickup truck spot Billy and Wyatt up ahead on their cycles and decide to scare them. One of the pickup riders points a shotgun at Billy and says, "Why don't you get a haircut?" In response, Billy gives him the finger.

Seconds later the man fires, blasting Billy off his cycle. Wyatt rushes to him at a grassy strip next to the road. "Oh my God," Billy says. "I'm gonna get him [the gunman]." But Billy is dying.

The pickup riders know they can't leave a witness behind, and they turn around. As Wyatt, seeking help, speeds by the truck, the hunter fires again. Wyatt, too, is killed, his motorcycle flying into the air, bursting into flame.

The camera pans from the burning wreckage and becomes an aerial shot. Credits roll, and we hear "Ballad of Easy Rider." "All I wanted was to be free," the song says, "And that's the way it turned out to be."

The end of the road for Wyatt and Billy.

Five Easy Pieces
(1970)

Directed by Bob Rafelson. Screenplay by Adrien Joyce from a story by Rafelson and Joyce. Photography, Laszlo Kovacs. Editors, Christopher Holmes and Gerald Sheppard. Music, Tammy Wynette and Pearl Kaufman. Produced by Rafelson and Richard Wechsler. Songs: "Stand by Your Man," B. Sherril, T. Wynette; "D-I-V-O-R-C-E," B. Braddock, C. Putnam; "When There's a Fire in Your Heart," W. Kilgore, S. Williams; "Don't Touch Me," H. Cochran. Songs sung by Tammy Wynette. Piano: Chopin, Fantasy in F Minor, Op. 49; Bach, Chromatic Fantasy and Fugue; Mozart, Piano Concerto in E-flat Major, K. 271; Chopin, Prelude in E Minor, Op. 28 No. 4; Mozart, Fantasy in D Minor, K. 397. Piano played by Pearl Kaufman. Columbia. Rated R. 96 minutes.

Robert Eroica Dupea	JACK NICHOLSON
Rayette Dipesto	KAREN BLACK
Elton	BILLY "GREEN" BUSH
Stoney	FANNIE FLAGG
Betty	SALLY ANN STRUTHERS
Twinky	MARLENA MACGUIRE
Recording Engineer	RICHARD STAHL
Partita Dupea	LOIS SMITH
Palm Apodaca	HELENA KALLIANIOTES
Terry Grouse	TONI BASIL
Waitress	LORNA THAYER
Catherine Van Ost	SUSAN ANSPACH
Carl Fidelio Dupea	RALPH WAITE
Nicholas Dupea	WILLIAM CHALLEE
Spicer	JOHN RYAN
Samia Glavia	IRENE DAILEY

"**I**'d like a plain omelet, no potatoes, tomatoes instead, a cup of coffee and wheat toast."

Jack Nicholson is giving his order to Lorna Thayer, a waitress in a roadside diner.

"No substitutions," says the waitress dryly.

"What do you mean?" he says, a bit put off. "You don't have any tomatoes?"

"Only what's on the menu," she answers. "You can have a number two—a plain omelet. It comes with cottage fries and rolls."

"I know what it comes with. But it's not what I want."

"I'll come back when you make up your mind." She turns to leave.

He grabs the hem of her uniform. "Wait a minute. I have made up my mind. I'd like a plain omelet, no potatoes on the plate. A cup of coffee and a side order of wheat toast."

"I'm sorry, we don't have any side orders of toast. English muffins or a coffee roll."

"What do you mean you don't have any side orders of toast?" Nicholson says, trying to control his mounting anger. "You make sandwiches, don't you?"

"Would you like to talk to the manager?" the exasperated waitress asks.

"You've got bread and a toaster of some kind?" Nicholson says, trying to demonstrate the utter simplicity of his order.

"I don't make the rules."

"Okay. I'll make it as easy for you as I can. I'd like an omelet, plain, and a chicken salad sandwich on wheat toast, no mayonnaise, no butter, no lettuce. And a cup of coffee . . ."

The waitress finally loses her patience. "You see that sign, sir?" The camera shows a sign on the wall that reads: "No Substitutions." The waitress snaps: "You'll have to leave. I'm not taking any

Jack Nicholson as Robert Dupea, a discontented drifter who keeps running from relationships.

more of that smartness and sarcasm."

"You see this sign?" Nicholson answers. With one fell swoop, he pushes all the water glasses and menus off the table.

This memorable sequence from *Five Easy Pieces*[1] has become a touchstone for generations of moviegoers. Some applaud at the end of the scene. Many have committed it to memory. They see Nicholson's outburst as a protest against the mindless rules of an overly organized society.

But *Five Easy Pieces* was more than just another counterculture movie pitting a misfit against the Establishment. It was a picture that tried to show man's eternal quest to find meaning in life by discovering his true self.

It did so by focusing on a classically trained musician who finds himself cast adrift—unable to live comfortably with his own cultured family or in the blue-collar world of oil rigs, country music, beer guzzling, and easy women. He is the rootless loner who keeps running because the only commitment he can make is to perpetual motion.

Many critics see the hero as a negative character. Director Bob Rafelson disagrees. "There are all kinds of great people who have moved from place to place in search of their identity," Rafelson said in an interview for this book. "They may be trying to find the one elusive adventure or romance or connection or relationship that will give them permanence and peace."

Nicholson's extraordinary performance had much to do with the success of the film. It was, in fact, his first starring role in a major movie. It was a long time coming. If any actor could be said to have paid his dues to the industry, that person would have to be Nichol-

Nicholson with Susan Anspach. She has the role of a talented classical pianist who attracts him.

son. In the 1950s and early 1960s, he played in dozens of B movies, many of them made on shoestring budgets by producer Roger Corman. Nicholson was, in fact, the only major actor to emerge from the so-called fringe Hollywood syndrome.

He played in such less-than-epic Corman films as *Cry Baby Killer* (1957), *Little Shop of Horrors* (1960), and *The Terror* (1963) with Boris Karloff. "Roger saved all our careers," Nicholson once said. "He kept us working when no one else would hire us. For this, we are all eternally grateful. For the fact that he was able to underpay us, he is eternally grateful."

After a while, Nicholson began appearing in pictures for large companies such as United Artists. Unfortunately, most were skimpy productions, too, and his performances were seldom mentioned in reviews. When *Variety* did call at-

tention to his role, as in *Hell's Angels on Wheels* (1967), it said his acting consisted "mostly of variations on a grin."

For a time, Nicholson turned to writing. He did several scripts, including *The Trip* (1967), a drama about drug abuse that he made with Peter Fonda, Bruce Dern, Susan Strasberg, and Dennis Hopper. He did another called *Head* (1968), which Rafelson directed, about a group called The Monkees. Nicholson felt it was "the best rock-'n'-roll movie ever made." *Variety* called it a "silly psychedelic pastiche."

Then things suddenly turned Nicholson's way. He almost got the role of C. W. Moss (which Michael J. Pollard played) in *Bonnie and Clyde* (1967). He lost out because he looked too much like Warren Beatty, the star.

However, when Rip Torn rejected an offer to play in *Easy Rider* (1969), Nicholson got a part. He played the likable, hard-drinking Southern lawyer. His charm and naturalness fascinated audiences and he got an Oscar

---

[1]It received Oscar nominations for best picture, best actor (Nicholson), and best actress (Black).

nomination for best supporting actor.

Recognizing his talent, Rafelson offered him a starring role in a picture yet to be written. The movie, which was to be *Five Easy Pieces*, was partly autobiographical and partly inspired by Senator Edward Kennedy.

Why Kennedy? "He was," said Rafelson, "the youngest son of a family of prominent people, upon whom had descended a great deal of pressure to be living up to his heritage."

Rafelson had written two scripts about this character before he got together with screenwriter Adrien Joyce. "She looked over the material and said, 'I think I know the character you want. Let's reinvent the story.'"

So they did. Rafelson suggested they start the character out as a roustabout in the oil business, then move the scene to the Northwest. "She proceeded to write the script as I drove to the Northwest and started to phone locations to her as I traveled. I decided to end up putting them on an island. That's pretty much how the script evolved some twelve weeks later."

Nicholson liked the finished product. It was, he said, "an honest statement about where a lot of people are who cannot act out their crisis to a successful conclusion." It took only thirty-three days to shoot.

Five Easy Pieces has been called a "road picture," a genre that is peculiarly American because it is about homeless people in search of something. In *Easy Rider*, the search was for a lifestyle, a place to settle down among like-thinking people and yet retain independence. But we never knew who the people really were and what made them the restless souls they turned out to be.

What sets *Five Easy Pieces* apart from other road films is that we come to know the hero's roots. He returns home. And his visit tells us why he left.

When we first meet Bobby Dupea (Nicholson), he is an oil-rigger in California, living with an empty-headed waitress named Rayette (Karen Black) who aspires to be a country music singer. She all but smothers him with affection.

But Bobby is a man suffering from an ill-defined malaise, and he can only tolerate her presence in small doses. When she sings along with a record, he tells her: "You play that thing one more time, and I'm going to melt it down into hair spray."

During the first half hour of the picture, we are in the world of the common man, the land of bowling alleys and mobile homes and honking cars.

Then the movie makes a 180-degree turn. We find that Bobby has a sister who is a concert pianist, that he comes from a family with a classical-music tradition, and that he too trained as a pianist but abandoned that life when he found he lacked the talent and dedication to be first-rate.

He visits his sister (Lois Smith) in a studio where she is recording, and she tells him that his father (William Challee), a former symphony conductor, has suffered two strokes. She urges him to go home to the family's island house in Puget Sound.

In one of the film's memorable scenes, Bobby tells Rayette she can't go along. As she sulks, he stalks out of their apartment. Her mood preys on him, and when he gets in his car, he can't drive off. He rages, screaming and cursing and throwing his body around the driver's seat. He knows she would be out of place among his family, but he hates to leave her so distraught. He quietly returns and invites her along.

Rafelson thought Black's performance in the movie was "extraordinary." At the same time, it typecast her. "She continued to play the character in the next five or ten movies," Rafelson said. "It was a real mistake, I think, not to try for something uniquely different."

Robert off for a day's work with his roustabout friend Elton (Billy "Green" Bush).

As Bobby and Rayette drive to Washington, the movie inserts some humorous sequences to break the somber atmosphere. They pick up two women whose car has broken down. One of them (Helena Kallianoites) is obsessed with junk littering the landscape. "People are filthy, that's what's wrong with people," she says. Launching into a neurotic diatribe, she adds, "I think they wouldn't be so violent if they were clean."

She is going to Alaska because someone has told her it is cleaner there. "That was before the big thaw," Bobby says, keeping a straight face.

The diner scene is the one people remember most, although Rafelson says he thinks it is not as good a sequence as those played off against Rayette or Bobby's father. But it is the only segment that came from Rafelson's original script. "Quite frankly, it's something I did for years myself," he said. "Every time I go into a restaurant, I rearrange the menu to get what I want."

Rafelson feels the scene makes an important statement about Bobby's nature. "It says that the rest of the world lives by rather ordinary and shallow rules. Part of what Bobby's life-style has become is to find the rules not only in something as meager as a restaurant but in all areas of life. . . . If you live by the rules, you don't go from one place to another drifting about. You get married or take on the job of being a rotten pianist in a family that has pushed the job upon you. The bolder thing is to reject your inheritance and to seek your own identity."

In Washington, Bobby leaves Rayette in a motel and goes to his family's home, a music-filled retreat on a wooded isle. There he meets his brother's fiancée (Susan Anspach), also an aspiring pianist. He sees her as a sexual challenge and seduces her. But he quickly becomes bored with his home environs and she becomes fed up with his moody disposition. She accuses him of being incapable of having any real feeling. "A person [who] has no love for himself," she tells him, "no respect for himself, no love for his friends, family, workers—how can he ask for love in return?"

The film probes no further into Bobby's background. And the weakness that I find in the picture is that we never discover the reason for his character flaw.

One day, Bobby goes off alone with his father. The old man is in a wheelchair. He can neither talk nor walk nor even feed himself. It is not clear whether he can understand anything, but Bobby talks to him as if he could, berating himself for failing to live up to his father's hopes. "I move around a lot," Bobby says. "Not because I'm looking for anything really. But I'm getting away from things that get bad if I stay. . . . The best thing I can do is apologize. We both know I was never really that good at it anyway. I'm sorry it didn't work out."

That emotion-charged scene produced the only disagreement between Rafelson and Nicholson. "It was over a transparency of emotions," Rafelson said. "I felt that if Bobby didn't reveal he had these emotions, then he would seem like a negative character, rather than a sympathetic character on a quest. He had to have some exposed nerve endings. Jack translated that into 'You mean you want me to cry?' He didn't want to do that.

"After a long, long discussion, he was utterly wiped out emotionally. That's when I shot the scene. We wrote it two minutes before we shot it. It was a static shot. I locked the camera, flipped the button, held the mike, and looked off in the opposite direction. So it was just Jack in the middle of the field. I did only one take."

One day, Rayette shows up in the family home, embarrassing Bobby by her lack of refinement. Nevertheless, after dinner when a pompous guest puts her down, Bobby explodes and leaves. He takes Rayette, but we sense they won't be together long.

Two ladies of the bowling alley (Sally Ann Struthers, *left*, and Marlena MacGuire).

Bobby and Rayette (Karen Black) in a tender moment.

The original script ended tragically. In the car, Rayette becomes a nuisance as she covers Bobby with kisses. He pushes her away, but she keeps distracting him and he turns the wheel violently. The car spins off the road into an embankment and plunges into the water. Only one person emerges, Rayette. She watches as several bubbles appear, then stop. "Bobby, you son of a bitch," she says and walks off.

"Something told me that wasn't the appropriate ending," Rafelson said. "This wasn't a character who was self-destructive in the obvious sense but someone searching for his identity. So I went off for several days and came up with sev-eral different endings. The one I ultimately used is the one you see in the movie."

In the film, Bobby drives off with Rayette. When they reach a gas station, she goes inside for some food. He steps into the men's room and peers at his features in a mirror. There and then, he decides to abandon Rayette. He leaves her with all his belongings—his car, his wallet, his money. He hops a northbound lumber truck. We see it pull off and disappear across a bleak horizon, taking Bobby toward the freedom and quest that make his life bearable.[2]

[2]Over the years, the picture has created an intriguing mystery—its title. Many have debated its meaning. Some say the five easy pieces refer to the five piano works played during the picture. Others insist it is the women in Bobby's life. Rafelson has finally given us the solution. "I had written a credit sequence. It showed a little boy in the same house we ultimately return to. In a panning shot, the camera comes to rest on the boy, sitting by his mother, playing from a well-known book of exercises called 'Five Easy Pieces.' It then becomes the full title of the movie. I decided not to shoot that," Rafelson explained, "because I wanted to keep the man's background elusive—as opposed to laying it out right there in the beginning of the movie. Then, I just couldn't come up with a better title."

The Graduate (1967)

Directed by Mike Nichols. 🎬 Screenplay by Calder Willingham and Buck Henry based on the novel by Charles Webb. Camera, Robert Surtees. Editor, Sam O'Steen. Music, David Grusin. Songs by Paul Simon sung by Simon and Garfunkel: "Mrs. Robinson," "The Sound of Silence," "April Come She Will," and "Scarborough Fair." Produced by Lawrence Turman. Embassy. 105 minutes.

Mrs. Robinson	ANNE BANCROFT
Ben Braddock	DUSTIN HOFFMAN
Elaine Robinson	KATHARINE ROSS
Mr. Braddock	WILLIAM DANIELS
Mr. Robinson	MURRAY HAMILTON
Mrs. Braddock	ELIZABETH WILSON
Carl Smith	BRIAN AVERY
Mr. Maguire	WALTER BROOKE
Mr. McCleery	NORMAN FELL
Second lady	ELISABETH FRASER
Mrs. Singleman	ALICE GHOSTLEY
Room clerk	BUCK HENRY
Miss De Witt	MARION LORNE
Berkeley student	RICHARD DREYFUSS

🎬 Academy Award winner

At a welcome-home party for a young man just out of college, a businessman sidles over, pulls him away and gives him some sage advice. "I just want to say one word to you . . . 'plastics.' There's a great future in plastics. Think about it."

This abbreviated formula for success comes from *The Graduate*, a film that drew hordes of young people to the movies in the 1960s. Older people followed to see what all the fuss was about.

The film's attraction was that it was saying something new—or so it was perceived. It attempted, among other things, to point up the burgeoning generation gap, a phenomenon that was preoccupying the youth of that decade. And so the movie quickly became a symbol of youthful rebellion. More than that, it took some telling swipes at the grossness of the upper-middle-class adult world. It was a study of coming of age and of alienation, of frustration, and of empty values.

The picture was based on a novel by Charles Webb, who, ironically, claimed he never went to see the film. "I was afraid if I saw the movie, I would have a nervous breakdown," he said. Webb was twenty-one when he wrote the book, his first novel. He got only a flat $20,000 for the movie sale, then another $5,000 when it became a runaway success and made millions. However, Webb's luck wasn't all bad. The reissue of his novel in paperback made well over a million dollars.

Webb's book read more like a screenplay. Most of it was straight dialogue. There was no physical description of the main characters. But Webb had nothing to do with the script. And he made no bones about attributing the movie's success to Dustin Hoffman and Mike Nichols.

Nichols, who had then directed only one other movie, went far out on a limb by putting Hoffman in the lead. Hoffman was unknown, and his test was anything but impressive.

In that test, Nichols asked him to sit on a bed and play a love scene with Katharine Ross. Looking at Hoffman, Ross remembered, her spirits fell. She thought: "He looks about three feet tall, so dead serious, so unkempt. This is going to be a disaster."

It was. He was so awkward and out of synch in their verbal fencing match that at one point when she turned around, all he could do was grab her backside.

"But," Hoffman said, "Nichols, clever guy that he is, saw something in me that he could use. Panic, maybe?" What Nichols really perceived was that Hoffman was perfect in the part of a confused young man groping to find his place in a society that repelled him.

Nevertheless, Hoffman's uncomfortable feelings during the screen test did not vanish during the filming. "I kept acting like on stage. Nichols would say: 'Very good, now do it again.' So I would

Ben (Dustin Hoffman) getting ready to storm the church and sweep away his sweetheart.

do what I thought was nothing. And it turned out to be enough."

Even though his performance made him a star, Hoffman thought the major credit for the movie's popularity should go to the director. "It's Nichols's picture, his victory, not mine. I look terrific up there—nobody will ever take such care with lighting on me again—but I don't have much feeling of personal accomplishment about it."

Part of that victory should go to the producer, Larry Turman. It was Turman who bought the rights to the little-known Webb novel, worked for a year to get the movie filmed, and hired Nichols. According to some accounts, it was also Turman who chose Hoffman.

A 1971 *New York Times* article said Turman picked Hoffman over Robert Redford for the title role. Turman said Redford made a screen test but was "too physically assured for the part. Redford gave a terrific test of a skillful, wonderful actor whose own qualities were totally wrong for the role. Dustin Hoffman was goony. . . . All the others we tested were playing at being goony."

Yet, successful though the picture was, it was a flawed movie. It broke into two distinct parts: the first a comedy, the second a romance. Those who hailed the movie insisted the parts had a unity. They felt that Ben's love for Elaine transposed him from a comic fumbler to a romantic figure.

Even so, the film was stylistically unbalanced. Most of the early interest was focused on Ben's inept affair with Elaine's mother, Mrs. Robinson. The melodramatic second half, in which he frenetically pursues her daughter, seems incongruous, even jarring. But Nichols keeps things racing at such breakneck speed he gets away with it—or almost.

Some film buffs were totally put off by the change of mood. The most colorfully phrased complaint came from a letter writer to the *New York Times*. "You can't change horses in midstream and expect this rider to keep up with you," said one William Herndon of New York City. "If I sit down to watch *The Importance of Being Earnest*, I don't expect the second-act curtain to reveal *A Streetcar Named Desire*."

Flawed or not, the film was a milestone of its era. For months, it was the prime topic of discussion at parties, no matter what the age group.

If you went to one of these gatherings and asked about the storyline, somebody might have told you something like this:

Ben Braddock, fresh from a successful college career in the East, returns to his upper-middle-class home in Los Angeles.

For all his credentials, Ben is really a kind of *nebech*, a harmless, inarticulate young man, confused about his values and the society he has been thrust into. At a homecoming cocktail party, he wanders about, flouncing from one fatuous group to another. "There's the award-winning scholar. . . . We're all so proud of you. . . . Proud. Proud. Proud. . . . Here's the track star. . . . What are you going to do now?"

The one relationship he makes is with Mrs. Robinson (Anne Bancroft), the neurotic wife of his father's partner. She lures Benjamin to her bedroom and casually disrobes while he looks on shocked, babbling moral platitudes.

But at their next meeting, he takes her to a hotel. What she sees in him remains a mystery. He keeps calling her Mrs. Robinson. He kisses her before she can exhale smoke from a cigarette. However, for better or worse, their affair begins.

Unlike most members of his sex, Benjamin tries to instill more meaning in their relationship than there is. Equally uncharacteristically, all Mrs. Robinson wants is a roll in the hay. "I don't think we have much to say to each other," she tells him.

Benjamin's mother and father begin to despair. When Benjamin isn't gone all night, he spends his time gazing in his tropical-fish aquarium or lounging on a raft in his backyard pool. His parents try to snap him out of his doldrums. Unaware of his true nocturnal activities, they arrange a date with Mrs. Robinson's daughter, Elaine, a former high school classmate.

Now the second part of the film starts. Benjamin falls hard for Elaine. "You're the first thing for so long that I like," he says. But their relationship is short-lived. When Mrs. Robinson finds her daughter is interested in Benjamin, she gives him an ultimatum: Either he leaves Elaine alone or she will tell her daughter everything.

Benjamin decides the best defense is a good offense. It turns out to be as costly a miscalculation as a blocked punt. When he confesses his affair with her mother, Elaine is outraged. She throws him out, goes back to college, and

Boredom sets in as Benjamin floats in his backyard pool wondering how to fit into an adult world that repels him.

The Hustler
(1961)

Produced and directed by Robert Rossen. Screenplay by Rossen and Sidney Carroll based on the novel by Walter Tevis. Art directors, Harry Horner ☆ and Albert Brenner. ☆ Sets, Gene Callahan. ☆ Photography, Gene Shuftan. ☆ Editor, Dede Allen. Filmed in New York City. 20th Century–Fox. B/W. 135 minutes.

Eddie Felson	PAUL NEWMAN
Sarah Packard	PIPER LAURIE
Bert Gordon	GEORGE C. SCOTT
Minnesota Fats	JACKIE GLEASON
Charlie Burns	MYRON McCORMICK
James Findley	MURRAY HAMILTON
Big John	MICHAEL CONSTANTINE
Preacher	STEFAN GIERASCH
Bartender	JAKE LaMOTTA
Cashier—Bennington's	GORDON B. CLARKE
Scorekeeper	ALEXANDER ROSE
Waitress	CAROLYN COATES
Young man	CARL YORK
Bartender	VINCENT GARDENIA
Willie	WILLIE MOSCONI
Turk	CLIFF PELLOW
Players	BRENDAN FAY, CHARLES DIERKOP, DONALD CRABTREE

☆ Academy Award winner

It wasn't made in color. It wasn't based on a best-selling novel to give it a presold audience. And it had no major financing.

In short, *The Hustler*[1] was the kind of movie you would expect on the second half of a double feature—a picture about a poolhall sharpie, a faded, tarnished bit of Americana.

But it was a sleeper, that unheralded, once-in-a-blue-moon film that exceeds the expectations of even its most optimistic backer. Shot at a cost of $150,000, it made over $8 million in its first year.

The fact is it was much more than the sleazy tale of a conman. With restraint and realism, the film told the absorbing story of an ambitious young man who learns some painful lessons about the true nature of life and love. Augmenting the picture's well-crafted plot was Gene Shuftan's imaginative photography that re-created the smoky world of the poolhall in harsh, shadowy images.

The movie benefited, too, from the craftsmanship of Robert Rossen, who had previously directed such dramas as *Body and Soul* (1947) and the Oscar-winning *All the King's Men* (1949). And it had solid performances from Paul Newman, Piper Laurie, George C. Scott, Myron McCormick, and Jackie Gleason.

Finally, its sparse but colorful dialogue added to its realistic portrait of the seamy side of life. Rossen and screenwriter Sidney Carroll wrote the scenario based on the novel by Walter Tevis.[2]

Here, for example, is the

The big match between Minnesota Fats (Jackie Gleason) and Fast Eddie Felson (Paul Newman).

[1]The movie had three name changes. It was called *The Hustler* during preproduction work. But Spyros P. Skouras, 20th Century-Fox president, thought the title might make audiences think of a prostitute. It became briefly *Stroke of Luck* and then *Sin of Angels*. However, the Motion Picture Association of America felt the latter title was too close to that of another current movie, *The Side of the Angels*. Rossen liked *The Hustler*. He thought it was a short, punchy title and persuaded the studio to go back to it.

Eddie and Sarah (Piper Laurie), an ex-alcoholic.

Sarah turns away from Eddie's new manager, Bert Gordon (George C. Scott), a shrewd gambler who loves to see men crack under pressure.

Fast Eddie makes the mistake of hustling one time too many. *From left:* Charles Dierkop, Newman, Donald Crabtree, Brendan Fay, Cliff Pellow.

hustler, Fast Eddie Felson, comparing the thrill he finds in shooting a game of pool to a jockey sitting on his horse:

"He's got all that speed and power underneath him. He's coming into the stall. The pressure is on him and he knows, just feels, when to let it go and how much. 'Cause he's got everything working for him—time and touch.

"Boy, it's a real good feeling when you're right and you know you're right. Like all of a sudden, I've got oil in my arms. The pool cue is part of me. It's got nerves in it. You feel the roll of those balls. You don't have to look. You just know. You make shots nobody's made before, and you play that game the way nobody's played it before."

Yet, for all its sterling features, the film did not win the kind of recognition it deserved. Nominated for nine Academy Awards, it had the bad luck to be made the same year as the musical *West Side Story*, a film that swept ten Oscars. *The Hustler* salvaged awards only for camerawork and design.

In addition to being disappointed at the Oscar derby, Newman was upset by the way 20th Century-Fox marketed the picture. To build prestige, studios usually restrict a big movie to a single first-run house in major cities and keep it there as long as it draws crowds.

But a succession of flops and the enormous budget overruns of *The Longest Day* (1962) and *Cleopatra* (1963) left Fox in a cash-flow bind. So it elected to send the film to the neighborhood theaters almost from the outset. Newman thought the picture should have run in a single art house in New York City, then been entered in the Cannes and Venice festivals.

"If we made a bad showing at the festivals that would be too bad," Newman said. "But I think we would have done well. Then, with this kind of buildup, we should have given the picture a general release. Fox was too greedy for a buck to do this."

Even so, the picture surmounted these drawbacks, due, in large part, to its interesting set of characters. Fast Eddie Felson is not just another poolhall conman. Out to beat the best player in the country on his own turf, Eddie approaches the game with reverence. When he and his manager, Charlie Burns (McCormick), step into the poolroom where Minnesota Fats (Gleason) holds sway, they look around for a minute.

"It's quiet," says Burns.

"Yeah," says Eddie. "Like a church. The church of the good hustler."

Later, when Fats makes his entrance at his usual time, promptly at eight o'clock, Eddie challenges him to high-stakes pool. The round man quickly wins Eddie's admiration. "Look at the way he moves—like a dancer. And those fingers, those chubby fingers. And that stroke—like he's playing a violin or something."

Eddie is sharp, too. He runs up an $18,000 lead as the game moves through the wee hours of morning.

In the hands of these virtuosi, the pool sticks wave like wands. The glistening balls make sharp, clicking sounds as they collide on the cloth of green.

The hours fly by and the pressure intensifies. And that is one thing Eddie has never learned to handle. While Fats keeps fresh by washing his face and dousing his hands with talcum powder, Eddie slowly gets drunk.

"Stay with this kid," Bert Gordon (Scott), a shrewd gambler, tells Fats. "He's a born loser."

Sure enough, Eddie begins to lose his touch. Fats starts gaining strength and gradually cleans Eddie out. His confidence shattered, Eddie starts going downhill. He leaves his manager and starts hustling alone, pretending to be a novice in games with local players, then making the key shot when the big money is down.

Eddie, a poolhall shark, discusses strategy with his manager, Charlie Burns (Myron McCormick).

In this netherworld of bars and taverns, he meets another drifter, an ex-alcoholic named Sarah (Laurie). They find a strange mutual attraction and begin living together. One night, four waterfront poolhall toughs break Eddie's thumbs when they catch on to his game. Sarah becomes a source of strength for Eddie. She nurses him and restores his pride.

His thumbs mended, he accepts gambler Gordon's offer to go on the road, taking Sarah along. As the days pass, she sees Eddie is only getting peanuts. Gordon is making the big money, although his real enjoyment comes not from winning big stakes but from watching others crumble and lose.

She tries to get Eddie to see what is really happening. But Eddie is too involved in his comeback. One night, Sarah, despair-ing of life and her relationship with Eddie, kills herself.

Stunned and hurt, but with his character toughened, Eddie gears himself for another match with Fats. This time he knows how to pace himself. Once he starts a roll, there is no stopping his sharpshooting spree. It is only a matter of time before Fats concedes.

With that challenge mastered, Eddie confronts Gordon. He breaks his contract with the sadistic gambler, finally aware that the only real winners in the poolhall world are the Bert Gordons who control the game.

Two decades after it was made, *The Hustler* holds up as a film that defines the antihero of the 1960s. He is a man who reaches the mountaintop only to find it wasn't worth the climb.

²Tevis was a gifted, if underrated storyteller. Born in San Francisco, he changed careers in midlife to become a free-lance writer in New York City after teaching Milton as a college English professor in Ohio. In addition to *The Hustler*, he wrote a second novel that was made into a movie, *The Man Who Fell to Earth*. The 1976 film starred David Bowie. Tevis wrote both books while working for the Kentucky Highway Department. "Originally, I wanted to be a poet," he said, "and I used to compose a daily sonnet on the way to the poolroom in Lexington, Kentucky. Actually, I learned about gambling after enlisting in the navy on my seventeenth birthday. I played poker for seventeen months on Okinawa. That was the background of the poolroom hustler. Milton came later."

After the success of these books, he became a professor at Ohio University. In 1978, he gave up teaching and rented a small apartment in New York City, where he began writing full-time, turning out two books a year. His work included: *Mockingbird, Far from Home*, a sequel to *The Hustler* called *The Color of Money, The Steps of the Sun*, and *The Queen's Gambit*, a story of a girl who becomes a contender for the world chess championship. Tevis died of lung cancer in 1984 at the age of fifty-six.

The Last Picture Show
(1971)

Directed by Peter Bogdanovich. Based on the novel by Larry McMurtry. Screenplay, McMurtry and Bogdanovich. Photography, Robert Surtees. Art director, Walter Scott Herndon. Editor, Donn Cambern. Songs sung by Hank Williams, Bob Wills and his Texas Playboys, Tony Bennett, Lefty Frizzell, Frankie Laine, Johnnie Ray, Eddy Arnold, Eddie Fisher, Phil Harris, Pee Wee King, Hank Snow, Johnny Standley, Kay Starr, Hank Thompson, Webb Price, Jo Stafford. Produced by Stephen J. Friedman. A BBS Production. Filmed in Archer City, Texas. B/W. Rated R. 118 minutes.

Sonny Crawford	TIMOTHY BOTTOMS
Duane Jackson	JEFF BRIDGES
Jacy Farrow	CYBILL SHEPHERD
Sam the Lion	BEN JOHNSON ★
Ruth Popper	CLORIS LEACHMAN ★
Lois Farrow	ELLEN BURSTYN
Genevieve	EILEEN BRENNAN
Abilene	CLU GULAGER
Billy	SAM BOTTOMS
Charlene Duggs	SHARON TAGGART
Lester Marlow	RANDY QUAID
Sheriff	JOE HEATHCOCK
Coach Popper	BILL THURMAN
Joe Bob Blanton	BARC DOYLE
Miss Mosey	JESSIE LEE FULTON
Bobby Sheen	GARY BROCKETTE

★ Academy Award winner

As first-time producer Stephen Friedman remembers it, his campaign to get backing for *The Last Picture Show* was an uphill battle.

"All the major studios told me that nobody would be interested in a film about the 1950s," Friedman said. "They said that the fif-ties were not yet a 'real period.' They said no one is very interested in pictures about teenagers. And they said nobody is interested in stories about Texas."

As it turned out, the studios were wrong—on all counts. But only Friedman's persistence and his faith in Larry McMurtry's novel made him see it through to the end. Nevertheless, it took three years from the time Friedman acquired the option on McMurtry's novel until filming began.

"The longer I spent trying to interest people in the story, the more difficult it became, because it seems that people are attracted to stories that are brand-new on the market."

In fact, Friedman's option ran out and he had to make a major decision: give up his quest or borrow a small fortune and buy the rights outright. Friedman's agent and lawyers advised him not to buy. Nonetheless, he decided to take the plunge.

Then, a few weeks later, he saw a first picture by a young filmmaker that sealed the fate of his venture. The movie was *Targets*. The director was Peter Bogdanovich.

Although *Targets* was a low-budget movie, Friedman was able to appreciate Bogdanovich's resourcefulness and ingenuity. Then things started to fall in line. BBS Productions agreed to finance the film, and Bogdanovich turned out to be familiar with the McMurtry novel and eager to direct it.

Bogdanovich's interest in films traced back to his youth. A New Yorker who went to Collegiate, a fashionable prep school, he became a movie addict in his teens, writing critiques for the New Yorker revival movie house. He went on to direct in stock and Off-Broadway before producer Roger Corman gave him his first big break in Hollywood. Corman put

Duane (Jeff Bridges) hitches his trousers after making love with Jacy (Cybill Shepherd) in a motel room.

him to work on the script of the B picture *The Wild Angels*, a Peter Fonda motorcycle movie, and let him direct some scenes.

Impressed with what he saw, Corman offered Bogdanovich a chance to direct *Targets*, a picture about a crazed sniper. There were two conditions. One was that he use Boris Karloff (because Karloff owed Corman two days of shooting). And two was that the film work in some sequences of *The Terror*, a picture Corman had shot earlier with Karloff. Bogdanovich not only met those conditions, but pulled off the project brilliantly.

Another two years went by—during which Bogdanovich had three failures—before he started *The Last Picture Show*. "I was really interested in McMurtry's novel because of the period," Bogdanovich said. "The idea of using old movie and TV clips and hit records excited me. I also saw the story as a Texas version of [Orson] Welles's *The Magnificent Ambersons*, which was about the end of a way of life caused by the coming of the automobile. This was about the end of a way of life caused by the coming of television."

Another chancy idea was the decision to pick a nonstar cast. Jimmy Stewart was considered for the part of Sam the Lion, Dorothy McGuire for Lois Farrow (in part because she resembled Cybill Shepherd, who played Lois's daughter), and Vera Miles as Ruth. But Bogdanovich insisted on unfamiliar faces. He wanted nothing interfering with the total identification of the characters with the story.

The gamble paid off. There were sensitive performances by Ben Johnson as the rural elder statesman, Jeff Bridges as a fun-loving teenager, Shepherd, in her film debut, as the prettiest, bitchiest girl in town, and Ellen Burstyn as her sexy mother. Most impressive was the acting of Timothy Bottoms, playing a youngster who learns the meaning of friendship as he grows into manhood.

Then there was the dusty town of Anarene, where all the action occurs and which itself became a central character. "Everything is flat here," says Lois Farrow. "There is nothing to do." It is in this windblown hamlet that young Sonny (Bottoms) grows up.

We first see him in his pickup truck, hillbilly music blaring, as he buckets into town to meet his girl, Charlene (Sharon Taggart), at the picture show. It is 1951, a Saturday, and Sonny, rushing from another losing effort for his high school football team, is late.

He's missed the cartoon and newsreel. "The main show has just started," says the theater owner, Miss Mosey (Jessie Lee Fulton). "So I'll just charge you thirty cents." That kind of treatment, of course, is down-home stuff. But it is also part of the reason the movie house is on the way out.

Inside, Sonny finds Charlene and they slip into the back row, pop out their bubble gum, and start smooching. It's their anniversary. They started going steady a year ago. But Charlene is a pale shadow of Elizabeth Taylor up on the screen in all her long-lashed, velvet-eyed glory in *Father of the Bride* (1950).

After the show, they park in a lover's lane where, in the midst of some heavier necking, Charlene nags Sonny about forgetting to get her an anniversary present. By now, Sonny has tired of Charlene and lets her know he wants to break up.

It's no great loss, she shrugs. After all, he's never been in style. He doesn't have a ducktail. And he doesn't play in the backfield, either. "You give me back my pictures, too," she pouts. "I don't want you showing them to all the boys and telling them how hot I am."

There's not much to Anarene, either, and so we see the kids pass the time at a poolhall run by Sam (Johnson). Sometimes they go to a diner and a fast-food drive-in while music of the day—songs like "Cold, Cold Heart"—strums in the background.

Sonny and his pal Billy (Sam Bottoms), a retarded youngster.

Sonny (Timothy Bottoms), a youth coming of age in the 1950s in a tiny Texas town, visits a friendly waitress (Eileen Brennan).

One day, Coach Popper (Bill Thurman) asks Sonny to take his wife (Cloris Leachman) to see the doctor. If Sonny does, the coach says he'll get him out of civics class. "That's the best offer I had all day," says Sonny.

After her visit, Mrs. Popper invites Sonny inside for a Dr Pepper, then begins crying. Sonny doesn't know quite what to make of her—actually, she is starved for affection—until one night he bumps into her in the dark outside a school dance. They kiss, and the next time he takes her to the doctor, they go to her home and make love.

Meanwhile, other threads of plot are spinning out. Duane is making a play for Jacy, spoiled and beautiful. But her mother eventually convinces her that there's no future here. "You ought to sleep with him a few times," her mother says. "Then you'd see there isn't any magic in it."

In fact, Jacy ditches Duane to swim nude at the posh home of a rich college boy (Gary Brockette). He likes her but can't get serious about her because she is still a virgin. "Come see me when you're not," he says. She decides to use Duane to take care of that technicality. Duane's first attempt fails—"I don't know what happened," he mumbles—but he comes through the next time with flying colors. His classmates park

outside the Cactus Motel, and he swaggers out with all the bravado of a macho man.

The father figure for Sonny is Sam, a knowledgeable old-timer. When Sonny goes fishing with Sam and his slow-witted boy, Billy (Sam Bottoms), Sam reminisces. "I brought a young lady swimming down here once. Me and this lady was pretty wild.... We used to come down here on horseback and go swimming without no bathing suits.... She bet me a silver dollar she could beat me across. She did."

"Why didn't you marry her after your wife died?" Sonny asks.

"She was already married. If she was here, I'd probably be just as crazy now as I was then in about five minutes. Isn't that ridiculous? Being crazy about a woman like her is always the right thing to do. Being a decrepit old bag of bones—that's what's ridiculous. Getting old."

A few days later, Sam dies suddenly. "Keeled over one of the snooker tables," a local good ole boy tells Sonny. "Had a stroke. He left you the poolhall."

Things start changing after Sam's death. Sonny takes Billy under his wing and tries his hand at running the poolhall. The senior class graduates. Duane leaves to join a wildcat crew. Jacy, bored because she doesn't have a beau, lures Sonny on an elopement,

which her enraged parents nip in the bud.

One day, Duane returns in uniform. He's off to Korea the next day. So he and Sonny spend the night at the movies. They are the only ones in the theater, and, in fact, business has gotten so bad it's the last picture show. The movie they see is *Red River* (1948).

"Nobody wants to come to shows no more," Miss Mosey says. "There's baseball in the summer and TV all the time."

When the bus pulls in, Duane and Sonny shake hands. "I'll see you in a year or two if I don't get shot," says Duane.

Minutes later, Sonny gets another shock. A truck hits and kills Billy as he stands in the middle of the road where he liked to sweep the street. "What was he doing there, anyway?" one of the townsfolk asks.

"He was sweeping, you sons of bitches," Sonny yells. And he carries him off. Alone and grief-stricken, Sonny drives to Ruth Popper's house.

At first, she turns him out, bitter at the way he dropped her for Jacy. But then she realizes how hurt he is. When he extends his hand, she grasps it. They hold each other, as the camera dissolves to a long shot of Anarene's deserted, sand-streaked main street and pans to the now closed Royal Theatre.

Cloris Leachman as Ruth Popper, a coach's wife who tries to escape her sterile life by having an affair with Sonny.

Sam the Lion (Ben Johnson) with his ward, Billy. Johnson won an Oscar for his performance as the bluff old Texan.

The Leopard (1963)

Directed by Luchino Visconti. Screenplay by Visconti, Suso Cecchi D'Amico, Pasquale Festa Companile, Massimo Franciosa, and Enrico Medioli. Based on the novel *Il Gattopardo* by Giuseppe di Lampedusa. Photographed in De Luxe color by Giuseppe Rotunno. Music by Nino Rota with an unpublished waltz by Giuseppe Verdi. Costumes, Piero Tosi. Produced by Goffredo Lombardo. 20th Century-Fox. A Titanus Production. Filmed in Sicily. 165 minutes (originally 205 minutes).

Fabrizio Corbero, Prince of Salina (the Leopard)	BURT LANCASTER
Tancredi, Prince of Falconeri	ALAIN DELON
Angelica Sedàra	CLAUDIA CARDINALE
Don Calogero Sedàra	PAOLO STOPPA
Maria Stella, Princess of Salina	RINA MORELLI
Father Pirrone	ROMOLO VALLI
Don Ciccio Tumeo	SERGE REGGIANI
Cavalier Chevally	LESLIE FRENCH
Concetta	LUCILLA MORLACCHI
Francesco Paolo	PIERRE CLEMENTI
Colonel Pallavicino	IVO GERRANI
Count Cavriaghi	MARIO GIROTTI (TERENCE HILL)
The Garibaldino general	GIULIANO GEMMA
Carolina	IDA GALLI
Caterina	OTTAVIA PICCOLO
Paolo	CARLO VALENZANO
The Little Prince	BROOK FULLER
Mariannina	OLIMPIA CAVALLI

When the Cannes Film Festival's 1963 Golden Palm Award winner, *Il Gattopardo*, crossed the Atlantic in August of that year in a shortened English-dubbed version as *The Leopard*, critics had a field day nit-picking.

No one questioned the film's visual beauty. But one reviewer blasted the star, Burt Lancaster, for speaking in a "blunt American voice that lacks the least suggestion of being Sicilian." Another found the English soundtrack "jarring and ultimately disturbing." Claudia Cardinale was either "voluptuously beautiful" or made up to look "like a gypsy." Finally, Father Pirrone's accents were clearly those of character actor Kurt Kaznar.

The director, Luchino Visconti, joined the critical chorus. Angry over 20th Century-Fox's dubbing and cuts, Visconti said, "It is now a work for which I acknowledge no paternity at all."

Audiences yawned and stayed home. The film was a box-office washout.

The Italian version, briefly revived in 1983, set off another round of grumbling. Lancaster's dubbed Italian was "raspy and rough." The colors of the shortened film, described twenty years before as "warm and dramatic," were now "muddy and garish." Its sound was "1960s Bronx."

So, the question may be asked: Is it worth it to sit for two hours and forty minutes looking at a slowly paced story of a Sicilian prince who lived in 1860 and came to terms with the destiny of his class? Indeed it is.

Seeing *The Leopard* is akin to going to an art museum or an opera. You get from it what you bring to it. It's better to read the book first. This elegant, humorous, and wistful novel was written in the mid-1950s by a Sicilian nobleman, Giuseppe Tomasi di Lampedusa. The book, published posthumously, is a thinly veiled biography of his great-grandfather, who lived through the Risorgimento when Garibaldi's Redshirts fought the Bourbon armies and succeeded in unifying Italy under Victor Emmanuel of Savoy. Its publishers thought it would interest only the intelligentsia. But the book captured international attention and acclaim. Historians noted that Lampedusa's story paralleled the final fall of the ruling classes under Mussolini.

It took another Italian nobleman, Luchino Visconti di Modrone, whose family came to Sicily with Charles of Anjou and dates back to Desiderius, Charlemagne's father-in-law, to bring it to the screen.

Lancaster, recalling Visconti in

The Leopard, Fabrizio Corbero, Prince of Salina (Burt Lancaster), reflects on the transience of life and the certitude of the stars.

Fed up with the hysterics of his pious wife, the Prince visits his Palermo mistress, Mariannina (Olimpia Cavalli). This scene was eliminated from the shortened English version.

Don Calogero Sedàra (Paolo Stoppa) introduces his daughter Angelica (Claudia Cardinale) to a smitten Tancredi (Alain Delon).

a rare 1983 interview with the *New York Times*, said, "The Visconti used to own Milan. He knew the leopards, those aristocrats, like the back of his hand. There was one scene where I had to open a drawer to take out some money. And when I opened it, I found magnificent silk shirts that had been made for me. I said to the cameraman, 'Does the camera see these?' He said, 'No.' I said to Visconti, 'Why are they there?' He said, 'You're the Prince. Is for you to touch.'"

And Lancaster is the Prince. Although he claims to have been third choice after Nikolai Cherkassov, who played Alexander Nevsky in Eisenstein's epic Russian film, and Sir Laurence Olivier, Lancaster's perceptive performance as Fabrizio Corbero, the Prince of Salina, whose coat of arms is a leopard rampant, is brilliant.

He is autocratic and belligerent, but also astute and thoughtful. Even Lancaster's physical attributes are faithful to Lampedusa. "Not that he was fat, just very large and strong. [His] rosy skin and honey-colored hair... betrayed the German origin of his mother."

The Leopard is a simple story.

All the clues come in the first few moments. As Nino Rota's bittersweet score plays in the background, a hot Sicilian breeze flutters the curtains of the ornate villa where the Prince leads his family and household in the daily ritual of the Rosary. Outside, in the garden, servants discover the body of a soldier killed fighting in nearby Palermo. A wind of change sweeps into a stronghold of traditional aristocracy.

The Leopard will deal with the ill wind in due time. First, he must calm his wife, the pious and hysterical Princess Maria Stella, played by Rina Morelli with all the nuances of a repressed and rejected mate. This union, begun as a love match years before, is now mostly boring and suffocating to Fabrizio, although laced with occasional moments of tenderness. He has done his duty to the House of Salina and has produced with Maria Stella seven amiable but nondescript offspring.

"Seven children I've had with her, Father," the Leopard brusquely retorts to Father Pirrone (Romolo Valli) after that worthy priest timidly attempts to rebuke him for visiting a local whore. "And I've never even seen her navel. I'm a vigorous man. How

can I find satisfaction with a woman who makes the Sign of the Cross before every embrace and cries, 'Gesumaria'?"

The bright spot in the Prince's life is his irrepressible and adventurous nephew Tancredi, the impoverished Prince of Falconeri, a dashing, young, and handsome Alain Delon. With the fire of opportunism in his eyes, Tancredi rushes off to join the Redshirts after telling "Big Uncle," "If we want things to stay as they are, things will have to change." The Prince recognizes this truth. His own luxurious life-style depends upon the domination of the peasants by either the aristocracy or the bourgeoisie. He knows his class is dying, and bids Tancredi goodbye with tolerant affection.

Now the family goes on its annual retreat to the summer palace at Donnafugata. In a magnificent scene, underscored again by Rota's splendid music, a convoy of carriages and horses makes its exhausting way through the sunbaked landscape of Sicily.

The vulgar, nouveau riche mayor, Don Calogero Sedàra (Paolo Stoppa), who has had the foresight to take advantage of changing times and has bought hundreds of olive groves, making him even richer than the Prince, meets this entourage. A scene of pure feudalism takes place. A jangling, off-key local band (another master stroke by Rota) plays as the House of Salina slowly alights from its carriages and greets the townspeople. The ancient major-domo of the palace, staff in hand, is pleased to hand over to the Prince "the Palace, in the same condition as it was left."

In the sweltering sunlight, the family proceeds afoot to the cathedral, where they sit in a long row, still and dusty as statues untouched by years, a final bastion of decaying aristocracy.

But the duties of the Salinas do not stop here. They must entertain the townspeople at a lavish party that very evening. Don Calogero arrives in an ill-fitting tailcoat, with apologies that his wife cannot come: she is indisposed. This is not big news. La Signora has not been seen for years except by those who attend the 5:00 A.M. Mass, where she wears a heavy veil. According to Don Ciccio Tumeo (Serge Reggiani), the organist and Fabrizio's hunting partner, she is so beautiful Don Calogero keeps her locked up. She is also the daughter of the unspeakable vulgarian "Peppe 'Mmerda."

In her place, Don Calogero produces his ravishingly beautiful and voluptuous daughter Angelica (Claudia Cardinale). It takes one look for the Prince to perceive that she and Tancredi are made for each other. She comes not only with beauty, but also with a handsome dowry which Don Calogero, beaming satisfaction, is bound to offer in the form of many olive groves and bags of gold coins. Although the Prince's daughter Concetta (Lucilla Morlacchi) has loved Tancredi in her passive way, Fabrizio Corbero knows she lacks the spirit Tancredi needs. So what if Angelica is the granddaughter of Peppe 'Mmerda? She will give Tancredi the fire he needs to become an ambassador.

So the Leopard agrees to this marriage against the snobbism of Don Ciccio and Father Pirrone and the hysterics of Maria Stella. In a plebiscite, Sicily opts for unification, and the citizens celebrate with fireworks as Don Ciccio cries, "I voted no, but they said yes." Fabrizio drinks a nasty-looking glass of white wine (background color of the Bourbon lily) under a hideous picture of Victor Emmanuel.

Don Calogero, overjoyed by this good fortune, forks over the

expected olive groves and bags of gold. He even confides that his family, too, comes from nobility— "Only one link missing." Amused and disgusted, but satisfied that Tancredi's precarious fortunes are now assured, the Leopard kisses Don Calogero.

The climactic scene is a sumptuous forty-minute ball, where Tancredi and the Prince introduce Angelica to society. Don Calogero, now attired in appropriate evening clothes, longingly wonders what the priceless antique candelabra might bring on the market. A boring general drives Fabrizio to refuge in the library, where he ruminates on the death of his class and his own impending death. Angelica finds him, and to a never-before-performed Verdi waltz, they dance. Age and youth, nobility and bourgeoisie, are united. Fabrizio puts his family into his carriage and walks home, reflecting on the transcience of life and the eternity of the stars.

The Leopard, admittedly, is not to every taste. But it is a fascinating evocation of the passing of a society and the displacement of one class by another. To those who are interested in history, it is a film not to be missed.

—**Sara Zinman**.

Don Calogero registers approval as the Prince casts his vote for the unification of Italy. Father Pirrone (Romolo Valli, hat in hand) keeps a poker face.

After the ball, the Prince asks Tancredi to see Maria Stella home. Recognizing the demise of his class, and knowing his death is imminent, he walks home alone.

Lonely Are the Brave
(1962)

Directed by David Miller. Screenplay by Dalton Trumbo based on the novel *The Brave Cowboy* by Edward Abbey. Music, Jerry Goldsmith. Camera, Philip Lathrop. Editor, Leon Barsha. Producer, Edward Lewis. Universal. B/W. 107 minutes.

Jack Burns	KIRK DOUGLAS
Jerri Bondi	GENA ROWLANDS
Sheriff Johnson	WALTER MATTHAU
Paul Bondi	MICHAEL KANE
Hinton	CARROLL O'CONNOR
Harry	WILLIAM SCHALLERT
Gutierrez	GEORGE KENNEDY
Reverend Hoskins	KARL SWENSON
First deputy in bar	BILL MIMS
Deputy Glynn	DAN SHERIDAN
Old man	MARTIN GARRALAGA
Prisoner	LALO RIOS
One-armed man	BILL RAISCH

*L*onely Are the Brave is not so much a cowboy story as it is a story of the struggle of a maverick who happens to be a cowboy.

That lends a broader appeal to the picture. It is really about the plight of any individual who has been left in the wake of advancing civilization—in this case, an aging prairie outdoorsman unwilling to relinquish his freedom to a society that fences him in and crisscrosses his sagebrush with superhighways.

In the end, the machine and "progress" prevail. But the picture celebrates the noble effort of a natural man to escape the technological age.

Unfortunately, the movie, whose simple story appealed to audiences at several levels, was a commercial flop. It got good reviews—New York's *Cue* magazine, for example, called it "an extraordinary motion picture"—but it failed to attract audiences after its opening. So Universal, its distributor, withdrew the movie,

causing no end of grief to its creators and its star, Kirk Douglas.

"What made me sad was how badly the studio handled it," Douglas said in an interview for this book. "I pleaded with them to try it in the smaller theaters, in the art houses, so people could discuss it.

"Instead, they just released it. It was out of circulation before the reviews from *Time*, *Newsweek*, and other publications that raved about it had a chance to create any interest. Then, because the egos of studio heads were at stake, they buried the picture."

Nevertheless, the film remains Douglas's favorite of the seventy-odd movies he has made. That includes such outstanding pictures as *Champion* (1949), *Detective Story* (1951), and *Paths of Glory* (1957).

"It [*Lonely Are the Brave*] pleases me," Douglas said. "The test of art is time. I see so many places over the world where this picture keeps coming up. There is even a cult about it."

Douglas was sixty-seven when he was interviewed in 1984, but he was still active. He headed his own production outfit, the Bryna Company, named for his mother, in Beverly Hills, and had just finished a western called *Draw*, with James Coburn, made for Home Box Office.

Why did he single out *Lonely* as the picture he liked best? First, he said, he identified with the role. "This guy was such an anachronism, especially now. One of

---

A barroom visit ends in a vicious brawl between Jack Burns (Kirk Douglas) and a one-armed man (Bill Raisch), who would later play the killer in the television series "The Fugitive."

Jack Burns, last of the old-time cowboys, scans the mountains he must scale in his bid for freedom.

the biggest problems we have is the lowering of our morals. Cheating in our society is taken for granted. Here, in *Lonely Are the Brave*, is a pure fellow who goes back to what was supposedly the ideal standards of the early-type cowboy. I loved the character. He was a modern Don Quixote. I was touched by him."

Even though he liked the part, Douglas thought the picture was poorly named. "I fought the title," he said. "The book [by Edward Abbey] was called *The Brave Cowboy*. I wanted to call the movie *The Last Cowboy*, which is what he was. Universal put it in the computer and out came *Lonely Are the Brave*. I hate pretentiousness in movies."

Nevertheless, the film had an important message. "To me, the movie says how tough it is to be an individual. Society squashes us down. It tells us, 'Don't stick your head up too far.'"

Equally important, Douglas said, is the fact that the picture's plot stood by itself as a story. "A movie is made for entertainment. The crucial thing it must do is take people out of reality, out of the tensions of the world they live in. It must make them live vicariously with what is happening on the screen. If they then can find a message, fine. But the statement has to be secondary."

Dalton Trumbo emerged from years of obscurity after he was blacklisted during the 1950s to do

Above left: Burns visits his best friend only to be told by his wife (Gena Rowlands) that he is in jail.

Left: In jail, Burns meets his old friend (Michael Kane) and a tough lawman (George Kennedy).

the script. It was a well-crafted scenario that set up the theme in the very first sequence.

The camera pans from a horse standing on a scrubby New Mexico range to his rider (Douglas) sleeping nearby. Overhead, jets screech by, waking the cowboy. He looks up at the vapor trails, then decides it is time to move on. But the range is being fenced in, and he has to clip wires and get his horse to dodge trucks on a highway before he can reach his destination—the modest home of an old friend, Paul Bondi (Michael Kane).

His pal isn't home. His wife (Gena Rowlands) says her husband has been jailed for harboring "wetbacks." That's not a crime to the cowboy. In his mind, his friend was merely helping others who crossed a fence between nations.

"Good for him," says the cowboy. "... Ever notice how many fences there are getting to be? Signs say, 'No hunting. No admission. Private property. Closed area.' ... Paul just didn't naturally see the use of it. So he acted as if it weren't there. When people sneaked across, he felt they were just people. So he helped them."

Paul's wife doesn't see the cowboy's point. "The world you and Paul live in doesn't exist. Maybe it never did. Out there is the real world. And it's got real borders and real fences. And real trouble. Either you play by the rules or you lose."

Her words have no effect. The cowboy gets himself thrown in jail by letting a one-armed war veteran (Bill Raisch) pick a fight with him in a bar. ("I was intrigued to see a one-armed guy who was a heavy," Douglas said. "Life doesn't always work the way you think.")

In jail, the cowboy offers to help his pal Paul break out. Paul isn't willing to risk doubling his sentence. So the cowboy escapes alone and becomes the target of

a modern posse—an army helicopter and jeeps mounted with walkie-talkies.

In a superbly orchestrated chase sequence, the cowboy leads Sheriff Johnson (Walter Matthau) and his deputies through craggy mountain passes and ravines. So expert and daring is the cowboy's flight that he soon wins the sheriff's silent admiration.

Yet, ironically, after the cowboy climbs the mountain and gallops away through a forest, his bid for freedom comes to a tragic end.

On a slick, rain-darkened highway, a heavy tractor-trailer driven by a sleepy driver (Carroll O'Connor) crashes into the cowboy and his horse. The final indignity is that the truck's cargo is toilets.

Lying on the ground, the cowboy winces as he hears the anguished whinnies of his dying mount. When someone shoots the

horse, the cowboy seems to relax. But there is a strained look on his face, and his eyes, open and unblinking, seem not to be making any connections.

An ambulance crew lifts him onto a stretcher.

"He ain't going to die?" the frightened truck driver asks.

"How do I know?" the ambulance driver says matter-of-factly and speeds away. The last shot shows the cowboy's hat left behind on the rain-spattered highway.

Douglas did not think the ending was ambiguous. "I could have played the scene where my head rolls and I'm dead," he said. "I purposely decided not to do that because the horse represented his kind of life. When that horse died, his world died, too. So he died. Whether he died figuratively or actually doesn't matter."

An angry Kennedy looks after the fleeing Burns.

Nashville
(1975)

Produced and directed by Robert Altman. Script, Joan Tewkesbury. Photography, Paul Lohmann. Music arranged and supervised by Richard Baskin. Executive producers, Martin Starger and Jerry Weintraub. Editors, Sidney Levin and Dennis Hill. Songs: "Keep a' Goin'" and "200 Years" by Henry Gibson and Richard Baskin; "I'm Easy," "It Don't Worry Me," and "Honey" by Keith Carradine; ☆ "Down to the River," "Bluebird," "Tapedeck in His Tractor (The Cowboy Song)," "Dues," and "My Idaho Home" by Ronee Blakley; "Yes, I Do" by Baskin and Lily Tomlin; "Let Me Be the One" and "One, I Love You" by Baskin; "Sing a Song" by Joe Raposo; "The Heart of a Gentle Woman" by Dave Peel; "The Day I Looked Jesus in the Eye" by Baskin and Altman; "Memphis," "I Don't Know If I Found It in You," and "Rolling Stone" by Karen Black; "For the Sake of the Children" by Baskin and Richard Reicheg; "Swing Low, Sweet Chariot" arrangement by Millie Clements; "I Never Get Enough" by Baskin and Ben Raleigh; "Rose's Cafe" by Allan Nicholls; "Ole Man Mississippi" by Juan Grizzle; "My Baby's Cookin' in Another Man's Pan" by Jonnie Barnett; "Since You've Gone" by Gary Busey; and "Trouble in the U.S.A." by Arlene Barnett. Paramount. An ABC Entertainment Presentation. Rated R. 159 minutes.

Norman	DAVID ARKIN	Tricycle man	JEFF GOLDBLUM
Lady Pearl	BARBARA BAXLEY	Albuquerque	BARBARA HARRIS
Delbert Reese	NED BEATTY	Kenny Fraiser	DAVID HAYWARD
Connie White	KAREN BLACK	John Triplette	MICHAEL MURPHY
Barbara Jean	RONEE BLAKLEY	Bill	ALLAN NICHOLLS
Tommy Brown	TIMOTHY BROWN	Bud Hamilton	DAVE PEEL
Tom Frank	KEITH CARRADINE	Mary	CRISTINA RAINES
Opal	GERALDINE CHAPLIN	Star	BERT REMSEN
Wade	ROBERT DOQUI	Linnea Reese	LILY TOMLIN
L. A. Joan	SHELLEY DUVALL	Sueleen Gay	GWEN WELLES
Barnett	ALLEN GARFIELD	Mr. Green	KEENAN WYNN
Haven Hamilton	HENRY GIBSON	Elliott Gould	ELLIOTT GOULD
Pfc Glenn Kelly	SCOTT GLENN	Julie Christie	JULIE CHRISTIE

☆ Academy Award winner

Barbara Jean, a country-and-western star, is performing at a political rally in Nashville. Without warning, a young man from the audience pulls out a gun and shoots her. As the ambulance rushes her away, an ambitious young vocalist takes her place on stage and leads the audience in another song.

Is the crowd so fickle that it has already forgotten Barbara Jean? Or is it so inspired that, despite the senseless tragedy, it can pick itself up? Who is the kooky man with the gun, anyway? Why does he want to kill the singer? Is she, in fact, dead?

These are some of the unanswered questions in just one scene of *Nashville*, a musical some critics have hailed as the most original film of the 1970s. But the loose ends in this kaleidoscopic

---

Country music stars Barbara Jean (Ronee Blakley) and Haven Hamilton (Henry Gibson) appear together at a political rally.

movie of twenty-four characters don't bother director Robert Altman.

"It is a section of life," Altman said. "We don't demand answers in real life." So why, Altman implies, should we expect them in movies? That is to say, in art.

It was their intention, says scriptwriter Joan Tewkesbury, "to make the audience the twenty-fifth character and give them room to form their own conclusion.... Whatever you think about the film is right, even if you think the film is wrong."

Whether one can follow all the nuances in *Nashville*, there is no denying that seeing it is a unique experience. Never has Altman exploited his cinematic trademarks so well—the overlapping dialogue, the improvisation, the background noise drowning out words.

He has, in fact, carried it off so professionally that there have been no complaints from Tewkesbury, even though her script is sacrificed in the process at several points. "That's how life is," she says. "There is mostly no dialogue in life. And in *Nashville*, espe-cially, there is always that music blaring constantly."

Despite its novelty, some feel that *Nashville* is, in the end, a putdown of country music and its coterie of characters. Altman denies this.

In an interview for this book, Altman said: "Those same people who say we put down country people are the same ones who will laugh their heads off at the good ole boys running around and wrecking cars. That is just one step removed from reality for them. So they can afford to laugh at it as a parody. But we came a little too close to reality. And that they didn't like."

To Altman, *Nashville* is really a state of mind, a metaphor for the place to be. "I was trying to show what happened in Hollywood in the thirties or in Nashville in the seventies. People are still getting off buses with a guitar on their back. When there is a dream of success, it is no different to become a rock star or a movie star or a toreador.

"It [*Nashville*] tried to show all the various elements and sides of that phenomenon. Was it worth it? How the successful people aren't necessarily happier than the unsuccessful.... It was really about the American dream or what is advertised about the American dream. It's a fairly universal theme."

Most critics responded positively. Pauline Kael of *The New Yorker* wangled an advance look at the picture and wrote, "I just sat there smiling at the screen in complete happiness. It's a pure emotional high...." Judith Crist, then of *New York Magazine*, called *Nashville* "an original work that stands not only as a milestone in creative filmmaking, but also as a remarkable perception of America in the mid-seventies."

Despite its flaws—and there are several—*Nashville* works because its panoramic vision of a cross section of Middle America is provocative, spontaneous, colorful, confusing, moving, and lifelike. It is a commentary on the tawdry, con-game aspects of the country music business and politics. At the same time, it is a comedy, a musical, a satire, and a melodrama all rolled into one. If there is little character development, it has some of the strongest performances of any film of its time.

Perhaps the most notable is that of Ronee Blakley, who made her film debut as the fragile Barbara Jean. A country-and-western composer-performer, Blakley wrote her own songs (as did a number of performers). She also created one of the picture's most effective scenes, in which Barbara Jean's mind wanders while she is before an adoring audience. She babbles incoherently about her childhood, a performance that puzzles and then sours her admirers.

Blakley wrote the breakdown scene the night before it was filmed. "The script called for Barbara Jean to collapse again," Blakley said. "I didn't want that because she had already fainted once in the film. And I thought it would take the whole rhythm of

BBC reporter Opal (Geraldine Chaplin) interviews rock star Tom (Keith Carradine).

the character's development.... I just wanted people to see what made her tick.

"The next morning, I asked Bob [Altman] if he could come and see me alone in my dressing room.... I know he thought, 'Oh God, what now?' I read to him what I had written. And he said, 'Do you know it?' And I said, 'Yes.' So we did it."

The idea for the movie evolved from a screenplay about country music that United Artists asked Altman to direct. It was to have been a vehicle for Tom Jones. Altman rejected it. "It was terrible. I said I would do a film about Nashville. But it would have to be an original."

He assigned the project to writer Tewkesbury, who had collaborated with him on *Thieves Like Us* (1974). "I sent her to Nashville. She was there eleven days. I said just keep track of everything that happens to you. Go around and fantasize a few things. And just come back with some characters. And the first thing that happened to her was she was stuck in a big multicar wreck on the freeway."

In fact, Tewkesbury made several trips to Nashville. And some of her characters are suggested by real country music stars: Loretta Lynn for Barbara Jean; Hank Snow and Roy Acuff for Haven Hamilton; and Charley Pride for Tony Brown, the black singing cowboy.

"When UA read the script, they were appalled." Altman said. "They wouldn't touch it. Then ABC gave me the money to make it. We made it for one point nine million. They took it to Paramount and kind of forced Paramount to release it because Paramount had a lot of TV business with them."

With Paramount in the fold, Altman undertook what has become the key step in his filming. "Casting is ninety percent of the creation," Altman said. He drew heavily from a group of actors who

Albuquerque (Barbara Harris) makes her singing debut at the Nashville Speedway but the roar of racing car engines drowns her out.

appeared in his earlier movies, offering fees of only $750 to $1,000 for eight weeks of work. Most jumped at his offer.

"In Europe, Altman is number one," said Geraldine Chaplin, who said she turned down a $130,000 role in England. Karen Black, hearing of the project, wrote two songs and persuaded Altman to let her play Barbara Jean's rival. Keith Carradine, who portrayed a promiscuous rock singer, said Altman's choices were uncanny. "He's looking for actors who are good enough so they don't have to act."

Once chosen, many rose to the occasion. Newcomer Lily Tomlin was, at first, unsure of her ability.

Sueleen (Gwen Welles) tries to prove her talents as a singer only to learn she has been hired to do a strip tease.

"But as I looked at everybody else and saw how perfect they were, I thought he couldn't be wrong about me." She gave one of the movie's most sensitive performances.

The picture's first assembly version ran eight hours. Then, it was reportedly cut to six hours, to be shown in two parts. A third version was three hours long. Finally, it evolved into its present length of two and a half hours.

In that final form, *Nashville* is a kind of modern-day *Grand Hotel* (1932), fusing multiple plotlines into one sprawling whole. The story of twenty-four interweaving characters, most of them people in the country music world, focuses around a political advance man's efforts to round up entertainers at a rally for a third-party candidate.

The candidate is a man named Hal Phillip, whose voice blares from a sound truck throughout the movie but who is never seen. From his platform he seems to be a Dixie anti-big-government politician like George Wallace.

Actually, the plot is Byzantine. Characters come and go so quickly it's hard to get to know them. One of them is Haven Hamilton (Henry Gibson), the grand old man of country music. It is 1976 and Hamilton is recording a salute to the nation's bicentennial—"We Must Be Doing Something Right to Last 200 Years."

Another one is Nashville's sweetheart, Barbara Jean, just returned from a tour. Exhausted and on the verge of a breakdown, she is hospitalized shortly after her arrival.

A third is Linnea Reese (Tomlin), a gospel singer married to a local lawyer (Ned Beatty). She has a one-night stand with a hot young rock singer (Carradine) who is really spending most of his non-working time with Mary (Cristina Raines), a female singer married to Bill (Allan Nicholls).

Linnea (Lily Tomlin), a white lead singer in a black gospel group, with Wade (Robert Doqui), who is struggling to make it in Music City.

And so the lines cross and re-cross until, in an operatic finale, most of them join at the rally. There, Barbara Jean, who has recovered, appears on stage with Hamilton until she is gunned down and another hopeful (Barbara Harris) takes her place.

That, more or less, is the bare bones of the plot. But it is not the movie, which is filled with memorable sequences. There is the scene where:

● Linnea talks with her deaf children and, in a touching exchange, teaches them with hand gestures the words to "Sing, Sing a Song." They tell their mother about their day in school while their father (Ned Beatty), who has not bothered to learn sign language, looks on uneasily.

● Sueleen (Gwen Welles), a tin-eared waitress who dreams of reaching the big time as a singer, is conned into doing a strip at a male smoker. The men cheer her on. But she is so inept and awkward—she even forgets to remove sweat socks from her bra before she goes on—that she

emerges a humiliated figure of pity.

● Haven's son Bud (Dave Peel) finds an audience in the glib BBC broadcaster (Chaplin) and begins telling her about the song he has written. She asks to hear it, and he starts crooning softly. In the middle of his song, she spots a movie star and bolts, yelling, "Elliott. Elliott Gould."

Some say the parts never meld into a whole. "*Nashville*," says Joel E. Siegel in the magazine *Film Heritage*, "fails because its view of people, individually and collectively, is so shallow, so lacking in depth and sympathy, it's like a series of bumper stickers— bright, flashy, paper-thin expressions of attitudes—soon past, soon forgotten."

But time is on Altman's side, because the movie has not grown stale. Altman is liberating film from old structures. *Nashville* is breaking new ground. Even though its storyline is diffuse and its plot unresolved, it is an innovative motion picture not soon forgotten.

Heroes
and
Villains

COOL HAND LUKE

ELMER GANTRY

THE GODFATHER

GOLDFINGER

Cool Hand Luke
(1967)

Directed by Stuart Rosenberg. Screenplay by Donn Pearce and Frank R. Pierson based on a novel by Pearce. Camera, Conrad Hall. Editor, Sam O'Steen. Music, Lalo Schifrin. Assistant director, Hank Moonjean. Produced by Gordon Carroll. A Warner Brothers Picture of a Jalem Production. 126 minutes.

Luke	PAUL NEWMAN
Dragline	GEORGE KENNEDY ☘
Society Red	J. D. CANNON
Koko	LOU ANTONIO
Loudmouth Steve	ROBERT DRIVAS
Captain	STROTHER MARTIN
Arletta	JO VAN FLEET
Carr	CLIFTON JAMES
Boss Godfrey	MORGAN WOODWARD
Boss Paul	LUKE ASKEW
Blind Dick	RICHARD DAVALOS
Rabbitt	MARC CAVELL
Tattoo	WARREN FINNERTY
Babalugats	DENNIS HOPPER
Boss Kean	JOHN McLIAM
Gambler	WAYNE ROGERS
Tramp	(HARRY) DEAN STANTON
Boss Higgins	CHARLES TYNER
Alibi	RALPH WAITE
Dog Boy	ANTHONY ZERBE
Dynamite	BUCK KARTALIAN
Girl	JOY HARMON
Sleepy	JIM GAMMON
Boss Shorty	ROBERT DONNER
Fixer	JOE DON BAKER
Sailor	DONN PEARCE
Stupid Blondie	NORMAN GOODWINS
Chief	CHARLES HICKS
John Sr.	JOHN PEARCE
John Jr.	EDDIE ROSSON
Patrolman	RUSH WILLIAMS
Wickerman	JAMES JETER
Jabo	ROBERT LUSTER
Negro boys	JAMES BRADLEY, JR., CYRIL "CHIPS" ROBINSON
Sheriff	RANCE HOWARD

☘ Academy Award winner

Stuart Rosenberg walked into the Pickwick Book Shop on Hollywood Boulevard in 1965, browsed through the pre-publication section, and came out with $82 worth of books.

He was looking for a story to film and having no luck. Then he started reading the novel *Cool Hand Luke*.

"I was fascinated," Rosenberg said. "It was the first time I had come across an existentialist hero in American literature. Here was a man not so much a rebel as a nonconformist, a man who didn't belong, committed to no external idea, but to himself, and desperately concerned to express that commitment."

And so began an idea that would evolve into a flawed but haunting movie that would win praise from critics, pack theaters, and earn a generous profit for Warner Brothers. It would also give a hefty boost to the careers of Rosenberg and two actors, Paul Newman and George Kennedy.

Until then, Rosenberg had been known primarily for his television work. He had directed hundreds of TV dramas, including some of the best episodes of "The Defenders," "The Untouchables," and "Naked City." *Cool Hand Luke* established him as a serious filmmaker, although subsequent movies like *The April Fools* (1969), *W.U.S.A.* (1970), and *The*

Paul Newman (opposite right) as Cool Hand Luke, a loner who becomes a legend in a Southern prison. Morgan Woodward plays a guard with mirrored sunglasses. Inmates call him "the man with no eyes."

Drowning Pool (1975) did not elevate him to such lofty cinematic heights again.[1]

Newman had been a promising actor with an uneven record. He did outstanding work in *The Hustler* (1961) and *Hud* (1963), then was miscast in productions like *Lady L.* (1964) and Hitchcock's *Torn Curtain* (1965). But he turned a corner in *Luke*. His dazzling performance earned an Academy Award nomination and anticipated still another virtuoso effort two years later in *Butch Cassidy and the Sundance Kid* (1969).

Cool Hand Luke was a milestone for Kennedy too. He won the film's only Oscar for his fiery and vivid portrayal of Luke's tough prison pal and went on to do dozens of character parts.

Yet, despite all this professionalism, the film fell short of the mark. It had many virtues—it was gripping, lyrical, tragic, and humorous all at once—and it was an ambitious venture. But its hero was not a major one because he lacked a cause.

To be sure, his ornery defiance of the prison system bolstered the morale of the other prisoners. But it was a defiance born not of any redeeming purpose but rather of sheer cussedness, machoism, and a mindless, devil-may-care attitude. His sad end is reduced by an almost willful drive to torment his persecutors, who torment him in turn.

Having said this, it must be noted that *Cool Hand Luke* is a moving story—a picture that winds inexorably and inevitably toward a violent end. All the while, we see visions of sensual, earthy beauty as the camera catches the road gang going out at first light, scything weeds and digging ditches in the oppressive noonday heat, then coming back in the cool summer twilight. The movie plays well in this apparently Southern milieu—actually the gently rolling acres of Stock-

George Kennedy as Luke's prison pal, Dragline. Kennedy won an Oscar for his performance.

ton, California—and the soft, mellow colors and slow, twangy accents ring true.

What makes it appealing to so many moviegoers is that its storyline exists on several levels. First, it is an updated version of all the old prison movies—closest, perhaps, to the 1932 melodrama *I Am a Fugitive from a Chain Gang*, in which Paul Muni starred.[2]

Neither *Fugitive* nor *Luke* shies away from the harsh conditions of the inmates and their brutal treatment. But *Luke* is less concerned with exposing conditions than with showing the effect that an in-

domitable spirit has on a despairing prison gang. After his death, they talk about him as if he were still alive, starting the legend of Cool Hand Luke.

In many ways, Luke seems like a modern-day Christ figure. He comes to an oppressed people, performs a miracle, is ridiculed and beaten, then martyred and entombed. The inmates become his disciples.

But the messianic analogy does not stand up. For one thing, Luke does not take himself seriously. At the outset, he is arrested and imprisoned for a silly offense

---

[1]"It's a strange statement to make." Rosenberg said, "but many directors will tell you, 'I don't want to be judged by the films I make.' Rosenberg explained by that he means that a director's qualities don't come to the fore when, through economic necessity, he contracts to do other people's pictures, movies over which he has little control. "They are exercises in professionalism. But they are really not my films unless they are films I choose and develop."

[2]Some critics have drawn parallels between *Luke* and Ken Kesey's *One Flew Over the Cuckoo's Nest* (1975). In fact, one can make the case that *Luke* is, in many ways, *Cuckoo's Nest* moved from a mental institution to a Southern prison camp. In both films, the protagonist, an outsider, comes into a group, raises its aspirations, but must sacrifice himself in the end. He doesn't change its conditions, but he gives it a dream. "In effect, this is the true hero," Rosenberg says. "You really aren't accomplishing a thing by changing a scene. You must change a personality."

Luke is tagged by a haymaker. But he shows his mettle and doggedly keeps getting up.

—drunkenly knocking off the heads of parking meters. And all through the movie, his wry humor and bent-for-hell high jinks make him less a mystic figure of piety than an old-fashioned good ole boy.

In fact, in an interview for this book, director Rosenberg said he was not trying to do a symbolic version of the Christ story. Many sequences that seem to have religious overtones were not even in the script. They were inserted as afterthoughts because they brought a touch to a scene or seemed right for a particular moment.

"There are elements of the crucifixion that certainly parallel Luke's whole story," Rosenberg said. "But it was not a conscious desire to do that when we started. It evolved in certain instances."

If there is one clearly defined quality that Luke has, it is staying power. We see this as soon as he is thrown in prison and Dragline (Kennedy) challenges him to a fight. The bout turns out to be no contest as Dragline's powerful blows drop Luke again and again.

But Luke won't stay down. One by one, the men, who came to cheer Dragline, leave, repelled by the gory, one-sided battle.

"Stay down," Dragline whispers. "You're beat."

"You're going to have to kill me," Luke says.

Confused by Luke's gameness, Dragline stops and walks off—leaving the fray to the bloodied but unbowed loser.

It is Dragline who later gives Luke his prison name in a scene where Luke wins a big poker hand by sheer bluff.

"A hand full of nothing," Dragline laughs when he sees Luke's cards. Then he turns to the losing cardplayer. ". . . He [Luke] beat you with nothing. Just like when he kept coming back at me—with nothing."

"Well," says Luke, "sometimes nothing can be a real cool hand."

"Move over," Dragline says, sliding alongside him. "I want to sit next to my boy—Cool Hand Luke."

From that moment, Luke becomes the road gang's leader. His free and exuberant nature inspires

the men to work at a frenzied pace to finish blacktopping a road two hours early. In a sense, they are beating the system by turning their enforced labor into fun.

Then Luke performs what seems like a miraculous feat. He accepts an inmate's challenge that he can't eat fifty hard-boiled eggs in an hour. With every dollar in the camp riding on the outcome, Luke wins the bet as Dragline shoves the last egg in his mouth. Afterward, Luke lies sprawled on a bed, stomach bloated, arms outstretched.

"It was not in my mind to do a cruciform number," Rosenberg said. "But when we finished shooting, Paul was lying on a table. I was on a ladder with my viewer, looking at him. I needed an end shot and I said, 'My God. You look like Christ.' I said, 'Let's push it. Strike the position.' And we did it."

The road gang bosses watch all these curious goings-on with puzzled expressions. Presiding over the prison camp is the captain (Strother Martin), a soft-voiced but menacing warden, and Boss Godfrey (Morgan Woodward), his crack-shot assistant, who wears mirrored glasses and never speaks. Dragline dubs him "the man with no eyes."

"Originally, when the script was written, he [Godfrey] spoke, like the others," Rosenberg said. "But I wanted to have a symbol of authority that was nameless, faceless, and impersonal. [He was saying] 'We don't hate you. This is just the way it is.' That was the whole idea of putting the glasses on and taking his lines away."

One day, Luke's consumptive mother (Jo Van Fleet) comes to say goodbye, propped up in the bed of an old pickup truck. In a memorable, understated scene, she tells Luke she always hoped to see him "well fixed [with] a crop of grandkids to fuss around with. . . . what went wrong?" He shrugs. "I always tried to live free and aboveboard like you. But I just couldn't find enough elbow room."

When she dies soon afterward, Luke pays his respects the only way he can—strumming a guitar in the barracks. The other prisoners give him the privacy of half the room, and he sings, "I don't care if it rains or freezes/ Long as I got my plastic Jesus/ Sittin' on the dashboard of my car. . . ."

The lines came from a jingle written for a company making religious ornaments, Rosenberg said. Newman took guitar lessons and practiced the song on his lunch break. Even though the scene was made in one take, Rosenberg said it took some manipulation to get it just right.

"Paul is such a professional that he learned the chords and lyrics so well it sounded too competent. So I told him I had a copyright problem and I changed the first two lines. I wanted to confuse him. It was coming out too clean, too clear. Then, we did a take. And if you look at the film, you'll see when he starts, he forgets a line. He looks at me off camera. And I made a sign for him to keep going. . . . He gets very pissed off. And that anger works. The camera keeps going on and he starts to weep. It was a very moving moment."

Then things start taking a different turn at the prison. Luke's actions worry his guards. So the captain puts Luke in the "box"—a windowless, cramped cubicle—to be sure he doesn't "get rabbit in his blood" and run off to his mother's funeral. That marks the beginning of the end for Luke. As soon as they let him out, he rebels against the gratuitous punishment and escapes.

A bloodhound posse quickly catches him. The captain slaps him in leg irons. "You gonna get used to wearin' them chains after a while, Luke," he says before all the inmates. "But you'll never

After a prison camp break, Dog Boy (Anthony Zerbe) lets loose the bloodhounds.

stop that clinkin' 'cause they're gonna remind you of what I've been saying for your own good."

"I wish you'd stop being so good to me, Captain," Luke says.

Enraged at Luke's boldness, the captain strikes him. "What we've got here," he says, looking up at the other convicts, "is a failure to communicate." The nine-word sentence is the picture's most remembered line. The generation gap was an issue when the movie was made, and young activists quoted it again and again to show how those in authority were ignoring their views.

Strother Martin, a veteran character actor who played the captain, had another interpretation. "The way I like to think of it," said Martin, "this captain—who probably had a sixth-grade education —read a sociological tract once. And this was the one phrase he remembered." Martin's annual income had a meteoric rise after the picture. It jumped from $20,000 to $50,000. And his per week fee —important for an actor—soared from $1,500 to $4,000.

Luke's running days are far from over. Even with his legs chained, he slips away in the brush the first time he goes out with the road gang. Months later, Dragline gets a picture in the mail showing Luke with his arms around two buxom bar girls. It's signed, "Playing it cool, Luke." While Dragline is showing the picture to other inmates the next day, Luke is dragged in again.

"You run one time, you get you one set of chains," the captain says. "You run twice, you get two sets. You ain't gonna need no third set 'cause you going to get your mind right."

Later, when the inmates gather around to find out more about his outside experience, Luke tells them the picture was a phony. He wants none of their praise. "Stop feeding off me," he yells.

Now the bosses start bearing down. They beat Luke and force him to dig ditches all night until he appears to break. "For God's sake," he pleads, "don't hit me anymore."

His weakness tarnishes his leg-

A stubborn Luke goes down under the blows of the Captain (Strother Martin), the camp boss.

endary reputation. He becomes a toady to the bosses, running favors for them on the road. But as soon as he gets his first chance, he jumps in a pickup truck and guns off. Dragline hops aboard.

"Those motherheads didn't know you was fooling," Dragline says.

Luke denies any heroics. "You can't fool about something like that."

"All the time you were planning on running again," Dragline insists.

"I never planned anything in my life," Luke replies.

Luke and Dragline are not to be together long. They part after they hide the truck and Luke makes his way to an abandoned country church.

"Hey old man. You home tonight?" he says, looking at the dusty rafters. "...I know I ain't got no call to ask for much. But, even so, you got to admit you ain't dealt me no cards in a long time. You got things fixed so I can't never win.... You made me like I am. Just where am I supposed to

fit in? What you got in mind for me? What do I do now?"

Luke asks for a sign of His presence. "On my knees, I'm asking..." Silence. "Yeah, that's what I thought. I guess I'm pretty tough to deal with—a hard case. Yeah, I guess I got to find my own way."

Dragline barges in. Police and the prison bosses have trailed him to the church. He tells Luke they've promised not to hurt them if they give up.

Luke walks to the door, looks into the police-car headlights, and smiles. "What we got here is a failure to communicate," he says mockingly.

The rifle of the man with no eyes cracks and a bullet thuds into Luke's throat. Dragline carries him out, but there isn't anything he can do. Luke dies without speaking as the bosses drive away with him. Their dusty car fades in the distance past a stop signal that blinks red in the rainy night.

What did he look like? the inmates ask Dragline the next day as they work under a bright, merciless sun. Were his eyes open or closed?

"He was smiling," Dragline tells them. The screen flashes back to scenes of Luke's prison life. Dragline's voice goes on. "That's right. You know that Luke smile of his? He had it on his face right up to the very end. Hell, if they didn't know it before, they knew it right then—that they weren't going to break him.... He was some boy. Cool Hand Luke. Hell, he's a natural-born world-beater."

The camera draws away and we see a crossroad, which, from afar, looks like a crucifix.

Some critics feel the last scene is redundant because the story really ends when Luke dies. Rosenberg agrees. "But the studio felt we were killing an international superstar and it was such a downer that they wanted an afterbeat," Rosenberg said. "There were quite a lot of arguments. But the producer sided with the studio. So we came up with what we thought was a compromise. I never really dug it.... I think it's fair to say that the picture is over when that stoplight turns red."[3]

---

[3]Nevertheless, there is something to be said for the studio-imposed finale. It gives the story a sense of continuity, because we see how Luke's disciples carry on his memory and turn him into a mystic figure. Even so, Rosenberg said that was not his intention. "As long as we were doing it [adding another sequence], I wanted to reestablish one area which I don't think anybody understood. And that was that a hero, because of his very presence and heroics, often stops a revolution. Here were these guys very happily sitting around the road with chains on because now they had something to talk about. That is one of the misgivings of leaders. And it is why many revolutionists say you should change leaders every few years. The importance of the hero is such that sometimes he nullifies any further movement. But I don't think anybody picked up on this."

Elmer Gantry
(1960)

Directed by Richard Brooks. Screenplay by Brooks 🎬 based on Sinclair Lewis's novel. Editor, Marge Fowler. Camera, John Alton. Art director, Ed Carrere. Music, Andre Previn. Producer, Bernard Smith. United Artists. 146 minutes.

Elmer Gantry	BURT LANCASTER 🎬
Sister Sharon Falconer	JEAN SIMMONS
Jim Lefferts	ARTHUR KENNEDY
Lulu Bains	SHIRLEY JONES 🎬
William L. Morgan	DEAN JAGGER
Sister Rachel	PATTI PAGE
George Babbitt	EDWARD ANDREWS
Rev. Pengilly	JOHN McINTIRE
Pete	JOE MAROSS
Rev. Brown	EVERETT GLASS
Rev. Phillips	MICHAEL WHALEN
Rev. Garrison	HUGH MARLOWE
Rev. Planck	PHILIP OBER
Rev. Ulrich	WENDELL HOLMES
Captain Holt	BARRY KELLEY
Friends	RAY WALKER, RALPH DUMKE, GEORGE CISAR

🎬 Academy Award winner

Hollywood doesn't often improve on books, but an exception to that rule came in the film version of *Elmer Gantry*. The movie brought to the screen Sinclair Lewis's searing novel that painted a scandalous portrait of a Midwestern clergyman.

Lewis's work became a best seller in 1927. In the process, it kicked up a storm of controversy. Its antireligious theme—Lewis made Gantry an opportunist and a fraud, a minister who mixed lechery with religion—was particularly jarring in the conservative Calvin Coolidge era.

The book riled church groups. It was banned in Boston. At least one minister was so outraged he suggested Lewis should be lynched.

Nobody took that extreme course. But many thought Lewis was too bitter, too broad and heavyhanded in his sweeping denunciation of organized religion.

Lewis must have realized this, too. Years later, when he met filmmaker Richard Brooks, he told Brooks that he would do well to heed the critics' advice. "Read the book reviewers. Don't make the same mistakes I did. Benefit from hindsight."

Brooks did just that. He was careful to set Gantry apart from the Establishment. He made him an unordained minister, a Bible-thumping spellbinder lured into the tent-show circuit by the business side of revivalism. As such, he created a prototype—a bad good guy, an engaging antihero who would reappear throughout the 1960s in such films as *The Hustler* (1961), *The Music Man* (1962), *Hud* (1963), and *Alfie* (1966).

So the movie's point of departure was that instead of attacking all those in the pulpit, it was attacking only those who use the ministry for self-serving purposes. Instead of attacking organized Christianity, it was attacking revivalism, an easier target because it lacked the political clout of established religion.

Brooks, who wrote and directed the movie, also added an appealing side to Gantry's character. Unlike Lewis, who turned Gantry into a sleazy opportunist, Brooks portrayed him as an engaging rogue. The Gantry of the movies was a good ole boy with a gift of gab and a healthy appetite for wine, women, and greenbacks. If the screen Gantry had flaws, he also had a basic decency and an innate respect for God.

Burt Lancaster as the hellfire-and-brimstone preacher Elmer Gantry.

The opportunistic Gantry joins evangelist Sister Sharon (Jean Simmons).

Brooks played down the corrupt nature of Gantry's character not only to avoid confrontation with religious groups but also because he had a special reason for wanting to bring Lewis's work to the screen successfully. Their relationship traced back a decade before the filming.

During World War II, Brooks, then a marine, was threatened with a court-martial. He had written a novel dealing with racial discrimination in the service without clearing it with his superiors. Lewis, who in 1930 had become the first American to win the Nobel Prize for literature,[1] was one of the prominent people who volunteered to come to Brooks's defense. The Marine Corps quietly dropped the matter.

The experience gave Brooks the idea of making *Elmer Gantry* into a movie. He wanted to present a realistic picture about contemporary revivalism. In an interview while the picture was being shot, Brooks said: "I felt then—and I still feel it—that religion is an integral part of American culture.

The subject of religion here is generally treated on film either from the point of view of the biblical period or as a sort of creative fantasy that has no direct relationship to religion today in the United States."

Hollywood did not warm quickly to Brooks's treatment of the sensitive subject. Brooks got the screen rights in 1954. However, he failed to interest any studio and had to pay another $2,500 each year for five years to renew his option. Finally, Burt Lancaster agreed to star in it. When he did, United Artists joined the venture.

Uppermost in Brooks's mind was the fact that he was turning a novel into a film. "Lewis exposed revivalism through the intellect. We are doing it another way—through emotion. In a book, the intellect comes first, and through it, the emotions. In a movie, you have to reach the intellect through the emotions."

One of the ways Brooks brought out the rousing feeling and raw emotions of the tent circuit was by concentrating on the audience. In

addition to using professional extras—a practice that union rules required—he hired 200 nonunion people, carefully selecting them for the character in their faces. He placed the elderly and middle-aged folk up front, so the camera could focus on their rapturous expressions. When the picture was released, reviewers remarked on the "faces that looked like they had never been out of the Bible belt."

In fact, Brooks shot the movie entirely in California, a state with no dearth of cults and sects. For location scenes, he used Los Angeles parks and streets. He also built special exterior sets at the Columbia Studios ranch. He staged the climactic holocaust sequence in the MGM backlot.

The movie, which is based on the book's middle segment dealing with Gantry's evangelistic career, picks up Elmer when he has become a traveling salesman. Even as a purveyor of vacuum cleaners, he shows a natural way with words. In a bar, he displays an ability to mesmerize with off-the-cuff sermons.

"You think religion is for suckers and easy marks? You think Jesus was some kind of sissy? Well, let me tell you, Jesus

In a tent meeting, a sinner repents to the shirt-sleeved Reverend Gantry.

---

[1]Lewis also won the 1926 Pulitzer Prize, for *Arrowsmith* (1925), a novel about an idealistic doctor. But he declined to accept it because he thought he should have gotten the award sooner.

The Godfather ※
(1972)

Directed by Francis Ford Coppola. Screenplay by Mario Puzo ※ and Coppola ※ based on Puzo's novel. Photography, Gordon Willis. Music by Nino Rota. Art director, Warren Clymer. Editors, Marc Laub and Murray Solomon. Produced by Albert S. Ruddy. Filmed in New York, Hollywood, Las Vegas, and Sicily. Paramount. Rated R. 175 minutes.

Don Vito Corleone	MARLON BRANDO ※
Michael Corleone	AL PACINO
Sonny Corleone	JAMES CAAN
Clemenza	RICHARD CASTELLANO
Tom Hagen	ROBERT DUVALL
McCluskey	STERLING HAYDEN
Jack Woltz	JOHN MARLEY
Barzini	RICHARD CONTE
Kay Adams	DIANE KEATON
Vergil Sollozzo	AL LETTIERI
Tessio	ABE VIGODA
Connie Corleone Rizzi	TALIA SHIRE
Carlo Rizzi	GIANNI RUSSO
Fredo Corleone	JOHN CAZALE
Cuneo	RUDY BOND
Johnny Fontaine	AL MARTINO
Mama Corleone	MORGANA KING
Luca Brasi	LENNY MONTANA
Paulie Gatto	JOHN MARTINO
Apollonia	SIMONETTA STEFANELLI
Amerigo Bonasera	SALVATORE CORSITTO
Neri	RICHARD BRIGHT
Moe Greene	ALEX ROCCA

※ Academy Award winner

Why did *The Godfather* become the biggest-grossing movie of its time? One can make some good guesses.

First, there is the film's open-ended celebration of violence. The picture reeks with gangland killings. Second, there are the strong performances. Everyone down to Salvatore Corsitto, as the Sicilian undertaker who opens the movie with a poignant monologue, is superbly cast.

But there are films equally violent or as well acted that have failed to capture the public's fancy. What, then, is the special quality that catapulted *The Godfather* to its enormous success?

It is, I think, the picture's intriguing glimpse of the behind-the-scenes subculture of the Mafia. The movie takes a more intimate look at the brotherhood of crime than any other modern film. In the 1930s, pictures like *Little Caesar* (1930), *The Public Enemy* (1931), and *Scarface* (1932) focused on criminals, too. But they were cocky hoods or ruthless, ambitious gangsters pushing their way to the top.

The Godfather is already at the summit. And the movie shows what life is like there. It takes the viewer into the inner sanctum, his private office in his home where he wields power and dispenses favors and patronage. It shows his uneasy liaisons with the police and the politicians and the other crime families.

And it shows how detached he and other Mafia figures have become from crime and its ramifications. Murder is a business transaction. To the Godfather, there is nothing hypocritical about executing a rival who has gained advantage and then appearing as a mourner at his burial.

It's a happy day for the Corleone family as Don Vito (Marlon Brando) celebrates his daughter's wedding. With him (*from left*) are sons Michael (Al Pacino), Sonny (James Caan), and Fredo (John Cazale).

69

Francis Ford Coppola has put all this on film and done it with such style and authenticity, it seems as if we are back in the 1940s watching the melodrama unfold before our very eyes. All this is the more remarkable when one realizes Coppola was the fourth choice to direct the picture.

A theater arts major at Long Island's Hofstra University, Coppola went to California to take his master's in fine arts at the UCLA film school. But he was little more than a promising director in 1971 when Paramount decided to film Mario Puzo's novel. Coppola had no successful film in his portfolio. And he was broke.

However, Paramount failed to interest Peter Yates (*Bullitt*), Costa Gavras (*Z*), and Richard Brooks (*Elmer Gantry*) in the project. So the studio lowered its sights. Primarily, it needed a director it could control, and who would not go over budget, because it was struggling to contain a deepening financial crisis.

Coppola seemed to fit the bill. Moreover, he offered a bonus. He was of Italian descent and spoke Italian. "He knew the way these men ate their food, kissed each other, talked," said Robert Evans, Paramount's production chief. "He knew the grit."

At first, the studio intended to make a low-budget production. It had been stung by *The Brotherhood* (1968), a failed effort at an inside-the-Mafia picture with Kirk Douglas. But when Puzo's book became a runaway best seller—the novel sold a million hardcover copies and twelve million paperbacks before the picture opened—Paramount changed its thinking.

After Puzo and Coppola finished the script, casting became the major concern. Several actors were considered for the prize role of the Don, including Laurence Olivier, George C. Scott, and Richard Conte. Even producer Carlo Ponti, Sophia Loren's husband, was suggested.

However, Puzo wanted Marlon Brando, and he convinced Coppola that Brando was the ideal choice. Convincing Paramount was another matter. Studio heads wanted no part of Brando. He had been in an acting doldrum in the 1960s. And he was notorious for his eccentric behavior during productions.

Evans did agree to look at a screen test, thinking that such a request would be humiliating to an actor of Brando's stature. But the test appealed to Brando's competitive spirit. His response has become a Hollywood legend.

The test took place in Brando's home. While Coppola and producer Al Ruddy set up a videotape machine, Brando applied crude makeup. He slicked back his hair, dabbed in white streaks, put shoe polish under his eyes. Then, he stuffed tissue paper in his cheeks and nostrils, puffed an Italian stogie, and scowled at the camera. "He looked just like my Uncle Louie," Coppola said.

Days later, after Evans saw the test, he said, "He looks Italian, fine. But who is he?" When he was told, Evans immediately gave Brando his vote.

Casting supporting roles was equally difficult. Paramount initially considered Robert Redford, Warren Beatty, and Jack Nicholson for Michael Corleone, the Don's youngest son and eventual successor. But Coppola, who proved to be a tough-minded director, held out for a cast of less familiar faces. In the end, he got James Caan as Sonny, Robert Duvall as Tom Hagen, the Corleones' *consiglieri*, and Al Pacino as Michael.

Pacino said the role was the most difficult one he has played. "The thing that I was after was to create some kind of enigma . . . so you felt you were looking at that person and didn't quite know him. When you see Michael in some of those scenes wrapped up in a kind of trance, as if his mind were completely filled with thoughts, that's what I was doing." In one interview, Pacino was quoted as saying: "They may have come to see Brando. But they left remembering me."

When the film was released, critics agreed that Coppola had transformed Puzo's potboiler into a gripping, richly textured film of great sweep and beauty. From the start, it was a financial success, pulling in $26 million only two weeks after the New York opening. In less than a year, it earned $82 million, replacing *Gone with the Wind* (1939) as the all-time box-office champion.

In the very first sequence, the film pulls the audience into the exotic world of the Mafia. "I believe in America. America made my fortune. And I raised my daughter in American fashion," says a heavily accented voice in the dark. As the camera pulls back, we see an elderly funeral director (Corsitto) talking to Don Vito Corleone (Brando). The undertaker's daughter has been raped. Her violaters have gotten off with suspended sentences. The outraged father, speaking with deference as if he were before a priest or a feudal lord, is asking vengeance.

The Don, despite his gruff voice, is a humane and gentle patriarch. He strokes his cat. Why, he wants to know, has the undertaker never even invited him over for coffee? In the end, the Don grants him the favor. Nothing is asked in return. But it goes without saying that one day there will be a price to pay.

All this takes place behind Venetian blinds in the amber-hued darkness of the Don's office. This is the closed masculine world of the Mafia in which business is conducted.

Next, the camera takes us outdoors into bright sunlight. This is another world, the world of women and children, a world of familial happiness and security where Don Corleone is giving away his daughter in marriage. Hundreds of guests are joyously dancing and drinking wine.

Here we meet the Don's three sons: the hot-tempered Sonny (Caan), the weak-willed Fredo (John Cazale), and young Michael (Pacino), the Don's favorite. Michael has returned from the war with a girlfriend, Kay (Diane Keaton). She is a non-Sicilian, an outsider, a Wasp who is unfamiliar with the ways of the family.

Who is that person? Kay asks, looking at Luca Brasi (Lenny Montana), one of Corleone's "soldiers," whose job is to do the rough stuff. (Montana, a former

The Godfather has the traditional first dance with his newlywed daughter, Connie (Talia Shire).

Luca Brasi (Lenny Montana), the Corleones' chief hit man, is himself dispatched Mafia-style, strangled while thugs hold down his hands.

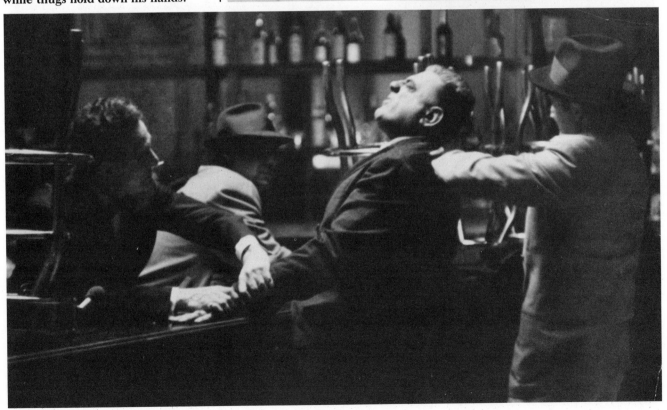

The Godfather and his youngest son, Michael, who will succeed him.

wrestler, was recruited by Coppola when he happened to see him while the company was on location in the streets of New York.)

Michael explains that Brasi once helped his father persuade a bandleader to cancel his singer's contract. It was holding back the career of Don Corleone's godson, crooner Johnny Fontaine (Al Martino). The bandleader turned down the Don's offer of $10,000 to buy the contract. But the next day, he accepted a $1,000 check.

Why? the puzzled Kay asks.

"My father made him an offer he couldn't refuse," says Michael, explaining that Brasi held a gun to the bandleader's head while Corleone told him either his brains or his signature would be on the contract. The line became a popular expression from then on.

Brando found the two-level aspect of Mafia life fascinating. The Don and other Mafia bosses regard themselves not as hoods but as businessmen not much different from corporation executives. "I don't think the film is about the Mafia at all," Brando said. "I think it is about the corporate mind." He compared the Don's ruthless methods to the tactics used by General Motors when it hired private investigators to try to discredit Ralph Nader.

Coppola saw this, too. When

Kay Corleone recoils after Michael tells her that his father is no different from any other powerful man—like a senator or a president—she says:

"Do you know how naive you sound? Senators and presidents don't have men killed."

Michael looks at her. Then he replies quietly, "Who's being naive now, Kay?"

The year is 1945 and times are a-changin'. Narcotics is the new racket, and the son of another family boss, Vergil Sollozzo (Al Lettieri), comes to the Don with a proposal about dope traffic. The old-fashioned Don wants no part of it. Gambling is okay. Heroin is dirty business. His attitude sets the stage for a bloody gang war.

Intent on power, Sollozzo has his men strangle Brasi and gun down Don Corleone. Even though five bullets have hit him, the tough old Mafia chieftain survives, hanging on to his life by a thread.

A week later, Michael visits him in his hospital room and finds his police guard gone. Sensing that another assassination attempt is about to take place, Michael rolls his father's bed to another room, then stations himself and another friend outside the hospital. They pose with hands in coat pockets as if they had guns. A dark limousine rolls up, spots them, then glides away.

Minutes later, an angry police captain named McCluskey (Sterling Hayden), friendly to the Sollozzo faction, charges up with his men and slugs Michael, breaking his jaw. But Hagen, the Corleone *consiglieri*, drives up with a platoon of private detectives. They surround the Don's hospital room, thwarting any further assassination attempt.

Now the Corleones want to retaliate. Sollozzo, who travels with McCluskey as his bodyguard, asks for a meeting with Michael to discuss a truce. It is at this point that Michael's fate as his father's successor is sealed. The young man goes unarmed. But Corleone soldiers plant a gun in the men's room of the restaurant that is their meeting place. Midway during the talks, Michael goes to the bathroom, returns with the weapon, and fires it point-blank into his family's enemies.

Michael flees to Sicily, where he falls in love with a Sicilian girl (Simonetta Stefanelli) and marries her. Still, the bloodbath goes on. His young bride is killed when she starts Michael's bomb-rigged car. Back in New York, Sonny, who has taken over the family leadership, is cut down at a toll booth.

At last, Don Corleone, weakened but recovered from his wounds, calls for peace. Eventually, Michael returns and marries his old love, Kay, then takes his father's place at the head of the family. The transition comes none too soon. In failing health, the old Don has a heart attack and dies.

The death scene takes place in the family garden, where the Don is playing with his grandchild. In an inventive bit of business, Brando put an orange peel in his mouth to scare the youngster, a trick that he had played in real life on his own children. The effect was perfect—first fright, then laughter from the boy.

At his father's funeral, Michael perceives another power try in the making. Acting quickly, he has his soldiers kill five gangsters to nip the coup in the bud.

Now Michael is firmly entrenched as the new Don. But there is still another facet of his character to learn before the movie ends. One of the hoods marked for assassination was the unfaithful husband (Gianni Russo) of his own sister (Talia Shire). Hysterical, she bursts into his home, screaming, full of hate for Michael.

Kay, a stunned onlooker, later asks Michael if, in fact, he has ever killed anyone. He tells her it is part of his business, therefore none of her business. Then he thinks better of his reply and says he will answer the question this one time.

"Is it true?" Kay asks.

"No," he says, deciding to lie rather than have her know the truth.

If Michael is two-faced, it is because he lives in two cultures. They are separate and distinct and must always be that way if he can sustain both simultaneously.

The point comes across at the end when Kay walks out of his den to do some housework in another room. The door is ajar, and into the office come gangsters, greeting Michael, bowing and kissing his ring. Then a henchman shuts the door, leaving Kay alone on the outside, again barred from the private world where her husband reigns supreme.

Dressed as a cop, a gunman from the Corleone family rubs out the bodyguard of a rival mob chieftain before gunning down his boss (Richard Conte, at rear).

Goldfinger
(1964)

Directed by Guy Hamilton. Screenplay by Richard Maibaum and Paul Dehn based on the book by Ian Fleming. Camera, Ted Moore. Editor, Peter Hunt. Production design, Ken Adam. Music, John Barry. Title song lyrics by Leslie Bricusse and Anthony Newley, sung by Shirley Bassey. Special effects, John Stears, Frank George (assistant). A United Artists release of an Eon (Harry Saltzman and Albert R. Broccoli) Production. 108 minutes.

James Bond	SEAN CONNERY
Pussy Galore	HONOR BLACKMAN
Auric Goldfinger	GERT FROBE
Jill Masterson	SHIRLEY EATON
Tilly Masterson	TANIA MALLETT
Odd Job	HAROLD SAKATA
"M"	BERNARD LEE
Solo	MARTIN BENSON
Felix Leiter	CEC LINDER
Simmons	AUSTIN WILLIS
Miss Moneypenny	LOIS MAXWELL
"Q"	DESMOND LLEWELYN

As James Bond leans over to kiss yet another conquest, he sees in the cornea of her eyes the reflection of a dark figure creeping up from behind.

Sooner than you can say "Hail Britannia," Bond swings the girl around so that her svelte back takes the crushing deathblow.

Still, the thug is not finished. He comes at Bond again. That proves to be a fatal mistake. Bond sidesteps, nudges the assassin into a bathful of water, and quickly drops in a handy live electric cord.

There may be suaver heroes, operatives with sharper intellect, men who have shown more bravery. But no one has ever put together all these elements as well as James Bond, indestructible British Agent 007. The rare double-oh prefix, of course, licenses him to kill on active duty.

The ultimate parody of the superhero, Bond has strong masculine features, iron nerves, and a difficult-to-define quality that comes close to what Ernest Hemingway called "grace under pressure."

But he is more than just tough and cool. He moves easily in the world of posh casinos, exclusive resorts, and elegant continental hotels. He appreciates good food and wine, and his precise, knowledgeable orders draw compliments from the most seasoned of *maître d*'s. They are all quite familiar with his favorite mixed drink—vodka martini, very dry, shaken, not stirred.

Then there is Bond's meaner side. He is a crack shot with a .25-caliber Beretta automatic (carried in his left arm holster) and a superb fighter who knows both judo and karate. He is, in short, a professional killer who never sentimentalizes over death.

Some have said he is an incomplete hero because he is lacking in morality. But death is an inevitable part of his job—as it is of that of a surgeon. Bond doesn't like killing. But if it happens, it happens. The next time, he could be the one on the wrong side of a bullet.

However, 007 is perhaps best known for Bondmanship, his ability to get beautiful women to jump into bed with him. Some of these desirable females are counterspies—that is, until they meet Bond and defect right into his rugged arms. His choice in women equals his gourmet taste in food. They are young, fresh and seduceable. The list includes:

● Pussy Galore (Honor Blackman), the man-hating aviatrix of *Goldfinger*. A judo expert, she delights in slamming 007 to the

James Bond (Sean Connery), indestructible British Agent 007, levels his gun.

ground—until he makes her forget judo. She ends up literally tossing in the hay with him and becomes his ally.

● Tiffany Case (Jill St. John), sultry member of an international smuggling ring in *Diamonds Are Forever* (1971). The sleek redhead abandons her illegal activities after she has an amorous encounter with Bond on a plastic waterbed filled with fish.

● Honey Ryder (Ursula Andress), the bronze nature girl he meets on Dr. No's mysterious island in the Caribbean. Her magnificent torso rises mermaidlike from the sea.

● Kissy Suzuki (Mie Hama), a Japanese beauty whom Bond marries in *You Only Live Twice* (1967) to lend credibility to his disguise as an oriental fisherman.

● Tatiana Romanova (Daniela Bianchi), the beautiful but vulnerable Soviet cipher clerk assigned to lure Bond into a trap in *From Russia with Love* (1963). Instead, she winds up in love with him.

● Jill Masterson (Shirley Eaton), the series' most opulent corpse. Goldfinger's henchmen brush her nude body with gold paint, closing her pores and suffocating her. All because this gilded beauty gave away Goldfinger's card-cheating tricks.

Auric Goldfinger (Gert Frobe), a solid-gold menace.

● Tracy Draco (Diana Rigg), an international gangster's daughter in *On Her Majesty's Secret Service* (1969). She marries Bond—for love—then is murdered.

● Miss Moneypenny (Lois Maxwell), the devoted secretary to Bond's boss, M. She has a crush on 007 that never seems to get very far. He's seldom around headquarters long enough to allow for a decent affair.

Maxwell, who appeared in all the Bond films through 1983, liked making the series. But the role typecast her. "Nobody would give me another part," she said. "Since my part was small, usually about twelve words, I would have only two days of shooting for each film. If I had to depend on my salary as Miss Moneypenny, I'd have died after two months."

Of all the Bond women, producer Albert R. (Cubby) Broccoli liked Andress best. "Diana Rigg was great, and Barbara Bach [who played Major Anya Amasova in *The Spy Who Loved Me*, 1977] and Honor Blackman were good. But Ursula stands out."

He picked her from a photograph to play Bond's first girl. "When I got to Jamaica," Broccoli recalled, "there was this beautiful creature. . . . I knew then she was the type of girl we should use for future leading ladies—an unknown with a new face who wouldn't demand an outrageous salary."

Except for Miss Moneypenny, none of these voluptuous gals stays on the scene very long. Bond hews to the lone wolf's motto—love 'em and leave 'em. And so no leading lady has ever appeared twice with 007.

Equally fascinating in a perverse sort of way are the archvillains who do battle with Bond. They include:

● Dr. No (Joseph Wiseman), the mad Chinese scientist and designer of a secret weapon capable of destroying Cape Kennedy. He operates from a subterranean base on a private Caribbean island

Pussy Galore (Honor Blackman) uses a judo twist to send Bond flying to a soft landing in the hay.

defended by fanatically loyal workers.

● Ernst Stavro Blofeld (Donald Pleasence, Telly Savalas, and Charles Gray), the shaven-head, saber-scarred chief of the international criminal organization Spectre (Special Executive for Counterintelligence, Terrorism, Revenge, and Extortion). An unforgiving taskmaster, he punishes failure with instant death, while stroking his white Persian cat.

● Emilio Largo (Adolfo Celi), Spectre agent and A-bomb hijacker who has a pool full of tiger sharks and a 95-mile-an-hour giant hydrofoil cocooned in a yacht.

● Auric Goldfinger (Gert Frobe), "the man with the Midas touch." Already a millionaire, he is nonetheless obsessed by bullion and a yen to turn Fort Knox's gold radioactive and unusable, so his own hoard will soar in value.

● Oddjob (Harold Sakata), Goldfinger's mute chauffeur-bodyguard. The squat, rocklike killer can crush a man's neck with one karate chop, or decapitate a foe with his razor-brimmed bowler hat, which he slings like a discus.

● Russian Colonel Rosa Klebb (Lotte Lenya), a toad of a woman. The torture queen of Spectre nearly does Bond in with a swift kick from one of the poison-tipped blades that flick out from her shoes.

This sadistic cast all come from the pen of Ian Fleming, whose thirteen books on Bond sold more than thirty million copies and brought him $3 million in royalties. It was often said that Fleming, who died in 1964 at the age of fifty-six, created Bond in his own image.

Son of a Conservative member of Parliament, Fleming was, in fact, a sports car enthusiast, gambler, firearms expert, and connoisseur of good food. Like Bond, he was once a Royal Navy commander. He went to Eton, Britain's most exclusive prep school, and Sandhurst, the military academy. However, Fleming felt he really had little in common with 007. "I do rather envy him his blondes and his efficiency," he once said. "But I can't say I like the chap."

Nevertheless, Fleming had a following that reached into the highest circle of government and royalty. President Kennedy and Allen Dulles, who headed the Central Intelligence Agency, were Bond fans. And so was Britain's Prince Philip.

But it was the movies that turned Bond into a household name—mainly because of the casting of Sean Connery. Son of a Scottish truck driver, Connery (his real first name is Tommy) grew up in Edinburgh. He quit school at fifteen, joined the navy at sixteen, but hated it and was medically discharged at nineteen with ulcers. He was considered 20 percent disabled and given a pension of nine shillings ($1.08) a week. Two tattoos, reminders of this part of his life, are on his right wrist. They say "Scotland Forever" and "Mum and Dad."

A succession of odd jobs followed his brief navy life. He was a plasterer's helper, bricklayer, coffin polisher, milkman, lifeguard, printer's devil. Then one day he read that a touring production of *South Pacific* needed chorus boys.

He took a cram course in dancing, went to London, and landed a part. "I couldn't think of any job but show business again," he said.

The virile, 200-pound, six-foot-two Connery went into stock, repertory, Shakespeare, and television. After small roles in four pictures in 1957, he played in a first-rate BBC production of *Requiem for a Heavyweight*. That led to a movie part in London opposite Lana Turner, who was then in her late thirties. Connery thought the film, *Another Time, Another Place* (1958), would be his big break. It wasn't. So he went back into stock. But there were those who would remember him from his television days.

Broccoli and Harry Saltzman, another American producer, had bought movie rights to most of the Bond novels. They were going into production with *Dr. No* and

Oddjob (Harold Sakata), Goldfinger's right-hand man.

eagerly searching for a leading man. Broccoli and Fleming favored a smooth old-school Establishment type like David Niven, Richard Burton, or James Mason. But Saltzman wanted fire and toughness. Despite these different conceptions, the two producers were sold on Connery as soon as they auditioned him.

"It was the sheer self-confidence he exuded," Broccoli said. "I've never seen a surer guy. Every time he made a point, he hit the desk with that great fist of his, or slapped his thigh. When he left, we watched him through the window as he walked down the street. He walked like the most arrogant son-of-a-gun you've ever seen. . . . 'That's our Bond,' I said."

The first film, *Dr. No*, drew long lines at the box office and grossed nearly $6 million on a $1.5 million investment. After that, there was no turning back.[1]

Though George Lazenby and Roger Moore played Bond after Connery's contract ran out, neither came close to equaling his performance.

If Bond fans are adamant on the superiority of Connery, they are split on his best film. Some cast their ballot for *From Russia with Love*. Still others say *Dr. No*.

My own favorite is *Goldfinger*,[2] because of its supervillain and its intriguing plot about the most ambitious break-in of all time. The plan to radiate Fort Knox's gold reserve is the brainchild of millionaire Auric Goldfinger (Frobe).[3] He wants to corner the market in gold for his cache in Switzerland.

---

[1]For the record, the Bond films are *Dr. No* (1963), *From Russia with Love* (1964), *Goldfinger* (1964), *Thunderball* (1965), *You Only Live Twice* (1967), *On Her Majesty's Secret Service* (1969), *Diamonds Are Forever* (1971), *The Man with the Golden Gun* (1974), *The Spy Who Loved Me* (1977), *Moonraker* (1979), *For Your Eyes Only* (1981), *Octopussy* (1983), *Never Say Never Again* (1983), and *A View to a Kill* (1985).

[2]It is also the choice of Roger Ebert and Gene Siskel, the Chicago film critics who are the hosts of the TV show *At the Movies*.

[3]The studio dubbed the voice of Frobe, a German character actor, even though he could speak English.

When Bond meets this tycoon by a pool in a posh Miami Beach hotel, Goldfinger is busy cheating at gin rummy. His method is almost as ingenious as his Fort Knox caper. Goldfinger has outfitted his blond girlfriend Jill Masterson (Eaton) with binoculars and planted her on a balcony overlooking the pool. There she discloses his opponent's hand via a wireless radio. Goldfinger picks up her transmissions with an earpiece that looks like a hearing device.

Bond not only foils Goldfinger's scheme—he slips up to the hotel balcony and snatches the mike from the blond—but he woos the bikini-clad lady. When a phone call from his American colleague interrupts his lovemaking, Bond treads the thin line of good taste by begging off with the excuse "Something big's come up."

Goldfinger, not one to tolerate defection, wreaks diabolical revenge on his lady friend. To make sure Bond has gotten the point, Goldfinger introduces him to Oddjob, his homicidal manservant with the build of a sumo wrestler.

That only increases the resolve of the British Secret Service. To give Bond some leverage, it issues him a $45,000 Aston Martin DB5 sports car specifically equipped with twin Browning machine guns mounted behind the parking lights. Its extras also include revolving license plates, retractable bulletproof window shields, a fog thrower, an ejector seat that hurtles unwanted passengers through the roof, and a radar screen.

With it, Bond traces Goldfinger to his Swiss hideout. But once there, Goldfinger captures Bond and nearly splits him in two. He spread-eagles 007 on a table and starts a lethal laser beam creeping up between his legs.

With the beam only inches away, Bond says he knows all about Operation Grand Slam, the code name for Goldfinger's diabolical plan to atomize Fort Knox. At

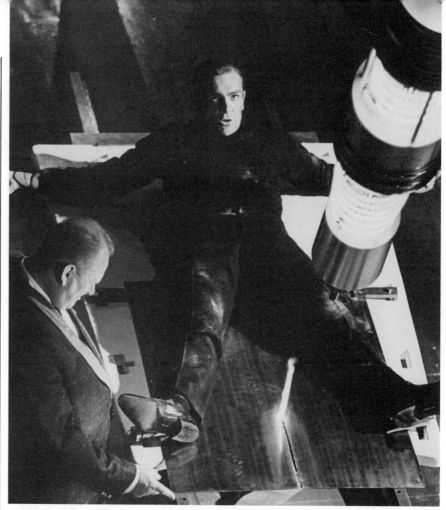

A deadly laser beam inches its way toward 007, tied to a laboratory table, while Goldfinger chortles.

first, Goldfinger appears unfazed. Then, concerned about how many more operatives might know about his scheme, he decides to spare Bond for the moment. Off goes the laser beam in the nick of time.

Hijacked to Goldfinger's Kentucky stud farm, Bond meets Pussy Galore (Blackman), a Goldfinger ally whose name intrigues Bond. To his dismay, he finds she is cool to him. But he is persistent. He tumbles her in a barn and eventually charms her into his camp.

The two join forces to spoil Goldfinger's caper—but just barely. Bond leaves himself only seconds before Goldfinger's A-bomb is timed to go off. Eventually, Goldfinger meets his fate when he is sucked out of a plane's window during a bare-knuckles bout with Bond.

There is one interesting footnote. When Blackman appeared on TV talk shows in the United States to publicize the movie, she was amused to find that many interviewers couldn't bring themselves to pronounce her character's name. Even those who did sometimes found their efforts fruitless, including Johnny Carson. Program officials bleeped out the offending word.

The film's producers, concerned that censors might object, had, in fact, given the character a second name, Kitty Galore. But their fears dissolved after Tom Carlisle, their publicity man, managed to have Blackman photographed with Prince Philip at a charity dance. Carlisle gave the exclusive story to a newspaper on condition that it use the caption "Pussy and the Prince." It did. No one objected after that.

Harold E. Stine. Music, Johnny Mandel. Song, "Suicide Is Painless," lyrics by Mike Altman. Editor, Danford B. Greene. Art directors, Jack Martin Smith and Arthur Lonergan. Produced by Ingo Preminger. An Aspen Production, later a TV series. 20th Century–Fox. Rated R. 116 minutes.

Hawkeye	DONALD SUTHERLAND
Trapper John	ELLIOTT GOULD
Duke	TOM SKERRITT
Maj. Hot Lips Houlihan	SALLY KELLERMAN
Maj. Frank Burns	ROBERT DUVALL
Lieutenant Dish	JO ANN PFLUG
Dago Red	RENE AUBERJONOIS
Col. Henry Blake	ROGER BOWEN
Radar O'Reilly	GARY BURGHOFF
Sgt. Maj. Vollmer	DAVID ARKIN
Spearchucker	FRED WILLIAMSON
Me Lay	MICHAEL MURPHY
Ho-Jon	KIM ATWOOD
Corporal Judson	TIM BROWN
Lieutenant Leslie	INDUS ARTHUR
Painless Pole	JOHN SCHUCK
Private Boone	BUD CORT

※ Academy Award winner

Maj. Frank Burns (Robert Duvall) and Maj. Hot Lips Houlihan (Sally Kellerman) are having a late-night tête-à-tête in her tent.

They are soul mates, two God-fearing, right-thinking officers commiserating about the louts whose boorish manners they must suffer at a lonely battlefield post.

"It's the disrespect for you. That's what I can't forgive them," says Hot Lips. Even while she speaks, she is undoing Burns's shirt buttons. His hand is disappearing beneath her skirt. In another instant, they are making mad love on an army cot.

As they do, another pair of hands is busy hooking up a microphone beneath the bedsprings. In a few seconds, the camp's loud-speaker system is booming every breathless sound of their act of love across the post to the startled ears of every soldier.

This is one of a series of irreverent, fast-moving scenes from *M*A*S*H*, a picture that made its point about war through humor rather than battlefield scenes. Not that the film lacked its share of gore. *M*A*S*H* stands for Mobile Army Surgical Hospital, and there was plenty of blood flowing. But the faces of the wounded were rarely seen, because director Robert Altman made satire his major emphasis.

Satire or not, the movie had a strong bite. Though it places the action in Korea, the picture was made during the Vietnam War. And it is clear the film is a commentary on the Vietnam fighting.

"Everyone associated it with Vietnam. That had a lot to do with the picture's success," director Altman said in an interview for this book. He sat in the living room of his midtown Manhattan apartment overlooking Central Park. Nearby was an oversize director's chair whose seat was about four feet off the ground. Altman said someone had given it to him as a joke. The chair was so big that anyone sitting in it would have to look like Lily Tomlin in *The Incredible Shrinking Woman*.

"Our byword was 'bad taste,'" Altman continued. "Anything that was in questionable taste was acceptable in the film. Then, by showing the results of war, those incredibly bloody operation scenes, we got people to think....A lot of people had the time of their lives in the theater. But when they walked out, they felt something was wrong. They remembered the endless parade of bodies in those helicopters. They saw the film was really an antiwar statement."

Altman was most interested in seeing that his message got through to the supporters of the war. "It isn't so easy to change people's minds who don't agree

Long-stemmed Major Hot Lips Houlihan (Sally Kellerman) makes a rather unmilitary entrance as she arrives via helicopter.

with you," he said. "We were really sneaking into the enemy's camp. We disguised what we were really saying with the humor. It took a little while for it to sink in. But it was in their computers."[1]

Still, Altman said it was a struggle to get 20th Century-Fox to let him make the movie the way he wanted. Studio boss Richard Zanuck did not like it. He wanted the blood and gore taken out.

"The only reason the picture got made and distributed was because they [Fox] had two other wars going on—*Patton* [1970] and *Tora, Tora, Tora* [1970]. Nobody [at Fox] paid much attention to our little film."

However, *M*A*S*H* got raves at a sneak preview in San Francisco, Altman said, and the studio couldn't ignore this. Just to make sure, Altman added, he grabbed Zanuck by the lapels after the preview and told him, "You have to listen. . . . You can't allow this picture to be cut."[2]

Ironically, this movie that drew millions of young people to theaters all over the country was the product of grandfathers: screen writer Ring Lardner, Jr., producer Ingo Preminger, and director Altman.

Which leads to an interesting question: Who gets credit for the picture's success? The answer sheds light on the *auteur* theory, that much-debated concept that

Nurse Dish (Jo Ann Pflug) slips out of the officers' tent a bit disheveled after some extracurricular activities.

Army medics Hawkeye (Donald Sutherland), *left*, and Trapper John (Elliott Gould) get in a round of golf between battlefield operations.

holds that it is the director, not the screenwriter or the producer, who is really the prime creator of a film.

The movie was based on a novel by Richard Hooker, a Korean War army surgeon. It provided both the style and philosophy of the movie, Lardner said, and quite a few of the jokes. The book was written by a professional writer who collaborated with Hooker. Even so, Lardner said he had to do a major overhaul to put together the screenplay. "The book wasn't very well organized and I did change it a great deal."

Altman, in turn, highlights his own effort. He said Lardner's manuscript went the rounds of several directors before Ingo Preminger sent it to him. Altman said he liked the script because he saw in it the opportunity to do something he had been working on for years.

"It was called *The Chicken and the Hawk*, a comedy in much the same vein [as *M*A*S*H*] about World War I flyers. It showed the

insanity, the bad taste, all the antics of war. But I never could get it off the ground. I never really had a good script. When I read *M*A*S*H*, I saw I could do the same thing with this vehicle."

Altman met with Preminger to discuss the script. "I told him that it would have to be very loose, very rambling. Anything that even looked like a plot would have to come out." Altman said Preminger agreed and held to that agreement. "And that's really how it got done."

According to Altman, the agreement left his actors free to improvise, one of the trademarks of his films. "I don't think anybody had ever done a film with that loose a structure. Every actor used a different comic style."

Lardner says he is not surprised that Altman, in effect, sees himself as the picture's *auteur*. Directors, by the nature of their job, must be self-confident authority figures to respond to rapid-fire decisions. As a result, Lardner says, they tend to overestimate

---

[1]For example, critic Rex Reed wrote: "I found myself angry at first for having such a good time watching such irreverence. Then, I got with it and I knew. War *is* obscene. War *is* offensive. War *is* a charade of vulgarity, an endless variety act of uncompromising stupidity. In short, war is a joke, and unless we can laugh at it, the joke's on us."

[2]As it turned out, *M*A*S*H* earned Altman an Oscar nomination, won the Grand Prize at the 1970 Cannes Film Festival, and was named Best Film of 1970 by the National Society of Film Critics.

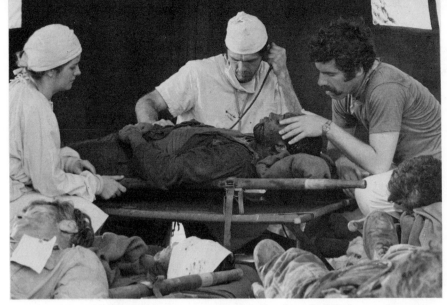
Another bloody battlefield victim is added to an already filled casualty tent.

their contribution to their films, often to the detriment of the author.

"What he [Altman] doesn't stop to think," Lardner said in William Froug's book *The Screenwriter Looks at the Screenwriter*, "is that there could have been no such picture if Richard Hooker had not written this book, setting those particular characters in this background. And that no matter how much it might have been changed from that, the basic authorship is there in the book. . . ."

Lardner, who won the movie's only Oscar for his screenplay, continued: "Bob's exaggeration of his role is quite sincere, because, and this probably applies to a lot of other directors, when we or they undertake to do a piece of material, they have to think that they are reconceiving it, shaping it, as they are, to their own particular tastes and imaginations. They just tend to forget how much has gone before, and that everything they're doing is based on other people's concepts. . . ."

In the end, Lardner says—and this is probably closest to the truth—the success of *M*A*S*H* is really a collaborative effort. Credit for the movie's authorship should be divided three ways: among Hooker, Altman, and Lardner.

If there is no unanimity over

major credit for the film's creation, there is little disagreement over the contribution of the actors. Elliott Gould and Donald Sutherland were brilliantly cast as Trapper John and Hawkeye Pierce, heretical army surgeons with an addiction for martinis, golf, and pretty nurses and contempt for authority and red tape. Also outstanding were Bible-thumbing, teetotaling Major Burns (Duvall) and long-stemmed, pompous chief nurse Houlihan (Kellerman).

*M*A*S*H* gave Kellerman her first big break. A big-boned blonde, almost six feet tall, she took eight years to win her first lead on a TV dramatic show ("Outer Limits"). Before *M*A*S*H*, she had appeared in thirty plays, twenty TV shows, and at least five movies without attracting much attention.

She was going nowhere when she appeared before Altman one day for the casting of *M*A*S*H*. Kellerman was actually sent in to test for the more glamorous part of Lieutenant Dish. But she said, "'I'll do anything. I can be funny. I can break loose, just let me try.' And I think I had hold of his [Altman's] pant legs or something because he took a long look at me and jumped up and yelled, 'Hot Lips!'"

In the movie, Hawkeye and

Trapper John work hard in surgery but party just as hard later and take more than a few liberties with nurses. In fact, the film made doctors seem like schoolboys in their reckless pursuit of pleasure. In one scene, there is a $20 bet to see if Hot Lips is a real blonde. Hawkeye and Trapper John pull down a tent curtain while she is showering—as the troops look on.

Altman had a novel way to get a genuine expression of surprise on Kellerman's face. "We had done the scene once. But Sally was very shy. I said [to the cast], 'Let's all take our clothes off. So we'll be standing naked when she looks out.' Gary Burghoff [Radar O'Reilly] said, 'I'll do it.' He dropped his pants and stood right next to the camera. When the tent collapsed, Sally just froze for that moment."

The picture abounds with outrageous gags. Doctors stash beer in a refrigerated blood bank. Hawkeye and Trapper John operate in golf shoes and Japanese kimonos. A Last Supper is held for Painless Pole (John Schuck), a suicide-bent dentist. Football players smoke grass on the bench and cheerleading nurses holler, "Sixty-nine is divine."

The episodic film moves so fast it's over before you know it. But its message lingers. *M*A*S*H* is an unique anti-Establishment film whose insouciance set new standards for comedy.

Trapper John and Hawkeye make an instant diagnosis of an X-ray.

The Producers
(1968)

Directed by Mel Brooks. Screenplay by Brooks. ✿ Photography, Joe Coffey. Music composed and conducted by John Morris. Songs: "The Producers" by Morris and Mort Goode; "Love Power" by Norman Blagman and Herb Hartis; and "Springtime for Hitler" and "Prisoners of Love" by Brooks. Editor, Ralph Rosenblum. Choreography, Alan Johnson. A Joseph Levine presentation produced by Sidney Glazier. Embassy Pictures Corp. 88 minutes.

Max Bialystock	ZERO MOSTEL
Leo Bloom	GENE WILDER
Franz Liebkind	KENNETH MARS
Old lady	ESTELLE WINWOOD
Roger DeBris	CHRISTOPHER HEWETT
Ulla	LEE MEREDITH
Carmen Giya	ANDREAS VOUTSINA
L.S.D.	DICK SHAWN
"Eva Braun"	RENEE TAYLOR
Nazi chorus boy	MEL BROOKS

✿ Academy Award winner

"He came to my office, a small guy who looked very nervous, and seemed to tell jokes, some of which weren't too funny, and I was a little uncomfortable."

That's how producer Sidney Glazier remembers his first meeting with Mel Brooks. Out of that meeting came the decision to make the hilariously irreverent comedy *Producers*.

The movie's taste is occasionally called into question, and, in fact, some critics put it on their all-time tacky list. But it won an Oscar for Brooks for best screenplay and an Oscar nomination for Gene Wilder for best supporting performance, and over the years it has become a cult favorite. It is, to my mind, a film that, like good wine and cheese, gets better as the years pass.

Still, it took some hard selling. Brooks, who was aspiring to become a director after years as a TV comedy writer, had tried to pedal the film for three years. Finally, he got an appointment with producer Glazier.

An inventive, freeform come-dian in his own right, Brooks played all the parts in Glazier's office. Glazier laughed until his sides hurt. In the end, Glazier agreed to produce the film. And that's how it all started.

In the book *the Shooting Stops ...the Cutting Begins* by Ralph Rosenblum and Robert Karen, Glazier recalled that the original name for the picture was *for Hitler* (which became the title of the musical within the movie).[1]

"If it had remained *Springtime for Hitler*," Glazier said, "it would have made several million dollars. But we had a Jewish distributor by the name of Joseph Levine who insisted that the Jews would be up in arms. So we reluctantly changed the title to a banal thing like *Producers*."

Actually, the plot is not as outlandish as it seems. It is based on an experience from Brooks's younger days when he worked for an unscrupulous Broadway producer who occasionally staged one-night flops so he could pocket the investment money.

Still, no theater story as wicked as this had ever been suggested for a movie. And few productions had been assembled with such clashing personalities as Zero Mostel and Brooks.

---

[1] It was one of Brooks's running gags. After his first TV series success, "Get Smart," Brooks answered all questions about what he was doing next by saying he was working on a picture called *Springtime for Hitler*. It was a takeoff on a long-running Edward Everett Horton comedy called *Springtime for Henry*. In this case, Brooks's joke became a reality.

Faded Broadway producer Max Bialystock (Zero Mostel) gets an investment idea from accountant Leo Bloom (Gene Wilder).

Ulla (Lee Meredith), the producers' secretary, demonstrating some non-secretarial talents.

Their personal zingers during the filming have become legend. Rosenblum, the picture's film editor, said the two traded insults on the set as if they were warring fishwives.

For one thing, Brooks, accustomed to the fast-shooting schedules of TV, found it difficult to adjust to the deliberate pace of movie productions. When Brooks worked for Sid Caesar's "Show of Shows," rehearsals began on Tuesday and climaxed with a ninety-minute live show each Saturday. By contrast, movie directors consider it a good day if they finish with five minutes of usable film.

"Is that fat pig ready yet?" Mel would sputter.

"The director?" said Zero. "What director? There's a director here? *That's* a director?"

The mood sometimes became tense on the set, Rosenblum said, and Brooks's flashing temper and mercurial moods alienated others besides Mostel. First he tactlessly chased producer Glazier from the shooting area. Then his relationship with photographer Joe Coffey deteriorated after Coffey tried to get Brooks to change some key camera angles.

Finally, after seeing Rosenblum's rough cut of the opening scene, he told Rosenblum in no uncertain terms not to do any more editing until all the filming was finished (and Brooks could be in the editing room).

Rosenblum quotes Brooks as saying: "I just finished with Coffey this afternoon. I told him I don't need his help. And I don't need your help either! I'll do it all myself. Don't you touch this film—

you hear?—don't *touch* it, until I finish shooting."

Perhaps because Brooks resisted professional advice so firmly, his picture drew many strong rebuffs. "Amateurishly crude," said *New Yorker* magazine. "Mostel is grotesque.... Brooks has almost no idea where to put the camera." Said *Vogue*: "The picture is warmly recommended for those who regard the following things as hilarious: Hitler, Nazis, queers, hysterics, old ladies being pawed, and infantilism."

Others couldn't make up their minds. "*The Producers* leaves one alternately picking up one's coat to leave and sitting back to laugh," said Renata Adler of the *New York Times*.

But over the years, the audience's reaction is clear. More people have opted to stay to be regaled by Mostel's outrageous antics and Brooks's irreverent lines. It has become a staple of revival houses and late-night television.

Unquestionably, it is its madcap plot and its motley collection of characters that win its legion of fans.

Max Bialystock (Mostel) is a faded entrepreneur reduced to conning little old ladies to invest in his dismal shows. He never dreams of fraud on a grand scale until mousy accountant Leo Bloom (Gene Wilder) one day innocently remarks that, given the right circumstances, a producer can make more from a one-night disaster than from a hit.

That rings a bell for Bialystock. He decides to sell 25,000 percent of a show that will be so terrible it is bound to fail. In that case, no one will expect any money back. The producers can declare a total loss and pocket huge profits.

To ensure failure, Bialystock and Bloom search out the world's worst play—*Springtime for Hitler*, written by helmeted Nazi Franz Liebkind (Kenneth Mars). When Bialystock and Bloom find Liebkind at his rooftop pigeon coop, the author mistakes them for the FBI. Cringing against his coop, Liebkind sputters: "I vas never a member of the Nazi party. I am not responsible. I only followed orders.... My papers are in order. I luf my adopted country." He salutes and starts to sing: "Oh, beautiful, for spacious skies, for amber waves of grain..." Brooks actually wrote the part with the idea of playing it himself.

Next, to drive more nails into the show's coffin, the producers seek the world's worst actor and director. They cast a far-out hippie (Dick Shawn) to play Hitler and a transvestite director (Christopher Hewett) who is so bad his productions usually close after the first rehearsal.

The show opens with goose-stepping dancers, a tenor in Gestapo uniform, and high-kicking chorus girls prancing in rotating swastika formations. "Don't be stupid, be a smartie, Come and join the Nazi party," says Brooks, coming out of the chorus as a jack-booted storm trooper.

The show-stopper is a hippie Hitler who sings rock-and-roll songs. Of course, the musical turns out to be so bad the audience sees it as one gigantic put-on and loves it. All of which puts Messrs. Bialystock and Bloom along with author Liebkind in the Big House.

If *The Producers* is sometimes vulgar and disjointed, it is more often wild and uproarious. It is a fast-paced, ribald comedy with enough slapstick energy to keep you laughing on the bleakest day of the year.

Above right: The *Springtime for Hitler* show-stopper with jackbooted Gestapo police and chorus girls decked out with beer steins and pretzels.

Right: It's bad news for the producers. Their show is a hit and they are financially ruined.

The producers interview Nazi playwright Franz Liebkind (Kenneth Mars) at his rooftop pigeon loft.

Dr. Strangelove: Or, How I Learned to Stop Worrying and Love the Bomb   (1964)

Produced and directed by Stanley Kubrick. Screenplay by Kubrick, Terry Southern, and Peter George, based on George's novel *Red Alert*. Camera, Gilbert Taylor. Editor, Anthony Harvey. Art director, Peter Murton. Production designer, Ken Adam. Music, Laurie Johnson. Columbia. A Hawk Film. B/W. 93 minutes.

President Merkin Muffley	PETER SELLERS
Dr. Strangelove	PETER SELLERS
Group Capt. Lionel Mandrake	PETER SELLERS
Gen. Buck Turgidson	GEORGE C. SCOTT
Gen. Jack D. Ripper	STERLING HAYDEN
Col. Bat Guano	KEENAN WYNN
Maj. T. J. "King" Kong	SLIM PICKENS
Ambassador de Sadesky	PETER BULL
Miss Scott	TRACY REED
Lt. Lothar Zogg, bombardier	JAMES EARL JONES
Mr. Staines	JACK CRELEY
Lt. H. R. Dietrich	FRANK BERRY
Lt. W. D. Kivel, navigator	GLENN BECK
Capt. G. A. "Ace" Owens, copilot	SHANE RIMMER
Lt. B. Goldberg, radio operator	PAUL TAMARIN
General Faceman	GORDON TANNER
Admiral Randolph	ROBERT O'NEIL
Frank	ROY STEPHENS
Members of defense team	LAURENCE HERDER, JOHN MCCARTHY, HAL GALILI

Merkin Muffley, the president, is on the hot line to Moscow. He has some embarrassing news for the Soviet premier.

"Hello, Dmitri. . . . I'm fine. . . . Now then, you know how we've always talked about the possibility of something going wrong with the bomb. . . . The bomb, Dmitri. The hydrogen bomb. . . . Well, now, what happened is that, uh, one of our base commanders . . . he went a little funny in the head . . . and he went and did a silly thing. . . . He ordered his planes to attack your country."

A comedy about an accidental nuclear attack? One that ends with total annihilation, thermonuclear apocalypse?

Preposterous.

That was the reaction of most Hollywood executives to Stanley Kubrick's proposal to do *Dr. Strangelove: Or, How I Learned to Stop Worrying and Love the Bomb*. Even Terry Southern, one of the picture's screenwriters, conceded that the project seemed far out. "If anyone submitted the script cold to a major studio, the reaction would have been, 'Are you kidding?'"

Kubrick thought otherwise. In the end, his thinking prevailed. He saw that, in the era of the nuclear arms race, *Dr. Strangelove* touched a raw nerve.

The film was based on a real situation, one that people live with every day, however subliminally, one they have learned to accept, however nervously. And the emotions of fear and laughter—though apparently poles apart—are really not that dissimilar.

Kubrick's dark comedy drew hordes of curious moviegoers. Almost from the start, they broke box-office records. At the same time, the picture touched off strong criticism. Some equated his plot with national disloyalty. "No Communist could dream of a more effective anti-American film to spread abroad than this one," said Chalmers Roberts of the *Washington Post*.

Kubrick thought his critics missed the point. He had no wish to make a taut drama based on our nuclear attack capability. He was

Peter Sellers as Dr. Strangelove, nuclear expert, works out a problem on his slide rule.

The huge war room where President Muffley (Sellers) calls an emergency meeting of his Pentagon chiefs.

fashioning a satire raking over every sacrosanct idea of the cold war and exposing human vulnerability and folly at the highest level of government.

Said Kubrick: "Why should the bomb be approached with reverence? Reverence can be a paralytic state of mind. For me, the comic sense is the most eminently human reaction to the mysteries and the paradoxes of life. I just hope some of them are illuminated by the exaggeration and the style of the film."

One reason Hollywood looked on Kubrick with suspicion is that, unlike most other directors, he did not rise through the motion-picture or television ranks. A native New Yorker, he started at age seventeen as a photographer for *Look* magazine. He soon branched out and shot a docu-

mentary short about a boxer called *Day of the Fight* (1951).

It failed to make money, but his family and friends encouraged him to continue. After producing two feature-length pictures with private financing—movies that also finished in the red—he did *The Killing* (1956), a picture about a racetrack robbery. The taut drama won critical acclaim. *Time* named it one of the year's ten best movies.

Because of that success, he was able to persuade Kirk Douglas to star in his next venture, the anti-war film *Paths of Glory* (1957), which became a classic of its genre. Kubrick's career took off from there. In quick succession he did *Spartacus* (1960) and the controversial *Lolita* (1962). Still in his twenties, his creative brilliance lay ahead.

Kubrick had wanted to make a film about the hydrogen bomb for several years. He had, in fact, read dozens of books on the subject. Nothing inspired him until someone called his attention to Peter George's book *Two Hours to Doom* (U.S. title, *Red Alert*).

George treated the attack as a suspenseful narrative. But the more Kubrick thought about it, the more he saw overtones of ironic comedy woven throughout the plot. The situation brought back memories of *Paths of Glory*. Kubrick recalled a sequence in which two French generals argue about how many deserters to shoot. The first says one would be enough. The other says 300. They compromise on three.

"That scene always brought a nervous titter from the audience," Kubrick said, "a reaction of shock, of recognition that things like that can happen within the context of the 'normal' world."

In the same light, Kubrick saw that many scenes in *Strangelove*, while essentially frightening, had a note of the ridiculous mixed in. So, in a 180-degree turnabout, he decided to do it as a comedy.

The mad saga revolves around a psychotic Strategic Air Command officer, Gen. Jack D. Ripper (Sterling Hayden), who lets loose his B-52 nuclear bomber squadron on the Soviet Union. Ripper takes this unilateral action because of his paranoid belief that Communists are sapping and contaminating "all our precious bodily fluids" as part of their plan to take over the world. Unbeknownst to Ripper, his attack will trigger the Russian's ultimate weapon, the Doomsday Machine, a diabolical retaliatory device set to blow up the planet.

The movie tells about the frantic but futile effort of the president (Peter Sellers) and his cabinet to stop the attack. The problem is that the cigar-chomping general is the only one who knows the code that will recall the bombers. And he's not telling.

Sterling Hayden, as Gen. Jack D. Ripper, unleashes a nuclear attack on Russia. Next to him is Sellers in his third role, RAF Group Capt. Lionel Mandrake.

George C. Scott as Buck Turgidson, the hawkish Air Force general.

Sellers plays three roles. In addition to the president, he is a British wing commander who tries to dissuade General Ripper, and Dr. Strangelove, a German scientist, now a U.S. weapons strategist, who in stressful moments forgetfully addresses the president as "mein Führer." Strangelove is a wheelchair-bound fanatic whose black-gloved prosthetic arm belies his loyalty. Every now and then, it goes out of control and snaps out a smart Nazi salute or starts strangling Strangelove himself.

Sellers was to have played a fourth role, Maj. T. J. "King" Kong, the patriotic Texas pilot. But Sellers broke his ankle and had to be replaced at the last minute by character actor Slim Pickens.

"I got a call from London, where they were shooting, at my farm near Fresno, asking if I was available," said Pickens. "I was." In fact, Pickens, who adopted his professional name—he was christened Louis Bert Lindley, Jr.—when he began a career as a professional rodeo competitor, was doing very little acting in those days. "I drove down to the courthouse and got me a passport —I'd never had one before—and I was on my way to England the next day.

"Kubrick wouldn't show me anything that he shot. He just said, 'Play it straight as you can. And it'll be fine.' I guess it was." As it turned out, Pickens nearly stole the picture.

One of the film's focal points is the Pentagon's underground war room, an imaginative set designed by Ken Adam. Its massive circular conference table is laid out before a giant global map. Blinking lights trace the progress of the ominous bomber flight.

To this room, the bald, bespectacled, rather ineffectual president summons his key advisers. They include Gen. Buck Turgidson (George C. Scott), head of the Joint Chiefs of Staff.

Roused from a motel room in mid-fornication, the hawkish Turgidson is elated by his pilots' at-

Debating nuclear strategy in the war room are Buck Turgidson and Dr. Strangelove.

tack. He enthusiastically urges all-out war, despite the massive U.S. casualties that would inevitably result. "I'm not saying we wouldn't get our hair mussed," Turgidson says. "I am saying only ten to twenty million people killed, tops, depending on the breaks." Turgidson's speech, Kubrick said, is not far removed from the prose of nuclear strategists in military journals.[1]

Eventually, the president and his men are able to call back all the planes but one, the bomber piloted by Major Kong. As he approaches Moscow, his H-bomb jams. But he frees it and rides it down to its target, straddling it like a bronco buster, yahooing and waving his hat. The explosion triggers a series of H-bomb blasts so extensive they will make the earth's surface as dead as the moon's.

Meanwhile, in the war room, Dr. Strangelove is babbling about survival miles below the earth where the nation's leaders would repopulate the nation (ten fertile women to every man) and animals could be bred and slaughtered. He grows in strength with this vision, and as the world blows up, he bounds from his wheelchair exulting, "Mein Führer, I can walk."

As a mushroom cloud spreads around the globe, Vera Lynn's soothing song "We'll Meet Again" tells us there is, indeed, no need to worry any longer.

Though *Strangelove* may disturb and dismay, it elevates comedy to new heights and remains a brilliant tract against nuclear war.

---

[1]There was also to have been a slapstick custard-pie-throwing scene involving the Russian ambassador, the president, and his advisers in the war room. It took nearly two months to shoot and cost thousands of dollars. Cooks baked hundreds of pies laced with shaving cream (because it shows up better on film than custard). "But," said Peter Bull, who played the Soviet ambassador, "Kubrick decided when he came to cut the film that it was completely at variance with the rest of it. Though admittedly sensationally funny and effective, it just didn't fit in."

Manners
and
Morals

CABARET

HESTER STREET

HUD

NETWORK

SATURDAY NIGHT
AND SUNDAY MORNING

TAXI DRIVER

TOMORROW

Cabaret

(1972)

Directed and choreographed by Bob Fosse ☆. Screenplay by Jay Allen based on the play by John Van Druten, the musical by Joe Masteroff, and stories of Christopher Isherwood. Photography, Geoffrey Unsworth. ☆ Sets, Herbert Strabl. ☆ Music, John Kander. Lyrics, Fred Ebb. Musical direction and orchestration, Ralph Burns. ☆ Art director, Rolf Zehetbauer ☆ and Jurgen Kiebach. ☆ Editor, David Bretherton. ☆ Sound, Robert Knudson ☆ and David Hildyard. ☆ Filmed in West Germany. Allied Artists. Rated PG. 118 minutes.

Sally Bowles	LIZA MINNELLI ☆
Brian Roberts	MICHAEL YORK
Baron Maximilian von Heune	HELMUT GRIEM
Master of ceremonies	JOEL GREY ☆
Fritz Wendel	FRITZ WEPPER
Natalia Landauer	MARISA BERENSON
Fraulein Schneider	ELISABETH NEUMANN-VIERTEL
Fraulein Kost	HELENE VITA
Fraulein Mayr	SIGRID VON RICHTHOFEN
Willi	GEORGE HARTMANN
Bobby	GERD VESPERMANN
Elke	RICKY RENEE
Cantor	ESTRONGO NACHAMA
Herr Ludwig	RALF WOLTER
Kit Kat dancers	KARTHRYN DOBY, INGE JAEGER, ANGELIKA KOCH, HELEN VELKOVORSKA, GITTA SCHMIDT, LOUISE QUICK (GORILLA)

☆ Academy Award winner

Few short-story collections have rolled up as much literary mileage as Christopher Isherwood's tales about the people he knew during his salad days as a British expatriate in Germany.

The collection, called *Goodbye to Berlin*, appeared in 1939, and its most celebrated story told of a brief encounter between an English university student modeled after Isherwood and a slightly kooky flapper who lived in the same boardinghouse.

In 1951, John van Druten turned the stories into a play called *I Am a Camera*, starring Julie Harris. Four years later, Jack Clayton and Henry Cornelius used them as the basis for a movie. Next, in 1966, John Kander and Fred Ebb resurrected them on Broadway as the musical *Cabaret*, which became the 1972 film.

Ironically, there really was not that much substance to this short-story collection that put into motion such an extensive multimedia recycling. But the stories were set against the tumultuous days of the beginning of fascism, and this charged atmosphere added a dimension to their plots.

Of the four versions of the original, Bob Fosse's film is clearly the best. It is an inventive, dazzling production that re-creates the sleazy atmosphere of bohemian Berlin through authentic sets, gutsy music, and creative camerawork. In the cabaret, for instance, the stage action is frequently seen from the level of the tables with waiters passing, briefly blocking the view, to give moviegoers a real sense of being in the audience.

Adding to this are superb performances by Liza Minnelli and by supporting players like Joel Grey. The two won the acting share of the picture's eight Oscars.

The biggest challenge the

Sally Bowles (Liza Minnelli) singing at the Kit Kat Club, the racy nightclub where Berliners forget their troubles.

Joel Grey won one of the picture's eight Academy Awards for his performance as the satanic-looking master of ceremonies.

Isherwood stories presented was how to re-create the mood of the times—the lack of concern of the German people for the repressive measures the Nazis had begun. Isherwood was trying to show that at a pivotal point in history, most Germans turned their heads, indulging themselves in pleasures of the moment.

Fosse and his screenwriter chose to make this point not by creating characters that would become spokesmen for this violence but, more obliquely, by showing flashes of the brutality itself—a Nazi beating up a nightclub *maître d'*, a Communist killed in the street, a crowd throwing a dead dog in front of a Jew's home. All the while, the movie keeps returning to the carefree cabaret, which becomes the symbol for decadent Berlin society escaping the harsh realities of the day.

This presentation is much too superficial and really never makes its point. It is not clear if the film is trying to say that this self-indulgent behavior was a symptom of the era or that it itself was responsible for Hitler's rise. The broad-brush treatment just doesn't demonstrate either thesis or enlighten us much.

If *Cabaret* is trivial as an interpreter of history, it is nonetheless far superior to any other musical of its time. It is a brilliantly evocative, unconventional movie that brings to the screen a fast-paced, boldly filmed story that keeps us mesmerized right from the colorful opening sequence.

"Leave your troubles outside," the satanic-looking master of ceremonies (Grey) tells the audience in the Kit Kat Club. "Life is disappointing? In here, life is beautiful."

As he introduces the entertainers and sings "Willkommen" ("Welcome"), the camera crosscuts to show Brian (Michael York) arriving in Berlin. A graduate student working on his doctoral thesis, Brian has come to write and earn money by giving language lessons. His first acquaintance at his boardinghouse turns out to be Sally Bowles (Minnelli), a garrulous entertainer whose liberated ways leave him slightly speechless.

"I may bring home a boyfriend, but only occasionally," Sally says. "I mean, I do feel you ought to go to the man's room if you can. I mean, it doesn't look so much as if one expected it. Does it?"

The next night, Brian visits her at the Kit Kat Club, where she sings in front of a bawdy chorus line. The dancers' grotesque makeup and slightly obscene choreography catch up the tawdriness and vulgarity of the times. "All the girls hated it because they had to grow hair under their arms," Minnelli said. "When we finished the musical numbers, we had a party and everybody gave them razors and soap."

Brian and Sally start spending time together, walking along the swastika-strewn streets, and Sally becomes romantically involved. But, to her dismay, she finds that Brian does not respond. "Maybe you just don't sleep with girls," she says angrily. Then she suddenly realizes the truth of her words.

Isherwood was, in fact, a homosexual, although he did not publicly disclose this until much later in his life. Nor did he make his hero one. In his story, the protagonist is more an observer of the drama than a participant. A homosexual in the 1930s, Isherwood felt, would have distracted the reader from his account of pre-Hitler Berlin. "If I had announced myself as a homosexual, I would have made the 'I' character too interesting," he said.

As the weeks pass, Brian is able to earn a living by giving English lessons to Fritz Wendel (Fritz Wepper), a gigolo, and Natalia Landauer (Marisa Berenson), the pretty daughter of a well-to-do Jewish merchant. In the stage musical, this subplot was given to Sally's landlady, played by Lotte Lenya, whose last-chance love affair with a Jewish shopkeeper is thwarted by anti-Semitism. But in the Fosse film, producers opted for a young couple. "Broadway theatergoers love to see elderly folks involved in romantic affairs," said producer Cy Feuer. "But on the screen, it's embarrassing."

Fritz sets his cap for Natalia, and they spend weekends bike riding and picnicking with Sally and Brian. To his surprise, Fritz finds he has genuinely fallen in love. On her part, Natalia confides to Sally that she doesn't know how to act toward him.

"Is this love or only infatuation of the body?" she asks in her somewhat awkward English syntax.

"Does it really matter as long as we're having fun?" Sally answers.

With the Nazis becoming more entrenched every day, Natalia decides not to accept Fritz as a husband because he is not Jewish. But the fact is Fritz is really a Jew who has only been masquerading as an Aryan. Once he tells Natalia the truth, the romance quickly leads to a wedding.

In time, Brian grows to be fond of Sally, too, and they become lovers despite his past sexual experience. However, their life is entangled with a third party when a German playboy, Baron Maximilian von Heune (Helmut Griem), lavishes gifts on both of them and takes them to bed—separately—in a weekend of debauchery at his country estate. "You, like me, are adrift in Berlin," Max says. "It's my duty to corrupt you."

On the way to his home, they stop at a country beer garden where young Germans sing the rousing song "Tomorrow Belongs to Me." It is an extraordinary scene. At first, the screen shows only the blond open-faced features of a teenager as he begins what appears to be a pleasant folk song. The camera cuts to the attentive German faces.

Then it returns to the boy and pans down to disclose his red-and-black Nazi armband. One by one, the others in the beer garden stand and join his anthem. Their voices swell until the words take on a more ominous meaning. So forceful was this scene that the producers cut it from the German version.

Max vanishes as suddenly as he appeared, leaving Sally pregnant. She isn't sure who the father is. But Brian assures her that he wants the baby and offers to marry her. Sally can't picture herself in a Cambridge cottage with a playpen in the bedroom. She opts for an abortion, and at that point Brian decides it's time to leave.

So Sally goes to the railroad station with him, says a teary farewell, and goes back to her old haunt, the Kit Kat Club. "Life is a cabaret," she sings. "Come to the cabaret."

Top: Sally and her friend; graduate student Brian Roberts (Michael York), partying with a German playboy (Helmut Griem).

Center: It's wedding bells for Natalia (Marisa Berenson) and Fritz (Fritz Wepper).

Bottom: By candlelight, Brian and Sally toast each other.

Hester Street

(1975)

Directed by Joan Micklin Silver. Screenplay by Silver adapted from the novella "Yekl" by Abraham Cahan. Photography, Kenneth Van Sickle. Music, William Bolcom. Editor, Katherine Wenning. Produced by Raphael D. Silver. Midwest Films. Rated PG. B/W. 90 minutes.

Jake	STEVEN KEATS
Gitl	CAROL KANE
Bernstein	MEL HOWARD
Mamie	DORRIE KAVANAUGH
Mrs. Kavarsky	DORIS ROBERTS
Joe Peltner	STEPHEN STRIMPELL
Fanny	LAUREN FROST
Joey	PAUL FREEDMAN
Rabbi	ZVEE SCOOLER
Rabbi's wife	EDA REISS MERIN
Peddler	LEIB LENSKY
Lawyer	MARTIN GARNER
Scribe	SOL FRIEDER
Greenhorn (café)	ZANE LASKY
Immigration officer	EDWARD CROWLEY

Jake, a Jewish immigrant garment worker, walks into his East Side tenement along with his bearded boarder, Bernstein.

Jake's wife comes out of the kitchen and Bernstein greets her in Yiddish. "Bernstein," says Jake, "you want you should be a greenhorn always?"

The boarder starts over. "Good evening, missus," he says in broken English. Then, he bows.

"Gitl," Jake says, signaling his wife to respond.

"Goot even-in-ing," she answers haltingly.

Jake smiles and pats his wife's backside.

Hester Street, a movie that sensitively depicts the struggle of new Americans trying to cast aside old world ways, had a bumpy ride on its way to the silver screen. For starters, its director was a woman, Joan Micklin Silver, then one of the few of her generation to aspire to this powerful film world post. Moreover, she was making her first feature-length picture.

Its theme—American immigrants—was one rarely seen in a commercial movie. The immigrants of *Hester Street* were not the hardy frontier type who tamed the vast open spaces. They were East European Jews who worked in sweatshops and lived in crowded walkup apartments in New York City.

Studios and distributors thought the story would have limited appeal. "Only old Jews would see it," one executive told Silver. It was not surprising, then, that Silver could find no one willing to bankroll the picture.

In the end, the movie was produced independently—a gamble whose outcome was not evident until opening day in New York City. It was a scene Silver would not soon forget.

"We had been told it's good for the weather not to be too warm because then some people want to go to the park," she said in an interview for this book. "But not raining or cold because then they want to stay home. It turned out to be pouring rain. We were immensely depressed. My husband said he wasn't even going to the theater. He did not want to put himself through seeing nobody looking at the movie.

"Then, someone called and said, 'I think you should come over.' So we went over. There was a line of people outside standing

Jake (Steven Keats) loses his temper and glares at Gitl (Carol Kane) because her old-world ways remind him of traits he is trying to put aside.

under umbrellas. . . . It had a long run there and ran successfully in lots of places all over America. For an independent film, it did marvelously."

On a budget of $370,000, *Hester Street* earned its costs in the first five weeks of release. It played in more than twenty countries and grossed over $5 million. Not only was it well received at the Cannes Film Festival, but it got favorable reviews in many U.S. publications like the *New York Times* and *The New Yorker* magazine. One of its stars, Carol Kane, got an Oscar nomination for best actress.

The upshot of all this was that it helped show there was no reason why women could not handle the demanding job of director—a fact that was not surprising to Silver.

An Omaha native who graduated from Sarah Lawrence, Silver began making a reputation in the industry by writing screenplays and directing short educational films. She got the idea for *Hester Street* from a novella called "Yekl." The story, built around the conflict between Jews from the ghettos of Eastern Europe and those who had preceded them to the new world, was written in the 1890s by Abraham Cahan. He would later become editor of the *Jewish Daily Forward*, the Yiddish-language newspaper.

Silver became interested in the subject of immigration because she was the daughter of two Russian Jewish immigrants—though they settled not in New York but in the Midwest. "Still," she said, "I felt a kinship with the New York immigrants with all the stories I heard around the table."

The tales fascinated her with their vivid descriptions of crossing in steerage, Ellis Island, and the painful adjustments in the new land. She wrote a screenplay, but she could not interest anyone in Hollywood in producing it, let alone hiring her to direct it. "Women," said one studio execu-

Joan Micklin Silver, whose first feature-length film, *Hester Street*, helped open doors to women directors in the movie business.

tive, "are one more problem we don't need."

So Silver's husband, Raphael,[1] a successful real estate developer, decided to back *Hester Street* independently—that is, to raise the money to finance it and distribute it himself. "I read her screenplay and loved it," he said. "I knew it wasn't a script any studio would fund. But I felt if that was the project she wanted, I wanted to be helpful."

Said Mrs. Silver: "It was a time of intense sexism in the industry. I could get screenwriting jobs but not directing jobs. . . . It was really a closed door. [My husband] was watching me flail around. He felt it was unfair. He felt everybody should have a chance at the brass ring."

[1]Raphael Silver produced the second film his wife directed, *Between the Lines* (1977), then directed a picture himself, called *On The Yard* (1979) with John Heard, Mike Kellin, and Tom Waites. In 1985, he directed *Walk on the Moon*, a movie about kids in the Peace Corps in Brazil. As the years passed, the film business became very much a family affair. In 1984, the Silvers' daughters Marissa and Dina wrote, directed and produced an independent picture called *Old Enough*.

After her husband committed himself to the movie, Silver's work just began. To keep costs down, she had to pick her cast from actors willing to work for scale. The most unusual choice was Mel Howard, who played the part of the boarder. He was a last-minute addition. He was, in fact, an assistant director. But with his oval face, soulful features, and beard, he looked right for the role.

"I remember telling my cameraman," Mrs. Silver said, "'I wish I could find a Bernstein that looks like him.' It turned out we hired an actor who dropped out four days before we started rehearsals. I was tearing my hair out. The cameraman reminded me that I thought Mel Howard had the right look. 'Yes,' I said. 'But I want an actor.' Howard turned out to be the only one in the cast who knew Yiddish. We brought him in and he read. He was very directable. And he did beautifully."

Because a good deal of the dialogue is in Yiddish, Silver had to get a Yiddish stage actor, Michael Gorrin, to coach the cast. "It wasn't as hard as it sounds," she said. "Actors' ears are very attuned." Yet, as it turned out in the movie, there seem to be several dialects going on all at once.

Silver picked Morton Street in Greenwich Village for location shooting because the block needed very few changes for the film. "There were no neon signs to take down and it was a 'T' street that dead-ended. So we didn't have to worry about looking down the street at skyscrapers."

Silver shot the picture in black and white not only to save money but to conform to photographs from the era. "With a thirty-four-day shooting schedule," she said, "half on sets and half on location, the filming went along in the usual manner. Which is to say, we had weather problems, personal squabbles, union pressures, lab

Bernstein (Mel Howard) teaching Jake and Gitl's son Joey (Paul Freedman) to write.

troubles, and always, always, money problems."

And yet, she not only surmounted these problems, but also transcended the low-budget production's limitations. The picture had a universal theme that appealed not only to elderly Jews but also to audiences of Gentiles and young people.

That was clear right from the beginning when we see Jake (Steven Keats) at a dancing school learning to socialize in his new country. In the background, we hear delightfully gay, ticky-tack music that will be repeated throughout the movie.

Silver had to be persistent to get just the effect she wanted for the film score. "Every composer I went to see produced Hebraic themes in A minor with cellos. I wanted the music to be what an immigrant would have heard on a Saturday night on the bandstand. In other words, the America he was yearning after and trying to adjust to."

William Bolcom, a college professor specializing in music from the period, finally came up with the score Silver was looking for.

The movie goes on to tell how Jake has preceded his wife (Carol Kane) and small son (Paul Freedman) to America. By the time he sends for them, his marriage is in trouble. Jake has a job in a sweatshop, a two-room flat on Hester Street, a boarder (Howard), a shy scholarly Jew who works next to Jake, and a girlfriend, Mamie (Dorrie Kavanaugh). She is a hardworking young Pole with a voluptuous figure and a burning ambition for success that exceeds even Jake's.

Gitl, Jake's wife, clings to her old-country ways, including wearing the traditional wig as was the custom with Orthodox Jewish wives. Embarrassed by his wife, Jake continues his pursuit of Mamie. Gitl, sad and bewildered, stays inside tending the house.

One day, a peddler (Leib Lensky) comes by. "How about a Sabbath tablecloth?" he asks in Yiddish.

Before an Orthodox Jewish rabbi, Jake and Gitl are divorced.

"No," she says.

"Maybe some new stockings? Mirrors? Brushes? Combs?"

"No."

"If you don't want anything," he says, perturbed, "why did you ask me in?"

"Maybe you have some medicine . . . for my man. . . . Maybe you have something that will make him love me again?"

"Ah," the peddler says, "you want a love potion."

But a neighbor, Mrs. Kavarsky (Doris Roberts), has a better idea. She goes out with Gitl and gets her some fancy clothes and a corset and starts lacing her up.

"It hurts," Gitl says.

"That means it's working," Mrs. Kavarsky answers. "You want to be an American? You gotta hurt."

But Gitl, who, in turn, is attracted by the quiet and intellectual Bernstein, finds that her efforts are too little, too late. She eventually sees that her husband is cheating on her, and, breaking out of her passive role, she sends him packing.

When a lawyer offers her $50 not to contest a divorce, she surprisingly rises to the occasion. She shows she is more than his match by quietly driving up the settlement to $300—all of Mamie's savings. Then she goes about the business of getting a husband, developing a business, and raising her child.

"I think she is forced to discover that she is a strong and valuable human being," said Carol Kane in an interview for this book. A Cleveland-born actress, Kane appeared in several major films, including *Carnal Knowledge* (1971), in which she played Art Garfunkel's hippie girlfriend.

"The fact that her husband has no place in his life for her forces Gitl to stand up tall and become her own person. It is something in all of us. But sometimes life's circumstances accelerate one's growth, and that is what happens to this little woman from the old country.

"The nicest compliment I ever got from a review was in this film. The *New York Times* talked about

Mamie (Dorrie Kavanaugh) and Jake are off to be married in their fancy clothes.

the fact that Gitl literally seemed to grow in size as the movie went on."

In the end, all the characters get what they think they want. Jake gets Mamie, and Gitl gets Bern-

stein. But Gitl is the biggest winner of all because her character has blossomed. She has developed into a mature woman ready to take her place in America.[2]

[2]Silver said people often ask her what happened to the couples afterward. She says she tells them: "Mamie ran an important Seventh Avenue dress house and Jake was her front man, the customer's man. Gitl and Bernstein were very happy, but, not unlike typical American parents, they had trouble with their son Joey as he grew up."

Hud
(1963)

Directed by Martin Ritt. Screenplay by Irving Ravetch and Harriet Frank, Jr., based on the novel *Horseman, Pass By* by Larry McMurtry. Photography, James Wong Howe.☆ Editor, Frank Bracht. Art decoration, Hal Pereira and Tambi Larsen. Music, Elmer Bernstein. Produced by Ritt and Ravetch. Paramount. B/W. 111 minutes.

Hud Bannon	PAUL NEWMAN
Homer Bannon	MELVYN DOUGLAS ☆
Alma	PATRICIA NEAL ☆
Lon Bannon	BRANDON DE WILDE
Hermy	JOHN ASHLEY
Burris	WHIT BISSELL
Jesse	CRAHAN DENTON
Jose	VAL AVERY
Thompson	SHELDON ALLMAN
Larker	PITT HERBERT
George	PETER BROOKS
Truman Peters	CURT CONWAY
Lily Peters	YVETTE VICKERS
Joe Scanlon	GEORGE PETRIE
Donald	DAVID KENT
Dumb Billy	FRANK KILLMOND

☆ Academy Award winner

Even before we see him, we have a good idea about his character. We see his pink Cadillac convertible parked like a calling card outside a married woman's house just after dawn.

This is Hud—cocky, aggressive, virile. The charming and handsome, but irresponsible and amoral rancher will, as the picture unfolds, leave a wash of human flotsam in his wake. He will break his father's heart, alienate his family's loyal housekeeper, and disillusion his adoring nephew.

And he will show no remorse. Nor will his personality change one whit. As far as Hud is concerned, the code of life is simple: Take or be taken. The law of the jungle prevails in the land. Those who ignore it are bound to come out second-best in the game of life.

Such a tough, cynical attitude is not often seen in a western. But, though the film takes place in Texas, *Hud* is really not a story of the old West. It is set in modern Texas. The main characters are ranchers and cowhands. The locale, though, could be any place.

Larry McMurtry's novel *Horseman, Pass By* was the basis for the screenplay. However, instead of focusing on Hud (Paul Newman), the book made the protagonist his young nephew (Brandon de Wilde), who had come to stay with him. In the end, put off by his uncle's ways, Lon decides to steer a different moral course in life.

On the other hand, the movie zeroed in on Hud, a complex man, who, despite all the problems he creates, never wavers. The key conflict comes when he and his father (Melvyn Douglas) clash over the old man's decision to destroy his cattle. They are suspected of having hoof-and-mouth disease.

"You gonna let them shoot your cows out from under you on account of a schoolbook disease?" argues Hud. "Now you lookee here. You've had twenty-four of my thirty-four years working here on this ranch. And Daddy, you have had top-grade cheap labor. . . . Dammit, I want out of this spread what I put into it."

Ever the pragmatist, Hud wants to sell the cattle before the government can condemn the herd.

"That would run the risk of starting an epidemic," his father answers.

Paul Newman as Hud, a playboy of the Texas plains.

"Why this whole country is run on epidemics," Hud replies. "Where you been? Big business, price-fixing, crooked TV shows, income tax finagling, souped-up expense accounts. How many honest men do you know?"

"You're an unprincipled man, Hud," his father tells him.

The fact is, Hud is only saying what every businessman fears: To be principled in the modern, highly competitive commercial world can jeopardize survival and invite self-destruction. But in the Camelot days of the Kennedy era, when this picture was made, Hud's down-to-earth philosophy was not what audiences wanted to hear from their heroes.

In making a lead character out of Hud, the bad good guy, the movie was following a trail blazed by foreign films and by *The Hustler* (1961), a picture about a pool shark that Newman made two years earlier. *The Hustler* was successful both in the critics' corner and at the box office. *Hud* faired even better. Two of its stars, Patricia Neal and Douglas, won Academy Awards, as did its

Hud (*front row right*) gets set to break fast from the line in a greased-pig-catching contest.

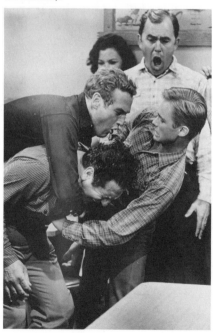

Hud joins forces in a barroom brawl with his young nephew Lon (Brandon de Wilde).

cameraman, James Wong Howe. And both Newman, who got an Oscar nomination, and de Wilde were outstanding.

In fact, the husky-voiced Neal did the best acting of her career. "Alma, the housekeeper, was real to me from the time I first read the script," Neal said. "Paul Newman sent it to me with a letter. I told Marty Ritt, our director, I'd do it.

"My best bit, and the thing I loved the most about Alma, hit the cutting-room floor. Naturally. It was a scene where the young boy comes out to her cabin and asks Alma what life is all about anyway. 'Honey,' she tells him, 'you'll just have to ask someone else.'"

One of the weaknesses of the script is that Hud's meanness is never explained. Some of it, we learn, stemmed from his guilt at having caused the death of his older brother in a drunken-driving accident. But that isn't enough to explain his father's total lack of love or affection.

In a climactic scene between the two, Homer Bannon (Douglas) explains his coolness by telling Hud that he is the antithesis of his father's philosophy. "You don't give a damn.... You don't value nothing. You don't respect nothing.... You live just for yourself. And that makes you not fit to live with." However, how and why Hud got that way is never explained.

The most interesting relationship is the one that develops between Lon (de Wilde) and Hud. The true core of the story centers on Lon and his reaction to Hud's life-style. Lon is seventeen, approaching a time when he has to decide what kind of life he aims to lead. One model is his grandfather: law-abiding, hardworking, sober. At the other end of the scale is Hud: hard-drinking, devil-may-care, unscrupulous, and a womanizer, to boot.

At first, the choice is a difficult one. Hud isn't all bad. Strong and fearless, he demonstrates his prowess to Lon by winning a greased-pig catching contest at a county fair. Then, when Lon is kicked into a fence during a cattle roundup, Hud carries him home to Alma (Neal) for a day's rest. Finally, Hud comes to Lon's rescue when a bully picks a fight at a saloon.

Days later when Lon sticks up for Hud in a talk with Hud's father, the old man says, "Little by little, the look of the country changes because of the men we admire. . . . You're just going to have to make up your own mind one day about what's right and wrong."

More characteristically, Hud is busy pursuing a playboy's life, chasing women, brawling and drinking, not giving a damn about the ranch his father spent his life developing. Yet, there are times when Hud's philosophy, however greedy, seems the better part of wisdom.

When his father's sick herd is slaughtered, the patriarch hears that oil prospectors have approached Hud. But as long as the old man is above ground, no one is going to be punching holes on his land.

Hud suggests that those oil checks might come in handy. The old man won't listen. He is inevitably tied to another era. He says: "What can I do with a bunch of rotten oil wells? . . . I can't ride out and prowl among them like I can my cattle. I can't breed 'em or tend them or rope them or chase them, or nothin'. I can't feel a smidgen of pride in 'em because they ain't none of my doing. I don't want that kind of money."

Yet, Hud goes too far to win our sympathy. He tries to get his father ruled incompetent. He never extends any kindness or compassion to the hidebound but proud old pioneer, even when his father dies of a heart attack.

Drunk and raging, Hud even tries to rape his housekeeper, Alma, one night. Instead, he drives her away. When she tells him it would have happened

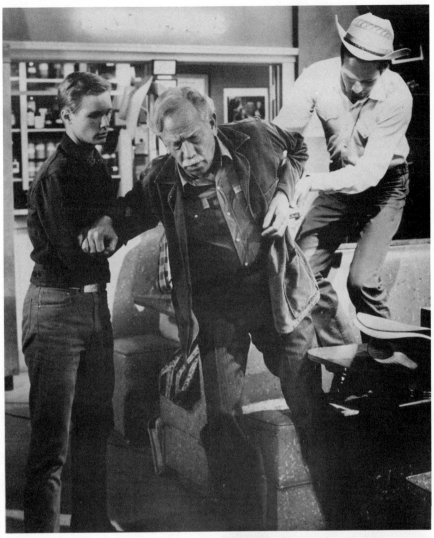

In a local diner, Hud and Lon help Homer Bannon (Melvyn Douglas), who has suffered a slight heart attack.

Alma (Patricia Neal) takes a last look back after leaving her job at the Bannon ranch.

eventually without the roughhouse, he just shrugs. "I'll remember you, honey. You're the one that got away."

Lon, fed up with his uncle's excesses, packs his bags and leaves, too. He will follow a different path.

In the end, Hud is left defiantly alone on the vast spread, shouting bitterly after Lon: "This world is so full of crap, a man's going to get into it sooner or later."

Network
(1976)

> Directed by Sidney Lumet. Screenplay by Paddy Chayefsky. ☒ Photography, Owen Roizman. Editor, Alan Heim. Music, Elliot Lawrence. Produced by Howard Gottfried. A Metro-Goldwyn-Mayer production released through United Artists. Rated R. 120 minutes.
>
> | | |
> |---|---|
> | Diana Christensen | FAYE DUNAWAY ☒ |
> | Max Schumacher | WILLIAM HOLDEN |
> | Howard Beale | PETER FINCH ☒ |
> | Frank Hackett | ROBERT DUVALL |
> | Louise Schumacher | BEATRICE STRAIGHT ☒ |
> | Nelson Chaney | WESLEY ADDY |
> | Arthur Jensen | NED BEATTY |
> | Great Ahmed Kahn | ARTHUR BURGHARDT |
> | TV director | BILL BURROWS |
> | George Bosch | JOHN CARPENTER |
> | Harry Hunter | JORDAN CHARNEY |
> | Mary Ann Gifford | KATHY CRONKITE |
> | Joe Donnelly | ED CROWLEY |
> | Bill Herron | DARRYL HICKMAN |
> | Narrator | LEE RICHARDSON |
>
> ☒ Academy Award winner

An aging TV newscaster, whose ratings have slipped, suffers a momentary breakdown on the air. He tells a shocked national audience he plans to blow his brains out on his show.

The next day, UBS, his fourth-place network, gets front-page headlines. That week, the half-mad newscaster's ratings improve so dramatically that his network, instead of firing him, makes the newsman a star. He rides the crest of his soaring ratings, and so does his network, until they start dropping again. Then, faced with economic disaster, unable to control him or figure a way to gently ease him out, network officials have him killed on camera.

That, in essence, is the wild plot of *Network*, a satire on the television industry that stirred a hornets' nest of controversy on New York's network row. At the time of its premier, *Christian Science Monitor* TV critic Arthur Unger got the following reactions from top industry executives and personalities.

CBS news president Richard Salant: "I read the script and got sick. . . . I have no intention of seeing it. It is a distorted fantasy and simply could never happen."

NBC newsman Edwin Newman said he did not understand it to be satire, however black. "I couldn't tell which parts were supposed to be taken literally and which parts were supposedly exaggerated."

M. S. Rukeyser, Jr., NBC's vice-president for public information: "Very boring. Nothing to do with our business."

Barbara Walters, ABC News: "As an entertainment, it is very good and people will enjoy it. As to what it says about network news, I must admit there is some truth in it . . . [but] what bothers me most about the film is when it becomes exaggerated. I worry that the public may be misled into believing that this is the way television news really is."

But screenwriter Paddy Chayefsky, who wrote such memorable movies as *Marty* (1955), *The Bachelor Party* (1957), and *The Hospital* (1971), thought he was right on target. "People say to me, 'Jesus, you moved into some pretty surreal satire.' I say, 'No. I still write realistic stuff. It's the world that's gone nuts, not me. It's the world that's turned into a satire.' We never lied. Everything in the movie is true—with some extensions."

Whoever is closest to the truth, the fact is, audiences found the film engrossing. They came in droves. At the Academy Award ceremonies, the picture won four Oscars.

Ironically, when the movie was offered to the networks, CBS executives forgot their ruffled feelings. They eagerly bought it, then showed a sanitized version on television.

The censored version eliminated a bedroom scene with Faye Dunaway and William Holden. On the screen, while making love,

Howard Beale (Peter Finch) suffers a breakdown on the air. The next week, he tells his audience to rebel against the sorry state of things.

Max Schumacher (William Holden), head of network news, is on the crisis phone as Beale urges viewers to shout out their windows: "I'm mad as hell and I'm not going to take it anymore."

she prattles on about bigger ratings and maybe putting on a homosexual soap opera. CBS also excised a lot of four-letter words, making MGM call back some of the actors to record new voice tracks. But it did leave in one eight-letter vulgarity—"bullshit" —which was shouted from coast to coast.

Even retaining that expletive took a bit of soul-searching. "The use of BS is a focal point of the movie," said Donn O'Brien, CBS vice-president of program practices. "A TV news anchorman has become unstable, gone off his rocker, and uses the word on his newscast. BS is not obscene. It's gutter slang and can mean many things. We would not allow BS to be used in movies we make ourselves. But *Network* is a movie of renown that won four Oscars." CBS also cut all use of "goddam." The network said that word, more than any other, usually brings the most protests from viewers.

The film all this controversy is about centers around newscaster Howard Beale (Peter Finch), a character who, according to trade gossip, was based on Ed Murrow.

Once the "mandarin of TV," Beale is now on the way out. In fact, he has just gotten two weeks' notice.

Drinking with his old friend Max Schumacher (William Holden), Beale threatens to kill himself "right in the middle of the seven-o'clock news." Schumacher makes light of the matter, suggesting it would give Beale a super rating. And he gives it no more thought. But the next night, Beale calmly announces on the air that he has been fired. He tells the audience: "I'm going to blow my brains out right on this program a week from today."

The next day, Beale is contrite. He asks network executives for a reprieve, a chance to apologize for his outburst. He gets his chance. Instead, when he goes on the air again, he roars: "It's all bullshit— the country, life in general, the world."

Schumacher wants to fire him. But Diana Christensen (Faye Dunaway), head of programming, notes how the ailing network's ratings have rocketed and proposes a glittering nightly "porno" news show. It would feature a soothsayer, a gossip columnist, and Beale billed as the "Mad Prophet of the Airwaves." She prevails.

In the weeks that follow, Beale transfixes millions of viewers as he rages over the network in angry monologues. He tells them to go to the window and shout, "I'm mad as hell, and I'm not going to take it anymore." Windows fly up from New York to Los Angeles. Beale's ratings jump to 60 percent. He becomes a national media hero.

Network bosses fire Schumacher, and Diana Christensen takes over the news division. Flushed by success, she plunges ahead and creates a show called "The Mao Tse-Tung Hour," hiring terrorists to rob banks and hijack planes while TV cameras grind.

A memorable scene shows the contract negotiations. The black revolutionaries and their agents quarrel not over the morality of

the idea but over money, residuals, and syndication. The scrap gets so loud one of them fires a gun to get silence.

While all this is going on, Schumacher and Diana start an affair, but not until his wife of twenty-five years (Beatrice Straight) reacts sharply. In jagged tones, she chastises him for a "last roar of passion" before settling into his "menopausal years." The four-minute scene, which won Straight a supporting Oscar, is a tense and bitter one. Straight, displaying an incredible range of responses, makes the most of it. "When she came in to read for the part," said producer Howard Gottfried, "she had us all weeping."

Eventually, Schumacher leaves home to live with Diana. In bed, lying on top of Schumacher, Diana prattles on about TV ratings until orgasm. "The love scene is the core of the picture," Chayefsky said. "...She represents television. He represents humanity."

As the weeks pass, it becomes obvious the autumn-spring romance won't work. One day, Schumacher, fed up, loses his temper. "I'm tired of being an accessory in your life.... You're one of Howard's [Beale's] humanoids. If I stayed with you, I'd be destroyed."

He goes on: "You are TV incarnate, Diana. Indifferent... insensitive to joy. All of life is reduced to the consummate rubble of banality. War. Murder. Death. All the same as a bottle of beer."

In the meantime, Beale's popularity grows. But he is unpredictable and uncontrollable. On one show, he warns against the growing economic power of the Arabs. "They're all over," he says. "The Arabs are simply buying the U.S." Beale points out that Arab interests are trying to get a big piece of the very corporation that owns his own network. He urges his audience to flood the White House with telegrams to block the deal.

"The show is a disaster," says

network chief Frank Hackett (Robert Duvall). "I'm finished."

Arthur Jensen (Ned Beatty), head of the conglomerate that owns UBS, summons Beale and delivers a sermon spelling out the corporate facts of life. "You get up on your little twenty-one-inch screen and howl about America and democracy. There is no America," Jensen says. "There is only IBM, ITT, AT&T, and Dupont, Union Carbide, and Exxon. Those are the nations of the world. . . . We no longer live in a world of nations and ideologies. The world is a college of corporations. . . . The world is a business. It has been since man crawled out of the slime. . . ."

Jensen urges Beale to preach the gospel of big business. And Beale does. Taking a 180-degree turn, he goes on the air and talks about dying democracy and dehumanization. His ratings start slipping. As they do, the network's economic position sags, too.

Hackett and Diana try to salvage the situation. They want to fire Beale. But Jensen is in his corner. He likes Beale's speeches, and Jensen's position is inflexible.

"So what do we do about Beale?" the question is asked in a staff meeting.

"I suppose we'll have to kill him," Duvall says offhandedly.

"I think I can get the Mao Tse-Tung people to kill him on one of his shows," Diana says. "It could be done right on camera. . . . I don't see that we have any option."

And so they arrange his assassination. Howard Beale becomes the first newscaster to die in full view of his national audience—an improbable ending to an improbable story, but one that raises disquieting questions about the evolution of television into a dehumanized extension of corporate America. "When the *Hindenburg* blew up," says author Chayefsky, "the reporter broke down on the radio. I can't imagine anything like that happening today."

Ned Beatty as Arthur Jenson, a business magnate, talks with Beale and network executive Frank Hackett (Robert Duvall).

Beale and Schumacher have a last-minute talk before airtime.

Diana Christensen (Faye Dunaway) and Schumacher become romantically involved until he realizes she is emotionally dead.

Saturday Night and Sunday Morning (1960)

Directed by Karel Reisz. Screenplay by Alan Sillitoe based on his novel. Camera, Freddie Francis. Editor, Seth Holt. Music, Johnny Dankworth. Produced by Tony Richardson. A Continental Distributing Inc. release. British. B/W. 89 minutes.

Arthur	ALBERT FINNEY
Doreen	SHIRLEY ANNE FIELD
Brenda	RACHEL ROBERTS
Aunt Ada	HYLDA BAKER
Bert	NORMAN ROSSINGTON
Jack	BRYAN PRINGLE
Robbe	ROBERT CAWDRON
Mrs. Bull	EDNA MORRIS
Mrs. Seaton	ELSIE WAGSTAFFE
Mr. Seaton	FRANK PETTITT
Blowsy woman	AVIS BUNNAGE
Loudmouth	COLIN BLAKELEY
Doreen's mom	IRENE RICHMOND
Betty	LOUISE DUNN
Drunk	PETER MADDEN
Mr. Bull	CAMERON HALL
Policeman	ALISTER WILLIAMSON

"What I'm out for is a time," says Arthur Seaton a jaunty, belligerent lathe operator in Nottingham. "All the rest is propaganda."

After a long, monotonous week at his machine, Arthur cuts loose on Saturday night, womanizing, boozing, and brawling with a vengeance. He is one of England's restless corps of angry working-class young men featured in books and films of the 1960s. They rebelled against conformity, poverty, and their barren lives. "Don't let the bastards grind you down," Arthur growls defiantly.

Saturday Night and Sunday Morning is a prime example of the work of a new generation of British writers and directors who brought to the screen an uncompromising view of industrial-town life. Their protagonists are not men on the rise, like the hero of *Room at the Top* (1959), but men in a rut, trapped by their narrow existences.

They are victims of a meager education, a class-conscious society, and their own lack of ambition and vision. They are repeating the dull, provincial lives of their fathers. Their horizons are limited by the grimy borders of the slums beyond which few dream of venturing. The landmarks of their lives are the factory, the local pubs, the cinema, the amusement park, the grubby neighborhood streets and canals, the telly, and the bedroom.

Playing the role of the frustrated nonconformist who lashes out against this dreary, unrewarding life is Albert Finney. He was then twenty-four, England's new acting sensation who had started his career in Shakespearean plays.

That surprised many moviegoers, because in the picture he spoke Nottinghamshire, a thick Midlands dialect, at times incomprehensible to Americans. It is a working-class accent that sounds as if the speaker had a mouthful of marbles.

"We had a bit of trouble with that," Finney said. "Not all of us spoke exactly the same accent at the beginning. And we wanted to export the film. So I had to reread two of the long soliloquies, especially the first one that opens the film, in a less accented version."

In the picture, Finney portrays a hardworking machinist who

Arthur (Albert Finney) and Doreen (Shirley Anne Field) have a night out at a carnival.

113

Arthur, one of Britain's angry young men of the 1960s, mired in a working-class life of boozing, brawling, and womanizing, and Brenda (Rachel Roberts), his girl of the moment.

A new love interest enters: Doreen. "The first kiss," a friend warns Arthur, "and she'll expect an engagement ring."

slaves all week at a mindless job for his 14 pounds in wages. Come Saturday night, he's off to the pub for a loud and rowdy beer session.

With him is Brenda (Rachel Roberts), his girl of the moment. Married to a fellow worker, she is nonetheless captivated by his rough good looks and happy-go-lucky air. She watches amused as Arthur challenges another pub patron to a drinking bout. Arthur outdoes him handily by downing ten pints, then passes out smiling as he falls down a flight of stairs.

Afterward, he staggers to Brenda's house, spends the night with her, then slips out the next morning before the return of her husband, Jack (Bryan Pringle).

There is not much diversion at home. Arthur's parents have settled into a dull, empty life—focused around their TV and the fire. He thinks of them as "dead from the neck up." He wonders, "Is there nothing more in life than what my mom and dad got—a telly and a packet of fags?"

So it's off to a bar for Arthur, where he spots a trim filly named Doreen (Shirley Anne Field) and makes a date for a picture show. "She's different," Arthur's cousin, Bert (Norman Rossington), tells him as they fish in a gloomy canal. "The first kiss and she'll expect an engagement ring."

"I take my tip from the fishes," Arthur says. "Never bite unless the bait is good. I won't get married till I'm good and ready."

In between dates with Doreen, Arthur sees more of Brenda, whose husband, Jack, has gone on the night shift. One day they almost run into him at a workingmen's club. Brenda rushes off while Arthur cheekily goes right up to Jack and coolly chats with the man whose wife he has just made love to.

"You know," Brenda says at their next meeting, "the trouble with you is you don't know the difference between right and wrong. I don't think you ever will."

"Maybe I don't," Arthur says. "But I don't want anybody to teach me, either."

A week later, Brenda announces she's pregnant. She tells Arthur he'd better "bring it off damn quick." Arthur can only take her to his aunt (Hylda Baker), whose old wives' remedy—a hot bath while Brenda pours down glass after glass of gin—fails pathetically.

Brenda needs 40 quid for an abortion, and Arthur promises to pay for it. By this time, his relationship with Doreen has ripened, and Brenda, hearing of it, confronts him. He denies everything. But it's obvious that their affair is all but over.

Meanwhile, Arthur, undaunted by his drab job, kicks up his heels at life. He doesn't know how to break away or reform the system. But at least he can pull off some monkeyshines now and then to show he still has some spirit. He shoots a neighborhood gossip in the backside with an air rifle, drops a dead rat on a woman coworker's workbench, and defends a hapless drunk who has busted a grocery-store window.

But these skirmishes are only minor diversions. His problem lies with Doreen, who upbraids him for being rude and never taking her out in public. Arthur, who has been trying to keep his romance with Doreen secret, gives in and takes her to a local fair. It turns out to be a bad idea.

Brenda, who has come with her husband and his soldier brother and another army comrade, runs into Arthur. They slip off long enough for her to tell Arthur she has decided to have the child and "face whatever comes of it."

Before she can get back, her husband spots her with Arthur. The two soldiers chase him to a dark lot and beat him savagely. It takes a week for him to get out of bed.

But he comes around soon enough when Doreen visits and consoles him after he confesses his

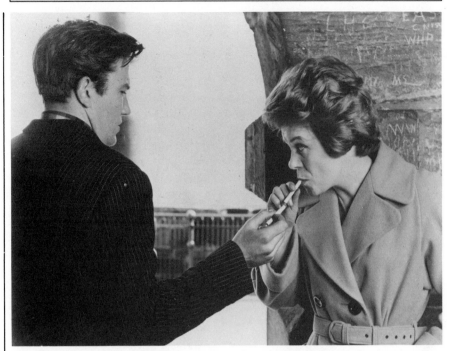
The fun is out of the affair because Brenda is pregnant.

Despite his defiant independence, Arthur opts for a domestic life with Doreen.

transgressions with Brenda. At the end, we see Arthur and Doreen on a hilltop. He has reluctantly succumbed to her taming influence and reconciled himself to settling down to a factory life.

Arthur is hooked, like the fish he casts for on Sunday mornings. But he still wants to be his own man. He tosses a rock at a nearby housing-development sign.

"Maybe one of those houses will be for us," Doreen says, scolding him mildly. "You shouldn't throw things like that."

"It won't be the last one I'll throw," Arthur answers, a defiant tone still very much there.

Taxi Driver
(1976)

Directed by Martin Scorsese. Written by Paul Schrader. Photography, Michael Chapman. Music, Bernard Herrmann. Art director, Charles Rosen. Editors, Marcia Lucas, Tom Rolf, and Melvin Shapiro. A Bill/Phillips Production. Produced by Michael and Julia Phillips. Filmed in New York City. Columbia. Rated R. 112 minutes.

Travis Bickle	ROBERT DE NIRO
Betsy	CYBILL SHEPHERD
Iris Steensman	JODIE FOSTER
Wizard	PETER BOYLE
Sport (Matthew)	HARVEY KEITEL
Tom	ALBERT BROOKS
Charles Palantine	LEONARD HARRIS
Personnel officer	JOE SPINELL
Passenger	MARTIN SCORSESE
Concession girl	DIAHNNE ABBOTT
Angry black man	FRANK ADU
Melio	VIC ARGO
Policeman at rally	GINO ARDITO
Iris's friend	GARTH AVERY
Stick-up man	NAT GRANT
Tall Secret Service man	RICHARD HIGGS
Easy Andy, gun salesman	STEVEN PRINCE

Even if *Taxi Driver* had not been linked to John Hinckley's mad attempt to kill President Reagan, the film would have been remembered for its frightening and disturbing impact.

As a dramatization of the bizarre world of a psychotic, it is a brilliantly evocative picture. It has created the nightmare odyssey of a tormented man moving through New York City's bustling crowds.

Alienated and untouched by it all, unable to connect with his fellow beings, Travis Bickle, the driver, is longing to be noticed. Yet he is powerless to make friends because he lacks the skills to maintain any meaningful relationship.

Screenwriter Paul Schrader, neither a New Yorker nor a taxi driver, gained insight into Travis's inner struggle after he himself underwent a major depression. During his emotional slide, he withdrew from the outside world, escaping into alcohol until he was hospitalized. "When the pain subsided and my stomach healed, it hit me. There was a perfect metaphor—someone living like a taxi driver, drifting through a sewer in an iron coffin, surrounded by people, but alone."

Schrader's offbeat scenario was not easy to sell. Studio executives thought the depressing theme of violence and loneliness was box-office poison. But when director Martin Scorsese and Robert De Niro became interested—and agreed to do it at cost—Columbia Pictures decided to back it.

Unquestionably, Scorsese's inspired direction and De Niro's sensitive acting help enormously to make the picture a memorable one. Shooting entirely on location in New York City, Scorsese filled the screen with nighttime scenes showing steam spouting from manhole covers, turning the city into an after-dark allegory of hell. His was a stylistic study of the city's garish netherworld of porno movies, pimps, and prostitutes.

De Niro's cab driver, a man whose pent-up emotions slowly unhinge his mind and turn him into a killer, was a major acting triumph. Some say he achieved it by the total concentration he gives a role. De Niro, playing a Vietnam veteran, read books on the Green Berets. He even asked Schrader to let him wear his belt because De Niro felt the movie was a personal statement and wanted to feel even closer to the role.

He also drove a cab, and therein lies a story. "One day," Scorsese said, "a guy gets in, a former actor who recognized his name on the license. 'Jesus,' he says, 'last year you won the Oscar and now you're driving a cab again?' De Niro said he was only doing research. 'Yeah, Bobby,' the actor says, 'I know. I been there, too.'"

Travis Bickle (Robert De Niro), a lonely Vietnam veteran, walks through the porno district in the midst of a city where he is disintegrating into madness.

Cybill Shepherd as Betsy, a political volunteer working in a presidential candidate's headquarters. With her is Albert Brooks.

Shelley Winters calls De Niro the most complete actor she ever met. "When we did *Bloody Mama* (1970), he played my youngest son, who was a junkie," Winters said. "By the time we got done filming, he had lost thirty pounds and broken out in sores all over his body. After he got killed in the script, I was afraid I'd look in the grave during the burial scene and find him."

One actor who worked with De Niro for three months found him highly professional, a polite and ingratiating coworker. "But I can't say I've really exchanged one full sentence with him about anything other than work," the actor said. "In fact, I don't know any more about him now that I did the first day he walked onto the set."

If De Niro is difficult to know as a person, so is the character he portrays. We know little about Travis—only that he has been to Vietnam, that he is attracted to unattainable women, and that he is slowly going mad. A loner and an insomniac, he gets a job as a taxi driver because he is willing to work nights and go into the city's sleaziest areas.

In his taxi, people ignore him, treating him as if he were an inanimate part of the machine as they make out in the backseat. On his travels, water and garbage spatter his windshield. A man walks down the street with his shirt pulled over his face. A fare, enraged by his philandering wife, pulls out a gun. He asks: "Did you ever see what a .44 Magnum pistol can do to a woman's face?"

Travis remains impassive and anonymous. During the day, he sleeps in his dreary tenement apartment, eating junk food, swilling peach brandy, popping pills to keep calm. At night, he cruises through the city's garish sections, riding through its demimonde of hookers. Like an Old Testament zealot, he is obsessed with the people whom he sees through his windshield.

"All the animals come out at night," he scribbles in his diary. "Sick. Venal. Someday a real rain will come and wash all the scum off the streets."

One day, he is drawn to a beautiful blond campaign worker (Cybill Shepherd), an aide to a presidential candidate. Travis manages to meet her and take her out to lunch. She is, at first, curiously attracted to him. She finds him only somewhat eccentric, and he flatters her ego.

But it soon becomes clear that he is painfully lacking in social graces. He takes her to a cheap porno movie, and, angry and embarrassed, she walks out on him. His mind is so confused, he wonders why she is shocked.

Fascinated by women but not knowing how to relate to them, Travis latches on to a twelve-year-old prostitute (Jodie Foster). She is a runaway, content to work for a macho pimp (Harvey Keitel). Her life revolts Travis, and he vainly tries to persuade her to give it up. He has gone full circle in women

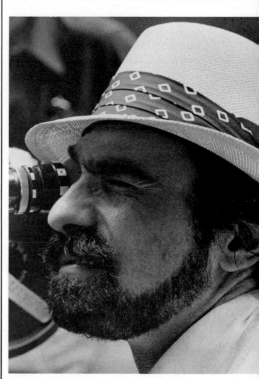

Director Martin Scorsese checks a camera angle.

from goddess to whore and found both inaccessible.

Foster, an actress since she was three years old, was thrust into the headlines after it was learned that Hinckley had been seeking to impress her when he tried to kill the President. Hinckley never met Foster, although he wrote to her. Federal investigators believe he developed a fantasy about her after seeing *Taxi Driver*. And, in trying to shoot President Reagan, he was acting out Travis's violent role.

Travis, growing even more alienated as the weeks pass, decides to commit a grandiose act: assassinate the presidential candidate. He buys a handgun, gets a Mohawk haircut, and stalks the politician. But the candidate's bodyguards spot him at a rally and he barely gets away. Frustrated, he goes to the block where the young prostitute works. There, in

Wizard (Peter Boyle), a fellow taxi driver, talking with Travis.

Jodie Foster as Iris.

an explosive shootout, he guns down her pimp and two of his gangster associates.

Many thought the picture would end here. It didn't. In an incredible aftermath, Travis emerges from the cold-blooded slaughter as a hero. One of the dead hoodlums turns out to be a wanted criminal. The tabloids treat the story as if Travis were a knight rescuing a damsel in distress. The girl's family writes him an emotional letter of thanks.

Later, back on the job, Travis picks up the blond goddess as a fare. Nothing really happens on the ride. She congratulates him for him noble deed. But she is wary and remains cool and distant. When she arrives at her destination, she gets out without inviting him to call her again.

The ending seems out of synch with the rest of the picture. But author Schrader argues that if the movie had stopped with the shootout, it would have been seen only as a slice of life. "It would have been less successful," he said. ". . . We forced people to go back into the text of the movie. Has he been cured by violence? Will he repeat his violence?"

Even though the finale seems jarring, Schrader does have a point. The ending perpetuates the nightmare. We watch the girl's uneasiness in the cab and her studied attempt to avoid riling Travis. And we see his eyes, dark and leaden, observing her in the rear-view mirror. There is no doubt that the pressures are still there, smoldering. Travis's fantasy world goes on. It will only be a matter of time before violence erupts again.[1]

---

[1]The last frames dedicate the picture to Bernard Herrmann, who wrote its moody, jazzy score. A prolific composer, he did the music for sixty-one films, including *Citizen Kane* (1941), *Vertigo* (1958), and *Psycho* (1960), and got an Oscar in 1941 for the music for *All That Money Can Buy*. Herrmann died on December 24, 1975, one day after he finished the score for *Taxi Driver*.

Tomorrow
(1972)

Directed by Joseph Anthony. Screenplay by Horton Foote from a short story by William Faulkner. Music, Irwin Stahl. Editor, Reva Schlesinger. Photography, Allan Green. Produced by Gilbert Pearlman and Paul Roebling. Filmed in and around Tupelo, Mississippi. A Filmgroup Release. B/W. 102 minutes.

Jackson Fentry	ROBERT DUVALL
Sarah Eubanks	OLGA BELLIN
Mrs. Hulie	SUDIE BOND
Isham Russell	RICHARD MCCONNELL
Lawyer Douglas	PETER MASTERSON
Papa Fentry	WILLIAM HAWLEY
Preacher Whitehead	JAMES FRANKS
Jackson and Longstreet	JOHNNY MASK

A jury in a small town in Mississippi is deliberating a murder charge against H. T. Bookwright, a man who shot a local ne'er-do-well who was eloping with his daughter.

Everyone on the panel is convinced the victim, who was drawing a pistol when he was killed, got what was coming—except one work-worn cotton farmer.

"I can't help it," says Jackson Fentry (Robert Duvall). "I ain't going to vote Bookwright free."

Why Fentry is the lone holdout, why he won't vote with his peers, is the story of *Tomorrow*.

Fentry's secret unfolds as the movie tells the tale of his lonely life after he leaves his father's farm to become a watchman at a sawmill. One day, his life changes. He discovers a sickly, pregnant woman (Olga Bellin) unconscious. He takes her in, and an innocent and tender love grows between them.

The picture is an adaptation of a short story that William Faulkner sold in 1940 to the *Saturday Evening Post* for $1,000. The story created a memorable character who loses a woman, not really his wife, and a child, not his own. Yet, they represented everything important to him in a hard, unrelenting life of toil.

Horton Foote, a Texan who had won an Oscar for writing the screenplay for *To Kill a Mockingbird* (1962) and would win another for *Tender Mercies* (1983), did an adaptation of "Tomorrow" for television. Richard Boone and Kim Stanley starred in the production on "Playhouse 90" in 1960.[1]

A few years later, *Tomorrow* appeared as an Off-Broadway play, this time with Duvall and Bellin in the leading roles. Herbert Berghof decided to put it on in his little theater, the H. B. Playhouse in Greenwich Village.

As Foote remembers it, he was living in New Hampshire and wasn't able to attend rehearsals until a few days before the opening. "Duvall's performance that afternoon is one that I will never forget," Foote said. "I watched the play as many times as I could during its run and I was on the set most of the time during the filming. I have seen the film many times since it was finished in 1972, and I never tire of Duvall's performance and always find something to marvel at."

Unlike Boone, who played the role without any accent, Duvall affected a deep backwoods drawl —a kind of bass monotone—that was so pronounced it seemed almost incomprehensible at times.

"Some people questioned what he was doing," Bellin said in an interview for this book. "They said it called attention to itself. But I thought it was wonderful. And when we went to Mississippi [to make the film], there was a handyman who worked at our motel.

Robert Duvall plays Jackson Fentry, a Mississippi sawmill caretaker, and Olga Bellin is Sarah Eubanks, an abandoned pregnant woman.

[1]Also in the cast were Chill Wills, Beulah Bondi, Elizabeth Patterson, and Charles Bickford.

He was exactly what Duvall sounded like"[2]

Duvall, who in 1984 still felt Fentry was his favorite part, said the characterization traces back to an Arkansas man he met on a trip from his St. Louis home when he was in high school. In the book *Tomorrow and Tomorrow and Tomorrow,*[3] Duvall said: "He didn't open his mouth until he had something to say. He talked straightforward. He talked like a cow. Fentry was such a guy, a closed guy. He was no retard. He was a simple man. And I wanted to keep him that way. I wanted him to be a stoic."

Bellin's husband, coproducer Paul Roebling, got interested in *Tomorrow* as soon as he saw the play's opening. "I said, 'God that's a movie. That could be the most stimulatingly beautiful movie of a Faulkner work that's ever been done.'"

Gilbert Pearlman, the movie's other producer, was also at that first performance and felt the same way. "What excited me about the work was the basic human relationships among all the characters, something I had missed a lot in recent films and plays."

They got in touch with Foote's agent and worked out a deal. It was a low-budget production—the final figure was $635,000: $435,000 to film and $200,000 for distribution and promotion. But financing wasn't easy because they had unknowns in the lead and because they shot in black and white.

"Everybody wanted me to shoot in color," Roebling said. ". . . [But] what very few people understood . . . was that the choice for color is the choice for style. They mistook the movie for a realistic film. It isn't at all. Faulkner writes in essences of character. *Tomorrow* is a style piece. . . . He brought out essences of what he saw in these people. His work had what Horton Foote called a mythic quality. . . . It had to be done in black and white."

Tomorrow, the movie, is told as a flashback. The narrator is the lawyer (Peter Masterson) whose case collapses when Fentry refuses to vote to acquit his client. "And so Jackson Fentry, cotton farmer, hung my jury. Who was he? . . . You see, that was my first case, and I had to find out why I lost it."

In the flashback, we see Fentry some twenty years earlier. He is living a solitary life at the mill, which is shut down for the winter. One day, he finds a gaunt, light-haired woman lying outside in the cold in an advanced stage of pregnancy. She is still weak. So Fentry feeds her with a spoon and lets her stay with him. She says her name is Sarah, and as the days pass, a bond develops. Weeks later, as Fentry is cleaning their clothes—boiling them outside in a large iron pot—he asks her to marry him. He says it matter-of-factly without looking at her. "Well, I can't marry you, Mr. Fentry," she replies. "I've got a husband."

Fentry persists. He reminds Sarah that her husband deserted her. "I can't help it," she says. "We're married in the sight of the law."

Weeks later, when a midwife delivers a baby boy, Sarah knows she will not survive the delivery. She asks Fentry to take care of the

Two farmers take their ease as Fentry walks past the general store.

---

[2]Foote said that Duvall has the ability, common to all great actors, of being able to change his voice, accent, and appearance from part to part. He totally immerses himself in a role, Foote said. For instance, in 1984 Duvall wrote a screenplay about a Southern preacher, then toured the South watching and talking to as many preachers as he could. "You might say for the last two years, he has been obsessed by preachers," Foote said. "He calls you on the phone and the first thing he tells you is about a new preacher he has come across. And he begins to talk like him, to preach to you like him."

[3]The work, which included the Faulkner short story as well as Foote's TV adaptation and screenplay, was published in 1984 by the University Press of Mississippi.

child and marries him on her deathbed.

After he buries her, Fentry takes the child back to his father's cotton farm and raises it on goat's milk. Fentry and the child become inseparable. When Fentry works in the field, he carries the baby in a satchel on his back.

Then one day three men ride up in a wagon with the sawmill owner's son. "We've come for the boy," one of them says. They are the Thorpe family, brothers of Fentry's dead wife. "He's our sister's boy. His daddy gave him to us. He's our kin."

"Run, boy," Fentry cries as he picks up an ax handle. "Run to the field to your grandfather."

The men wrestle Fentry to the ground. Fentry struggles with the strength of a wounded animal, thrashing and clawing. "They can take the boy, Fentry," says the mill owner's son. "It's the law. Her husband is alive and he gave the boy to them." Finally, Fentry gives in. "I knew it. I been expecting it," he says. "I reckon that's why it took me by surprise."

We hear the narrator's voice again as we see Fentry hoeing in the fields, picking cotton, plowing —alone. The narrator says his search for the boy ended when he learned that the Thorpes had taken the child and raised him as their own.

The camera takes us back to the present inside the courtroom, and the narrator tells about the boy, now called Buck Thorpe, always in trouble—drinking, stealing cattle. There was even talk that he had killed a man.

We go into the jury room, hear the panel imploring Fentry to change his vote, hear him refuse again. Then the judge declares a mistrial and adjourns the court. Fentry comes out and unhitches his mule.

"Of course, Fentry wasn't going to vote Bookwright free," the narrator says, "because somewhere in

Fentry washes soiled clothes by boiling them in an iron pot.

Fentry holds a handmade crib for Sarah's baby. With him is Isham (Richard McConnell), the mill owner's son.

Buck Thorpe, the adult, the man that Bookwright slew, there still remained at least the memory of that little boy...."

We watch Fentry get on his mule.

"I could never have guessed Fentry's capacity for love," the narrator continues. "I suppose I'd figured, coming from where he came from, even the comprehension of love had been lost out of him back down the generations where the first Fentry had to take his final choice between the pursuit of love and the pursuit of keeping breathing."

As Fentry rides down a muddy dirt road to his farm, the narrator sums up the inexorable will to survive, in the face of misfortune, that is the touchstone of all the common people of the world. "The lowly and invincible of the earth [continue] to endure and endure and endure—tomorrow and tomorrow and tomorrow."

The picture is understated and moving. But even though it makes a powerful statement, it falls short of Faulkner's short story, in my opinion. In its middle part, it is slow and static—most of the action takes place in the cramped confines of Fentry's miserable shack. This is all right for a play. But it is a problem for a movie because the medium is designed for movement, action and changing vistas.

Duvall said he thought the picture was "a good film, even a great film." Yet, he said, it was less than what it could have been. "I have to say I was stunned when I saw it. They had cut out the scenes I did with the boy after he grew up. In my opinion, the audience had to see Fentry see the boy grow up. And then Fentry's decision to convict the man who killed the boy would have more meaning, make more sense...."

As it turned out, *Tomorrow* got generally excellent notices. It had an eight-week run at the 68th Street Playhouse in Manhattan. But the *New York Times* panned it, and a favorable review in that paper was critical for a low-budget film without major distribution.

"It was an art film and it had authenticity," said Bellin. "Most people said, 'Oh, I don't want to be depressed.' It was a bit too stark. But it was what Paul [Roebling] wanted, which was a movie true to the spirit of Faulkner's story."

Over the years, *Tomorrow* has developed a loyal following. When Joseph Papp began showing film revivals at the Public Theatre in New York City, it was among the top three movies requested in an audience poll. In 1984, the American Playhouse showed it on television over the Public Broadcasting System.

"I think there is something very elemental about it," said screenwriter Foote. "It is actually the unselfishness of this guy, not asking for anything. And it is this ability to love, which is a surprise in this kind of man.... I don't want to treat this sentimentally, but there is something essential and very fulfilling about a love for a child. It is a deep, abiding love when it happens.

"Of course, Fentry goes on living [after he loses the boy]. This is very Faulknerian, this sense of endurance. But the price of endurance is enormous."

With his adopted son (Johnny Mask) in the cotton field.

Butch Cassidy and the Sundance Kid (1969)

Directed by George Roy Hill. Original screenplay, William Goldman.✵ Photography, Conrad Hall.✵ Music composed and conducted by Burt Bacharach.✵ Song "Raindrops Keep Fallin' on My Head" by Bacharach and Hal David.✵ Sung by B. J. Thomas. Editors, John C. Howard and Richard C. Meyer. Art Directors, Jack Martin Smith and Philip Jefferies. Produced by John Foreman. Presented by Campanile Productions/Newman-Foreman/George Roy Hill–Paul Monash Productions. Filmed in Utah, Colorado, Wyoming, and Mexico. 20th Century–Fox. Rated M. 110 minutes.

Butch Cassidy	PAUL NEWMAN
The Sundance Kid	ROBERT REDFORD
Etta Place	KATHARINE ROSS
Agnes	CLORIS LEACHMAN
Sheriff Brady Bledsoe	JEFF COREY
Percy Garris	STROTHER MARTIN
Bike salesman	HENRY JONES
Woodcock	GEORGE FURTH
Harvey Logan	TED CASSIDY
Marshal	KENNETH MARS
Macon	DONNELLY RHODES
Large woman passenger	JODY GILBERT
News Carver	TIMOTHY SCOTT
Fireman	DON KEEFER
Flat Nose Curry	CHARLES DIERKOP
Bank manager	FRANCISCO CORDOVA
Sweet Face	PERCY HELTON

✵ Academy Award winner

Butch Cassidy and the Sundance Kid is the western that New York critics loathed but audiences throughout the nation loved. It was an offbeat film that made good guys out of bad guys and injected humor into a genre not noted for levity. Just for good measure, it added jazzy music.

All this was an untested recipe in the 1960s—which made the movie an unlikely gamble. In fact, selling the script took more than a good measure of perseverance.

The idea was conceived by screenwriter William Goldman, who had been intrigued by articles about the two turn-of-the-century outlaws. Goldman researched their checkered career on and off for eight years before writing his screenplay. His agent, Evarts Ziegler, showed it to Jack Lemmon and others. When it failed to kindle interest, Goldman did several revisions. Still, there were no takers.

One day, Ziegler sent the script to Paul Newman and Steve McQueen. The story captivated both of them. From that moment, everything changed.

Ziegler, knowing he was now dealing from strength, started a studio auction. When the bidding stopped, 20th Century-Fox had bought the script for a record $400,000. The price was considered a breakthrough because only a few screenwriters had even been paid in six figures.

Goldman went on to win an Oscar for best screenplay, a feat he duplicated in 1976 when he wrote *All the President's Men*.

Despite these accolades and the prosperity they brought, Goldman says he is proudest of being a novelist. He feels writing movies can be depressing—because a screenwriter loses control of his script once he submits it. Even if the film becomes a hit, he rarely receives acclaim. "Screenwriting," he told one interviewer, "is the equivalent of what the women's movement people call—and you'll excuse the term—shitwork.[1] It's a craft that is very occasionally raised to the level of art."

Nevertheless, Goldman chose to convert his ideas for *Butch Cassidy* into a film rather than a novel. Why? "Because it came to me as a movie," he said in an interview that appeared in John Brady's book *The Craft of the Screenwriter*. "The feel of it was a movie."

The film's original title was *The Sundance Kid and Butch Cassidy*, because Newman was going to be the Kid. But Newman had prob-

Butch Cassidy (Paul Newman) and the Sundance Kid (Robert Redford) in their fatal shoot-out in Bolivia, the freeze frame that ended the film.

lems playing the character. So when McQueen bowed out (over a dispute on the billing), Newman jumped at the chance to switch to the lighter role. Robert Redford, whose career was starting to accelerate, joined the production and the title changed. However, Goldman says he still prefers the original. "It's a difference where the rhythm on the word 'Cassidy' comes. I always liked 'The Sundance Kid' first."

Most of the story is based on history. Butch and Sundance were desperadoes whose exploits spanned two continents. Butch was, in fact, an affable, easygoing outlaw. He and Sundance did lead a gang that held up banks and trains. And Sundance did bring his sweetheart, Etta Place, on their derring-do episodes.

Still, some threads of the story were spun by Goldman's fertile imagination. There was a posse. However, Butch and Sundance left the United States before it could chase them. They went to South America. But Goldman made up the bumbling scene where they rob a Bolivian bank without knowing how to speak Spanish.

Goldman guessed that Etta was a teacher, though she may have been a whore. Butch and Sundance did try to go straight in real life. But Goldman made up the ironic sequence in which they defend a mine owner's payroll from bandits. And he fabricated the scene where the Kid discloses he can't swim just before they dive from a cliff to escape their pursuers.

Even though these touches all strengthened the storylines, critics still felt the picture lacked action. They also felt the humor was too thin to sustain it as a comedy.

What most of them did not take into account was Newman and Redford's enormous popularity. *Butch* is a winner because it is a vehicle first and a story second. It is primarily a picture about Newman and Redford playing cow-

Sundance and Butch lose some of their confidence when they look back to see a posse still hot on their trail.

boys. Besides its box-office appeal, the picture has a spry, self-mocking tone that holds up through the years. And it is filled with playful, inventive touches.

For instance, take the opening scene, in which Butch and Sundance are in a saloon. As Sundance wins at blackjack, a cardplayer accuses him of cheating. The cardplayer pushes away from the table, ready for a shootout. Then Butch mentions his partner's name.

The cardplayer's face turns ashen. "I didn't know you were the Sundance Kid when I said you were cheating," the cowed gunman mutters. He recants and apologizes, but, as Butch leaves, the cardplayer suddenly questions the Kid's skill. Sundance whirls and shoots off the man's gunbelt.

The scene was put in to show Sundance's credentials from the outset. Though Sundance has appeared in other films—such as *Return of the Badmen* (1948), in which Robert Ryan played him—he has not been nearly as celebrated as other Western badmen like Jesse James or Billy the Kid.

Butch and Sundance prove to be skilled and elusive robbers, leading their gang to a successful holdup of a Union Pacific train. Butch wants to head for Bolivia, where he hears that silver, tin, and gold mines bring big payrolls. First, Sundance pays a visit to his

schoolteacher sweetheart, Etta (Katharine Ross).

The picture's most famous scene comes at this point, one that was introduced as an afterthought. Director Hill realized something was lacking in the scenes between Ross, Newman, and Redford. He told Newman, "There's no relationship between you and the girl, and we need it." So Hill dreamed up the engaging sequences in which Newman stunts on a bicycle as Ross watches, chuckling from a barn.[2]

Newman did most of the tricks himself, because, as it turned out, the stunt man kept falling off. Though Conrad Hall's photography was inspired, Hill felt the scene still needed something else. He dubbed in music and asked Burt Bacharach to come up with a

Butch and Etta try out the latest in transportation—the bicycle.

song with a similar beat. Bacharach did. "Raindrops Keep Falling on My Head" became everybody's favorite song except for one unimaginative studio executive. According to legend, he looked at the rushes and said, "No. No. It has nothing to do with the plot."

Buoyed by the ease of their earlier train robbery, Butch and Sundance decide to hold up the same train. This time, however, a posse is aboard and rumbles out of a freight car. Day after day, the duo stay a jump ahead of their dogged stalkers. We never see the posse close up, but it is led by a sheriff in a white hat named Joe Lefors. One day the posse corners its ex-

Redford and Newman in the title roles.

hausted quarry high above a swiftly running river.

The river is Butch and Sundance's only escape. As they hang over the edge, the Kid confesses he can't swim. He jumps anyway, then grabs Butch's gunbelt as they are swept downstream out of the clutches of the posse.

Not wanting to push their luck, the boys head for Bolivia, via New York City, taking along Etta. Bolivia doesn't turn out to be the land of milk and honey that Butch had in mind. But Butch promises they will all feel better after they rob a bank. They do, even though the language barrier presents a problem. Butch can't read his notes translating "Stick 'em up" or "Nobody move." However, the bank officials get the point, and the two soon become infamous as the *bandidos yanqui.*

They make an attempt at going straight. A tin-mine operator hires them as payroll guards. Unfortunately, the job proves to be more violent than holding up banks. Bandits try to rob the payroll, and Butch and Sundance have to cut them down in a gunfight. In slow motion, Hill shows the bandits reeling backward in a grisly slow-motion ballet reminiscent of the slaughter that ended *Bonnie and Clyde* (1967).

"Well, we've gone straight," the Kid says. "What do we try now?"

Etta, tired of their life on the run, tells them she doesn't want

to see them die and decides to go back to the States. In the screenplay, they go to a movie. On their last night together, they see actors playing Butch and Sundance die in the film. Goldman felt it foreshadowed their impending violent death. Hill thought the scene came too near the end and was too coincidental. So he cut it after the first sneak preview.[3]

With Etta gone, Butch and Sundance resume their old ways. Their luck soon runs out. Several hundred Bolivian soldiers surround them in a patio. The two try to scramble to safety, but both are hit. Bleeding badly, they manage to drag themselves inside a building.

"I got a great idea where we should go next," says Butch, retaining his zany personality to the end.

"I don't want to hear it...I don't ever want to hear another one of your ideas," says Sundance, reloading his pistol.

"Australia..."

"That's no better than here. Name me one thing better."

"They speak English. So, smart guy, we wouldn't be foreigners.... [It has a] good climate. Nice beaches. You could learn to swim."

"What about the banks?"

"They're easy, ripe and luscious."

Both have now loaded their shooting irons.

"You didn't see Lefors out there, did you?"

"Lefors? No."

"Good. For a moment, I thought we were in trouble."

Guns blazing, they dash out together into the soldiers' withering rifle fire.

To preserve their memory as gallant, carefree characters, Hill ended the picture in the now-famous freeze frame. The audience never sees their bloody corpses. Instead, the last frame preserves their images as gutsy, devil-may-care adventurers, shooting with abandon as they charge their adversaries.

---

[1]Goldman says many have misunderstood this quote, thinking he is saying that scriptwriting is "shitty" work. That is not his view. In an interview with the author, Goldman explained that in the women's liberation movement "shitwork" is the name for work that is ignored when done well but commented on when done badly. Housework is one example. "In the same sense," Goldman said, "when a movie is a well-reviewed film, the contribution of the screenwriter is often not mentioned. They'll talk about how wonderful the star is. How glorious the director's vision is. But the bottom-line truth is a movie is a group endeavor. Everybody in the business knows it. But everybody out of the business doesn't want to know it."

[2]In a 1971 auction of 20th Century-Fox's props and memorabilia, there was spirited bidding for the bike. Burt Bacharach and his wife, Angie Dickinson, stayed in the bidding up to $3,000, then dropped out. Television producer David Winters and Bert Rose got it for $3,100. They said they bought it as a gift for Newman's wife, Joanne Woodward.

[3]Also revised was the beginning overline: "Not that it matters, but most of what follows is true." The preview audiences laughed. Hill felt there already was enough levity in the film. It became "Most of what follows is true."

Deliverance
(1972)

Produced and directed by John Boorman. Screenplay by James Dickey based on his novel. Photography, Vilmos Zsigmond. Editor, Tom Priestley. Song "Duelling Banjos" arranged and played by Eric Weissberg with Steven Mandel. Special effects, Marcel Vercoutere. Warner Bros. Filmed in northern Georgia. Rated R. 110 minutes.

Ed Gentry	JON VOIGHT
Lewis Medlock	BURT REYNOLDS
Bobby Trippe	NED BEATTY
Drew Ballinger	RONNY COX
Mountain man	BILLY MCKINNEY
Toothless man	HERBERT "COWBOY" COWARD
Sheriff Bullard	JAMES DICKEY
Old man	ED RAMEY
Lonny (the banjo boy)	BILLY REDDEN
First griner	SEAMON GLASS
Second griner	RANDALL DEAL

Camping out and riding white-water rapids is a ritual that each summer draws adventurers of all ages into the backwoods. There, deep within a breathtaking primeval wilderness, they test their manhood and flex their muscles, celebrating their triumph over nature.

The four weekend adventurers in *Deliverance* observe this time-honored custom, but only for the briefest moment. Nature quickly becomes the enemy. Even more threatening are the hostile mountain people who live in this paradise gone askew.

For some reason, not made entirely clear, they turn the tourists' outing into a weekend of terror. Instead of enjoying an innocent sojourn, the explorers encounter sodomy, maiming, murder. In the end, they struggle fiercely for deliverance from a world more frightening than anything they have known in civilization. What starts as an escapade ends as a nightmare.

Nightmares and struggles are nothing new to director John Boorman. His films frequently involve people battling the forces of society. "Society seems to be a hostile thing.... And also there is the relationship between the individual and nature, natural forces," Boorman once said when asked to explain this recurring theme in his work. ". . . For me, the world, the planet, is a very dangerous place to be. We're lulled into a sense of security by our daily lives. But we are hurtling through space at a tremendous speed in a very unstable piece of ground."

In *Deliverance*, Boorman shot the unstable part of nature along the Chattooga River in northern Georgia. He made the spectacular cliff scenes nearby at Tallulah Gorge, which the Great Wallenda once crossed on a tightrope.

Everyone treated the treacherous gorge with respect. James Dickey, author of the best-selling book on which the film was based, said Jon Voight had "more guts than a burglar." But even Voight declined to climb the gorge's cliff freestyle. His stand-in used a safety net, which was erased from the film.

This striving for realism—Boorman also made the film almost in continuity—does much to capture the essence of man's vulnerability in the wild. Also helping was the melding of sound and image. "The sound of the river is very menacing," said cinematographer Vilmos Zsigmond, "almost more menacing than the image itself."

To give the river a threatening aura, he filmed when the sun was gone. "Water on a sunny day doesn't look menacing at all. It just looks nice.... So we decided to shoot the first part [of the film] with sun and the second part in overcast."

The plot is simplicity itself. Four businessmen go on a canoe trip through the Appalachian Mountains. They are really stock characters. Lewis (Burt Reynolds),[1] the leader, is a kind of virility cult figure with an obsession about the people who will take charge after a nuclear blast destroys civilization. He persuades his pals to come because a dam under construction will soon wipe out the natural beauty of hundreds of thousands of acres of wilderness.

The second is a comic figure, Bobby (Ned Beatty), a fat crybaby type. A third is a dyed-in-the-

Jon Voight canoeing through white-water rapids of the Chattooga River in the wilderness of northern Georgia.

131

wood liberal, Drew (Ronny Cox). The last is the most complex character, Ed (Voight). He has a little of each in him. He is also the most thoughtful of the bunch. When the group is attacked and their survival depends on someone risking his life, it is Ed who shows strength of character.

Dickey, in an interview for this book, said he had the idea for *Deliverance* after he got a letter from an agent who liked his poetry. The agent asked Dickey if he had an idea for a novel about the Appalachian Mountains and the rivers that he had written about.

"I told him, 'I don't,'" said Dickey, who became a writer-in-residence at the University of South Carolina in Columbia. "I said that my main thrust was poetry and literary criticism. I remember going up and taking a siesta and thinking about it. I asked myself, 'If I were going to write a novel about Appalachia, what would I write about?' Nothing came through. Then, as I was fixing to go to sleep, I said, 'Uh-oh, what about the time...' And I knew the whole story in five minutes."

Dickey remembered that he had made several weekend outings in the wilderness. "Nothing quite like (what took place in *Deliverance*) happened. But I saw that it could have. I remember coming up on a couple of rough people on the riverbank. I got to wondering, 'Suppose those guys had been rather bad people. What would we decent people have done if forced to the wall?' Out of that came the thrust of the story."

On the way to the woods, Lewis lectures his friends about the corruption of modern civilization. "They're raping the whole goddam landscape," Lewis says. The unspoiled land will soon be gone. But the story will contradict everything Lewis has said. Nature turns out to be chilling and destructive.

Their first encounter with the primitive people who live in the

backwoods is brilliantly handled. Ed starts playing chords on his guitar. A half-witted boy (Billy Redden) answers them on his banjo. Gradually, Ed coaxes the boy into playing a duet and they strum away, mocking each other, playing the lively captivating piece "Duelling Banjos."

It is a rare moment that is pure cinema. It is as if the instruments were singing to each other and the souls of the two players were merging. But then, when the song is over, a discordant note sounds. As Drew goes to shake hands, the boy turns his head sharply, seemingly rejecting the town dwellers, whom he sees as interlopers, alien to his land.

Boorman uses the scene to establish the suspicious nature of the hill people—creating a mood of tension that extends through the rest of the movie. Later, as the sportsmen drift downriver, the boy watches from a bridge, silent and inscrutable, as if he were clairvoyant and were harboring a secret that would soon be made known to them.

Their first experience with the river is euphoric as they master the dangerous twists and turns of the rapids. "We beat it, didn't we?" Ed shouts. Lewis replies softly but sternly: "You don't beat it. You don't beat this river."

Soon, things take a different turn. When Ed and Bobby pull their canoe out of the river, two menacing mountain men (Billy McKinney and Herbert "Cowboy" Coward) emerge from the silent forest.[2] At shotgun point, the mountaineers tie Bobby to a tree, then beat and bugger him. The act is surprising because there is no provocation and not enough to prepare the audience for something this vicious. But Dickey takes issue with this criticism. "I suggest it was simply the worst way to humiliate an intruder."

While the hillbillies are brutalizing their two captives, another canoe pulls up. Lewis creeps out, draws his bow, and shoots an

Voight rehearses a scene on location.

arrow through the chest of one of the mountain men. The other flees.

Now the group must decide what to do with the corpse. Drew says what they have done is justifiable homicide. Lewis and Bobby are convinced that the local people would never accept their explanation. It remains for Ed to cast the deciding vote. He decides in favor of burying the body. The four will now become forever bonded by their awful secret.

In the morning, they glide downriver again, and the calm,

James Dickey, the poet-novelist, plays a sheriff in his story of four city men who plan a fun-filled outdoor weekend but instead meet with death and violence.

idyllic water suddenly changes. It starts churning and boiling. Without warning, Drew pitches overboard and disappears in the maelstrom. It is not clear if he lost his balance, jumped, or was shot from afar. Minutes later, they all spill into the rushing waters. By the time they can swim to the rocky shoreline, Lewis has broken his leg.

High on a bluff, a mountaineer stands with his rifle. But Lewis is reduced to a mewling wimp. Bobby is incapable of scaling the precipice. It is up to Ed to do battle with the stalking phantom.

Now comes a transition in the movie. Reynolds did an eight-minute scene in which he gave Voight the courage to make the climb. However, Boorman cut it from the movie. When Reynolds asked why, Boorman said: "Because the first half of the film is

yours. The second half of the film is Voight's. It has to be that way. With that scene, he never gets it from you. He *has* to take the picture from you."

Even before the sun comes up, Ed goes after his foe. Inch by inch, Ed scales the sheer cliff. At the last second, when he confronts the rifleman—never quite knowing whether it is the man who assaulted him—his hands shake so hard he can scarcely hold his bow straight. But he does, and his shot is true.

So it is Ed who delivers the two to civilization. They are finally safe, free again, yet not without a cloud of suspicion. The county sheriff (Dickey) and his deputies are skeptical of the group's story. The men say only that they lost a comrade in a canoeing accident. There is no mention of the mountaineers.

In the end, the sheriff lets them go. Each carries away a guilt-ridden memory. The trip has changed them all. But it is Ed who is the most affected, haunted even in his sleep. He wakes from nightmares in which a hand rises from the new artificial lake that covers the unseen wilderness.

What are we to make of this hair-raising tale? Is it just a pure adventure story to keep our attention rapt? Or does it have some other meaning, a muted undertone that we should perceive and ponder on?

Dickey said the picture must work as a narrative. If it does, then the symbolic meaning can be whatever the viewer or reader wishes.

But what does the story mean to the author?

"I think only one thing," Dickey said. "That men—it is probably true of women, too—settle for too little in their lives. And this chance encounter in the river was for the narrator, Ed Gentry, some kind of opening to a dark place in his psyche that, otherwise, he never would know was there. And that is necessary for him to know was there.

"John Berryman [the poet] once said that a man can live his whole life in this country without knowing if he is a coward or not. I think it is necessary for him to know."

---

[1]The part was the first big break for Reynolds. But his selection had nothing to do with any previous screen appearance. As Reynolds recalled it in Judith Crist's book *Take 22* (Viking): "John Boorman called me and said, 'I want to see you about this film.' I was terribly excited. I was in New York at the time, hosting the "Tonight" show. I flew back to Los Angeles, went to see him, and asked what he'd seen me in. He said, 'I saw you on the "Tonight" show.' And I said, 'How could you think of me for this picture because of the "Tonight" show?' He said, 'Because there were five people there, and you were in control. I want a guy who's in control.'"

[2]McKinney, a native of Memphis, was a part-time actor who earned his living as a tree surgeon in Los Angeles. Coward was recruited by Reynolds, who remembered him from a wild west show in North Carolina where the two had once worked as stunt men. For his audition, Coward showed up in bib overalls, no shirt, no shoes—his standard attire. As soon as he said his lines, Boorman told him, "You've got the part." Boorman added that he would be playing a backwoods character who would rape another man. There was a silence. Then, Coward said, "Well, that's all right. I done a lot worse than that."

Clutching his leg broken in the rapids, Burt Reynolds writhes in pain as Ned Beatty comes over to help him.

Afloat on a heavy-duty life raft, director John Boorman (short sleeves) waits for cameraman Vilmos Zsigmond to get ready for a river scene.

Planet of the Apes (1968)

Directed by Franklin J. Schaffner. Based on the novel *Monkey Planet* by Pierre Boulle. Screenplay, Michael Wilson and Rod Serling. Music, Jerry Goldsmith. Photography, Leon Shamroy. Art direction, Jack Martin Smith and William Creber. Editor, Hugh S. Fowler. Special makeup design, John Chambers.☆ Filmed partly in Utah and Arizona national parks. Produced by Arthur P. Jacobs. An APJAC Production. 20th Century–Fox. 112 minutes.

George Taylor	CHARLTON HESTON
Cornelius	RODDY MCDOWALL
Dr. Zira	KIM HUNTER
Dr. Zaius	MAURICE EVANS
Assembly president	JAMES WHITMORE
Honorious	JAMES DALY
Nova	LINDA HARRISON
Landon	ROBERT GUNNER
Lucius	LOU WAGNER
Maximus	WOODROW PARFREY
Dodge	JEFF BURTON
Julius	BUCK KARTALIAN
Hunt Leade	NORMAN BURTON
Dr. Galen	WRIGHT KING
Minister	PAUL LAMBERT

☆ Academy Award winner

A spaceship, sailing through intergalactic infinity, crash-lands on an unfamiliar planet apparently beyond the solar system.

The craft had taken off from Cape Kennedy some twenty centuries earlier. But since it has traveled at the speed of light and its astronauts have sealed themselves in airtight sleeping tubes, the crew has lived in suspended animation. They have aged only eighteen months.

Aging turns out to be only one of their problems. They have landed in a strange simian world where Earth's evolutionary processes have been reversed. Man is a brute—wild, unintelligent, naked. The ape is civilized—capable of speech, clothed, cultured. It is the ape who rules man.

He keeps man in cages, dissects him for research, stuffs him for museum display. He is careful to see that humans do not grow in numbers and strength and ultimately overrun and destroy ape society.

And so begins the engrossing saga of *Planet of the Apes*, a film based on a novel that was so fanciful, even its author never considered it for screen adaptation. Said Pierre Boulle, who also wrote *The Bridge on the River Kwai* (1957): "I didn't think a picture could be made of it."

Producer Arthur P. Jacobs, a former public relations executive who once represented Marilyn Monroe, thought otherwise. He bought the screen rights when *Planet* was still in manuscript form and in French (Boulle's native language). But for a while, it looked as though Jacobs had acquired a white elephant.

"The *Apes* property was stubbornly circulated around the studios by Jacobs for nearly two years," said Charlton Heston in an interview for this book. "It was turned down at least twice by everyone."

The reaction at each studio was similar. "How can you put a bunch of talking chimps in a serious drama?"

Jacobs refused to give up. He had Rod Serling write a screenplay. He persuaded Heston and Edward G. Robinson to make a fifteen-minute test in simian makeup, and got Franklin Schaffner to join the project as director. With this formidable team assembled, 20th Century-Fox got interested—at least to the extent of putting up $50,000 for a test.

"I give Dick Zanuck, then the head of Fox, great credit," Heston said. "He was intrigued. But he recognized the problem that audiences could have with the apes. 'Suppose they laugh at the makeup?' It was a good question."

The task of producing realistic makeup went to Fox makeup

Determination etched in their features, guards charge after George Taylor (Charlton Heston), who has escaped.

specialist John Chambers, a former surgical technician who had once helped repair the faces of wounded soldiers.

Chambers had to create a cast in which almost all the leading characters would appear as apes. They would have to come through not as masquerading actors but as if they were living, breathing chimpanzees, gorillas, and orangutans.

This meant that despite an elaborate disguise, a player would have to project the subtlest reaction. He would have to be able to move facial muscles and change expression for camera closeups.

It took Chambers three months to create the special makeup. But he rose to the task. Said Heston: "It was possible to change expression, although with great difficulty, and register emotion." For his efforts, Chambers won a special Oscar for original makeup—only the second such award in Academy history.

Pleased with the test, Fox went ahead with the picture. Out of his $6 million shooting budget, Jacobs allocated $1 million for makeup. Nearly eighty makeup artists—possibly the largest such force in movie history—were assigned to the picture.

Each morning, actors spent hours in makeup chairs while a special-effects crew applied foam rubber, plastic noses, anthropoid jaws, and hair. The actors had an extra set of teeth set in jaws that protruded beyond their own facial bones.

The production had an impact all over Hollywood. When large-scale scenes involving 200 or more apes went before the camera, so many makeup men were pulled in that other films and TV shows found their productions paralyzed.

"It took three hours to apply the makeup and another half hour to get it off," said Heston. It created some unique social situations. Heston had never met Kim Hunter and did not get to see her face during the shooting. At the premiere, she came over to greet him. "I drew a total blank," Heston said.

Despite the ingenious cosmetic job, the key to *Planet*'s success is its biting irony. At times, the film's attempts at satire go askew. For example, an ape's eulogy at a funeral awkwardly recalls Will Rogers: "The dear departed told me, 'I never met an ape I didn't like.'" A monkey says, "Human see. Human do." A three-judge tribunal strikes a pose resembling see no evil, hear no evil, speak no evil.

Overriding these hokey scenes is a first-rate science fiction fantasy embellished with penetrating commentary on human values. The picture strikes out against suppression—(a timely subject in the 1960s), the intransigence of established authority, and the vanity of ambition. And it provides a chilling allegorical prophecy about man's destiny.

Its moral lessons are plain even to children. *Life* critic Richard Schickel said it taught his young daughter that "animals, and by implication all creatures different from her, are capable of feeling. It taught her . . . that they can be scared of the unfamiliar and therefore be as foolish and as prejudiced as more familiar beings can."

However, the biggest surprise was the picture's longevity. Even with four first-rate actors—Charlton Heston, Kim Hunter, Roddy McDowall, and Maurice Evans—no one had given the slightest thought of the film's evolving into a series. But when the box-office returns came in, they showed that *Planet* earned a hefty $25 million before the year was out—more than four times the studio's investment.

So, reacting to the public's response, the studio went on to do a sequel, *Beneath the Planet of the Apes* (1970), and eventually a series. The others were *Escape from the Planet of the Apes* (1971), *Conquest of the Planet of the Apes* (1972), and *Battle for the*

Astronauts land on the Planet of the Apes. *From left*: Heston, Jeff Burton, and Robert Gunner.

George Taylor, held in captivity along with his fellow humans, tries to get the attention of Dr. Zira (Kim Hunter) and Dr. Zaius (Maurice Evans), the apes' Minister of Science.

Planet of the Apes (1973). Heston played in only one more picture, a brief appearance in the second film. "We've done it," he told Zanuck. "You can't do it again. The rest will be just more adventures with the monkeys."

That proved to be the case. As with most series, the best was the first film, where we initially come to know this topsy-turvy world, Right from the start, the film piques the audience's interest as astronaut George Taylor (Heston), disenchanted with the human species, leaves the earth on a trip into deep space.

"The irony," said Heston, "is that this misanthrope will find himself in a civilization where he becomes the sole defender of mankind as a valuable, rational species."

Centuries later, Taylor and his two companions land on what seems to be a barren planet. They soon find they are mistaken. The spacemen wander into the midst of a primitive tribe of humans who are pursued by mounted apes with guns and nets.

Evolution has apparently taken a different course on this planet. Man has no identity. He cannot talk. He can be taught a few tricks, but he is wild and untamed. The apes regard man as a nuisance. "He eats up his food supplies in the forest," says Dr. Zaius (Maurice Evans), the simians' Minister of Science. "Then, they migrate to our greenbelts and ravage our crops. The sooner he is exterminated, the better."

Zaius's hatred is prompted by an ulterior motive. He has discovered—and concealed the fact—that man once ruled the planet. This is at odds with simian culture as expounded in the ape Bible, called the Twelve Scrolls. The Scrolls would lose their credibility if the facts of evolution were known. In fact, the whole foundation of the ape culture would be undermined. Zaius, wearing his second hat as Defender of the Faith, feels he is duty-bound to suppress this information.

Meanwhile, Taylor, captured by the apes, is befriended by Dr. Zira (Hunter), a lady ape researcher, and Cornelius (McDowall), her fiancé. In time, they learn that the human has both speech and intelligence. Cornelius, an archaeologist, has unearthed evidence of an older human civilization in an excavation in the so-called Forbidden Zone. So far, he has not been able to convince anyone. Now, Taylor is living evidence of his discovery.

However, as soon as Zaius learns of Taylor's verbal ability, he puts him on trial to dispose of him. To seal the verdict, Zaius threatens Zira and Cornelius with scientific heresy and contempt of the tribunal if they aid in Taylor's defense.

The penalties fail to deter them. Zira and Cornelius help Taylor flee to Cornelius's excavation site. When Zaius follows, he is confronted with one of their prize findings: the remains of a talking doll from an older civilization of humans. Taylor asks: "Would an ape make a human doll that talks?"

Zaius will not concede anything. "If man were superior, why didn't he survive?" No one can answer that.

But the puzzle is solved in the picture's last sequence. Taylor and his lovely companion, Nova (Linda Harrison), win their freedom and ride away along a deserted stretch of shoreline.

"What will he find out there?" Zira asks.

"His destiny," Zaius replies.

Far away, Taylor and Nova come across the ruins of a massive structure. It turns out to be the Statue of Liberty. Suddenly, everything falls into place.

"Oh my God," Taylor cries, realizing his trip has taken him through time but not space. "I'm back. I've been home all along."

Raging on, he yells to his vanished race, "You finally did it. You murderers. You blew it up."

Collared on a leash, Taylor goes on trial for his freedom. Zira and Cornelius (Roddy McDowall), *right foreground*, are sympathetic.

Taylor and Nova (Linda Harrison) exchange a searching look before they flee into the Forbidden Zone.

2001: A Space Odyssey
(1968)

Directed and produced by Stanley Kubrick. Screenplay by Kubrick and Arthur C. Clarke based on the short story "The Sentinel" by Clarke. Photography, Geoffrey Unsworth. Additional photography, John Alcott. Production design, Tony Masters, Harry Lange, Ernie Archer. Editor, Ray Lovejoy. Space effects designed and directed by Kubrick. ☆ Special-effects supervisors, Wally Veevers, Douglas Trumbull, Con Pederson, Tom Howard. Wardrobe, Hardy Amies. Music, Richard Strauss, Johann Strauss, Aram Khachaturian, Gyorgy Ligeti. A Metro-Goldwyn-Mayer Picture. 141 minutes.

David Bowman	KEIR DULLEA
Frank Poole	GARY LOCKWOOD
Dr. Heywood Floyd	WILLIAM SYLVESTER
Moonwatcher	DAN RICHTER
HAL 9000	DOUGLAS RAIN
Smyslov	LEONARD ROSSITER
Elena	MARGARET TYZACK
Halvorsen	ROBERT BEATTY
Michaels	SEAN SULLIVAN
Mission Control	FRANK MILLER
Stewardess	PENNY BRAHMS
Stewardess	EDWINA CARROLL
Poole's father	ALAN GIFFORD
Floyd's daughter	VIVIAN KUBRICK

☆ Academy Award for best visual effects

Few films have had such long and careful preparation—six years in the making (at a cost of $10 million). Yet, despite the painstaking preliminaries, there were as many moviegoers who disliked the film as there were those who thought it was a science fiction classic.

It is, in fact, a difficult picture to fathom. Its format is bizarre. Almost a half hour goes by before the first word is spoken. In all, less than half the movie has dialogue—much of it mundane. And the plot, or what there is of it, seems disjointed and murky.

Audiences wondered what the first part—the long segment about the man-apes—had to do with the rest. What was the meaning of the reappearing monolith? What was the last scene about—the surrealistic sequence in which the astronaut grows old in the room with the Louis XVI furniture?

Many critics threw up their hands and wrote devastating reviews.[1] But months later, some went back and found they had a totally different experience. Pieces began to fall into place. On second sight, they felt they had been too hasty in their judgment. Many now realized they had seen a great film.

Time, for example, at first wrote off the movie. In August 1968 it said *2001* failed as drama. Though it called the picture's special effects "fabulous," the magazine said Kubrick's "message was obscure." One year later, *Time* did an about-face. It said Kubrick's "epic film . . . assumes awesome metaphysical consequences. Kubrick is one of the best American filmmakers and *2001* may be his masterpiece."

A terse second-sight review came from Sam Lesner of the *Chicago Daily News*. "At first, I thought Kubrick had flipped his lid. Now, I believe he's a genius."

These reactions were not totally unexpected. Kubrick was breaking new ground. In place of a

Keir Dullea as David Bowman piloting the spaceship *Discovery* through the void of space.

---

[1]A notable exception was Penelope Gilliatt of *The New Yorker* who called the movie "some sort of great film."

movie with a conventional beginning, middle, and end, he was presenting pure cinema, a sensory spectacle, a picture that tried to communicate more to the emotions than to the intellect. "There's a basic problem with people who are not paying attention with their eyes," Kubrick said. "Those who won't believe their eyes won't be able to appreciate this film."

Lots of kids, taking Kubrick at his word, flocked to the first rows of theaters to get a visual high. But 2001 was more than a movie to groove on. It could be, and should be, seen on another level, because it had perceptive things to say about the possibility of extraterrestrial life and the evolution of man.

Like a cubist painting, it is a film that grows in meaning the more the viewer brings to it. The movie is based on Arthur C. Clarke's short story "The Sentinel," and a reading of the story—or of the novel 2001 published after the movie opened—adds immeasurably to the understanding of the picture.

Of course, one could ask whether an audience can be expected to do homework. Shouldn't a picture stand or fall on its own merits? One

could answer that if a film, or any work of art, can give a viewer a deeper and more meaningful experience—in exchange for outside reading—that extra effort is worthwhile.

Ironically, for a film that started such a lingering controversy, 2001 had a quiet beginning. In February 1965—three years after Kubrick conceived the idea—Metro-Goldwyn-Mayer announced without fanfare that it would finance a new film called Journey Beyond the Stars.

For the next two years, Kubrick and Clarke transformed "The Sentinel" into a novel, then into a film script. Clarke's short story had explored the notion of higher civilizations existing elsewhere in the universe. It postulated that beings from another planet may have come here millions of years ago.

The story told of extraterrestrial scouts that landed on earth and left a signaling device to alert them when intelligent life finally evolved. Then they deposited a similar device on the moon to tell them when man's intelligence reached the point where he could conquer space.

Kubrick supervised every aspect of the picture from the design of futuristic clothes to the selection of background music. The story of the thousands of production details and how they evolved into the finished product makes fascinating reading. The details were, in fact, compiled by Jerome Agel and put into a paperback called The Making of 2001. Here are some samples:

● For the film score, Kubrick commissioned Alex North, who had composed music for Kubrick's film Spartacus (1960). North was excited because a movie about the future seemed an opportunity for a strikingly original composition. Working frantically to meet a deadline, he composed forty minutes of music—only to find that in the end, Kubrick used not a single note. Instead, he relied on existing musical works.

● There was a mixed reaction to the score. One composer whose work was excerpted, Gyorgy Ligeti, successfully sued, claiming that use of snippets of his Requiem distorted the piece. The film's most memorable music was the spine-tingling opening fanfare from Richard Strauss's tone poem Thus Spake Zarathustra. During the voyage to the moon, Kubrick used "The Blue Danube" despite its associations with courtly Viennese ballrooms. He felt there was a new young audience who would be free from this stereotype, and the waltz tempo would convey the grace and freedom of spaceflight.

● The Vickers Engineering Group built the spacecraft, a huge ship with a centrifuge large enough for astronauts to live in full-time. The craft, which took six months to construct at a cost of $300,000, looked something like a Ferris wheel. Equipment was bolted to the floor so that Kubrick could show the effects of zero gravity. In the sequence where space travelers are transported to the moon, a stewardess walks on the ceiling. Kubrick did the shot by putting an actress on a treadmill while the spaceship's interior rotated behind her.

● The realistic-looking man-apes

Bowman and fellow astronaut Frank Poole (Gary Lockwood) check their equipment.

Director Stanley Kubrick on the set. The movie drew harsh critical reactions, but many recanted after seeing the film a second time.

An outside view of one of the giant spaceships.

were actors, mimes, and ballet dancers who had slim builds so they would not seem like bulky people stuffed inside monkey suits. They wore apelike masks that allowed them to bare fangs, snarl, eat, and drink. The eyes did the acting. Intermingling with them were two chimpanzees directed by their trainers. Despite the extraordinary job that was done, the movie failed to win an Oscar for makeup. Clarke thought the Academy Award judges did not know the apes were human actors.

● HAL was the voice of Douglas Rain, a Canadian-born Shakespearean actor originally hired to be the narrator. When the narration idea was dropped, Rain was chosen over Martin Balsam to do HAL's voice. Balsam's voice, Kubrick felt, was too American, while Rain had the kind of bland mid-Atlantic accent that the part needed. Rain did his work without seeing a foot of the film.

● For the role of the ground control landing officer, Kubrick hired Franklin W. Miller, a U.S. Air Force traffic controller stationed in England. British Actors Equity protested. But Kubrick felt that British actors could not duplicate the mission controller's voice so familiar to Americans from the Mercury, Gemini, and Apollo voyages.[2]

Even its strongest defenders would concede that *2001* was a slow-paced, almost plotless film. Its first section, called "The Dawn of Man," shows a band of man-apes, hard pressed to survive in a desolate landscape because they had not learned to consume meat. They are battling to overcome extinction. The apes discover a strange ebony slab which serves as a mysterious catalyst in their transition to reason. They soon learn to use fossil bones as weapons and to eat the animals they slaughter. They quickly dominate their animal world. And so begins their move to more sophisticated tools and their evolutionary transition to *Homo sapiens*.

Frederick J. Ordway, the movie's scientific and technical consultant, felt it was a mistake to delete the narration from this long scene. "No one with whom I talked understood the real meaning of this visually beautiful and deeply significant sequence," Ordway said when the picture was released. "Its intended impact was lost."

In 1980, twelve years after the film was made, Ordway's position remained the same. "Many people, who have now read the novel, might think that my comment is no longer valid," he said in an interview for this book. "But I still feel that the narration, which really was splendid, would have been a big plus."

A brilliant transition takes the film into the second part. One of the apes tosses his weapon skyward, where it suddenly changes to a space shuttle hurtling toward the moon. A single cut has telescoped four million years of evolution—the longest flash forward in cinema history.

The second section begins in the first year of the twenty-first century, 2001. Man has started colonizing the moon and discovered a second slab buried beneath the lunar surface. It is a cosmic burglar alarm, put there to alert an unknown civilation that man

---

[2]Because he was not an actor, Miller remembers Kubrick did everything possible to put him at ease. "Once, I was tapping my foot which no one could see beneath the console where I was sitting. It was a nervous habit that produced quite a thump on the tape. Instead of asking me to stop, Kubrick got me a blanket, put it under my feet, and I tapped all I wanted."

The picture's surrealistic ending, in which Bowman ages and is born again.

has progressed to an advanced intelligence.

In the third section, man sets out to find the origin of the alien culture that has planted the monoliths. A supercomputer named HAL 9000 pilots the great ship *Discovery* through the black void of space.[3] A chatty, fussy robot brain, HAL eventually succumbs, like a human, to a personality failing and decides to kill the crew. HAL cuts off the life-support system of three astronauts in deep freeze and sends another (Gary Lockwood) flying off into space.

There remains only astronaut Dave Bowman (Keir Dullea), who barely manages to save himself by lobotomizing HAL's brain. As HAL dies, the computer's voice grinds down like a defective record. "Dave. Stop. Stop . . . My mind is going . . . I can feel it. There is no question about it. I can feel it. I'm afraid."

Bowman sails on alone, flying to the outer reaches of Jupiter, where he finds still another monolith and speeds through a world beyond space and time. Many viewers thought Bowman was plunging deeper into the atmosphere of Jupiter. What actually

was happening was that the monolith was, in effect, an interstellar accelerator catapulting Bowman through the universe to the place where the supercivilization lived.

In the famous last scene, the one that gives moviegoers the most trouble, Bowman finds himself growing old in a white-on-white bedroom with rococo furniture. The bedroom is a kind of cage outside of which the beings of this distant world are looking in. They are deciding if man should go on to the next stage of development.

In the end, they feel he is worthy. Once again, the monolith appears and transmits its powers.

Now we see an X-ray image of Bowman, reborn as a "star child" with sad, enigmatic eyes. The child, a new superspecies, is on the way back to Earth to prepare the planet to enter the cosmic community.[4]

Not everybody agrees with this interpretation. Dullea, for one, feels the last sequence is deliberately vague. "It's like a giant Rorschach test," Dullea said in an interview for this book. "An atheist and a highly religious person can be equally at home with the film. I don't think any person's idea is more valid than anyone else's. It's like different reactions to a piece of abstract art."[5]

---

[3]The computer's name was originally Athena, after the goddess of wisdom, and spoke with a woman's voice. But Kubrick and Clarke thought this would lead to misleading sexual interpretations about its interactions with the astronauts. Someone suggested that "HAL" was coined by moving back the letters "IBM" one position in the alphabet. Clarke and Kubrick denied this, but were delighted by the coincidence. Actually, HAL is an acronym of the two principal learning systems, "heuristic" (in which a student is trained to find out things for himself) and "algorithmic" (computing with numerals).

[4]After the original print was finished, Kubrick trimmed nineteen minutes. The cut sequences included "The Dawn of Man," Orion (the space station), and Poole exercising in the centrifuge and exiting from the spaceship. Kubrick, who insisted he made the cuts without pressure from the studio, said he did not think they detracted from the picture.

[5]*2010* (MGM, 1984), a sequel directed by Peter Hyams—with Roy Scheider as Floyd, HAL as a good guy, and Dullea playing Bowman in a cameo—continues the story. It's slick and it has neat special effects. But it lacks the poetry and mystery of the original.

Suspense
and
Intrigue

THE MANCHURIAN CANDIDATE

PSYCHO

CHINATOWN

The Manchurian Candidate

(1962)

Directed by John Frankenheimer. Screenplay by George Axelrod based on the novel by Richard Condon. Camera, Lionel Lindon. Editor, Ferris Webster. Music, David Amram. Sets, Richard Sylbert. Produced by Axelrod and Frankenheimer. United Artists. B/W. 126 minutes.

Bennett Marco	FRANK SINATRA
Raymond Shaw	LAURENCE HARVEY
Rosei	JANET LEIGH
Mrs. Iselin	ANGELA LANSBURY
Chunjin	HENRY SILVA
Sen. John Iselin	JAMES GREGORY
Jocie Jordon Shaw	LESLIE PARRISH
Sen. Thomas Jordon	JOHN McGIVER
Yen Lo	KHIGH DHIEGH
Psychiatrist	JOE ADAMS
Holborn Gaines	LLOYD CORRIGAN
Corporal Melvin	JAMES EDWARDS
Colonel	DOUGLAS HENDERSON
Zilkov	ALBERT PAULSEN
Secretary of Defense	BARRY KELLEY
Berezovo	MADAME SPIVY
Soldier	TOM LOWELL

A group of GIs is seated in a semicircle at what they think is a garden club lecture. They believe they are listening to a tedious talk on horticulture.

They are not. They are really on a stage before a group of Russian and Chinese psychiatrists trained in Pavlovian conditioning techniques. On command, one of the GIs gets up, puts his hands around the neck of a buddy, and calmly strangles him. Then, responding to another order, he picks up a gun and shoots down a second soldier.

This is the ultimate in brainwashing as seen in the gripping thriller *The Manchurian Candidate*, a film based on the novel by Richard Condon.

The movie had everything going for it—an innovative storyline, a first-rate cast headed by Frank Sinatra, and a brilliant young director, John Frankenheimer. Yet, it failed at the box office.

Audiences did not know how to react to the surprising twists and turns of its macabre plot. They were not sure they were watching something so far removed from reality that it was ridiculous, or something so close to the truth it was unnerving.

The Manchurian Candidate was a film ahead of its time. The country had not seen the assassinations of John and Robert Kennedy. And the thought that an American president could be shot to death —an event that had not occurred since McKinley was murdered by an anarchist in 1901—or that a foreign power could program someone to kill seemed, to put it mildly, farfetched.

No one has ever proved this ever happened. But we know that Lee Harvey Oswald spent time in Russia. And many writers have speculated on the possibility that he was brainwashed there and trained to kill.

True or not, the idea that a government could create a robot who kills without fear or guilt has more credibility today then when *The Manchurian Candidate* came out. So it is not surprising that the movie has attracted a cult following and gradually won critical acclaim.

John Frankenheimer received instant recognition for his direction—he was then only thirty-two—and it remains his best movie in the public mind. Ironically, he himself thinks he has

Laurence Harvey is about to be programmed to kill as Leslie Parrish enters in a party costume as the queen of diamonds.

made finer films. In fact, he once was quoted saying that he thought *The Manchurian Candidate* was "overrated" and that there were some "terrible" scenes he would take back if he could.

But in an interview for this book, Frankenheimer tried to set the record straight. "I think it's a pretty good movie. I've done better. I'm not sure which is my best. It could be *The Gypsy Moths* [1969] or *The Iceman Cometh* [1973] or *The French Connection II* [1975]. But I like *The Manchurian Candidate* very much. It was an easy movie to do. There were no problems. It was shot in only forty-two days."

As for taking back scenes, Frankenheimer said he never thinks of his work that way. "What's done is done. I don't want to go back and redo it. That's just an exercise in futility," he said.

"I think *The Manchurian Candidate* is a startling movie. It is a bold movie. And, as a result of the things [assassinations] that hap-

Harvey with Parrish, who plays his ill-fated screen sweetheart.

In a surrealistic brainwashing scene, Frank Sinatra and Harvey believe they are at a tea party.

pened, it became a very prophetic movie."

Frankenheimer, who got his start in television, became involved in *Candidate* by making the most of an unhappy incident. "George Axelrod and I worked together on the screenplay of *Breakfast at Tiffany's* [1961], and we were looking forward to working together on the picture. Then the producers cast Audrey Hepburn, and I was paid off because she had never heard of me. I was upset. But that was the way it was."

However, he and Axelrod had impressed each other and decided they wanted to collaborate. Axelrod had heard of Condon's newest book and urged Frankenheimer to read it. He read it that day and liked it.

"We called Axelrod's agent, Irving [Swifty] Lazar, on the coast, and he bought us the rights," Frankenheimer said. "We did a screenplay—I helped but Axelrod wrote most of it—and then we got Sinatra. It was not hard to do. He loved the book, knew Condon, and always wanted to do it. That's all we needed."

Or almost all. The fact is, once the picture was made, Frankenheimer needed some cooperation on the part of the audience. First, they had to accept the premise that a group of American GIs, captured during the Korean War, could be so ingeniously brainwashed they would forget all the details of their harrowing imprisonment.

Second, the audience had to believe that one of the GIs could be turned into an assassin and programmed to obey instructions without remembering his deeds after seeing the playing card the queen of diamonds.

But so brilliantly did all this come out on the screen that moviegoers were quite willing to accept this demonic plot as plausible. Once they did, the picture worked beautifully as a spy movie.

At first, the film moves slowly. The story really begins when Raymond Shaw (Laurence Harvey) comes home from the war to receive the Congressional Medal of Honor for leading a successful action against the Reds. The award delights his domineering, politically power-mad mother (Angela Lansbury). She sees Shaw's notoriety as a way to further the career

Psycho
(1960)

Directed and produced by Alfred Hitchcock. Screenplay by Joseph Stefano from a novel by Robert Bloch. Photography, John L. Russell. Special photographic effects, Clarence Champagne. Music, Bernard Herrmann. Editor, George Tomasini. Titles, Saul Bass. Location work: Arizona and California. A Paramount Picture. B/W 109 minutes.

Norman Bates	ANTHONY PERKINS
Marion Crane	JANET LEIGH
Lila Crane	VERA MILES
Sam Loomis	JOHN GAVIN
Milton Arbogast	MARTIN BALSAM
Sheriff Chambers	JOHN McINTIRE
Dr. Richmond	SIMON OAKLAND
Tom Cassidy (the millionaire)	FRANK ALBERTSON
Marion's coworker (Caroline)	PATRICIA HITCHCOCK
Marion's boss (George Lowery)	VAUGHN TAYLOR
Mrs. Chambers	LURENE TUTTLE
Car salesman	JOHN ANDERSON
Policeman	MORT MILLS
Police guard	TED KNIGHT
Man in cowboy hat outside office	ALFRED HITCHCOCK

Seventy-eight takes in seven days. That's what Janet Leigh remembers most about the frightening shower sequence in *Psycho*, perhaps the most famous murder scene ever filmed.

"I was wearing moleskin, a flesh-colored material that adheres to the skin," she said in an interview for this book. "Dancers use moleskin a lot. There were pieces over my front and bottom . . . except in one take when I felt the moleskin slipping. The steam from the warm shower was pulling it away. But the take was going well, and it was a difficult shot. So I said, 'The hell with it.' And the crew saw more than they bargained for."

Such was the dedication of performers when they appeared in a picture by Alfred Hitchcock. Actors considered it a unique experience to work with the master of suspense. For one thing, Hitchcock, whose name on a marquee virtually guaranteed a box-office success, had his own *modus operandi*. Unlike directors such as Robert Altman who often follow the script loosely, Hitchcock worked like a symphony conductor carrying a score to the podium.

Before each movie, there was a long period of preparation. He wrote down every sequence in detail, usually working with the writer before the dialogue was created. "It is as though you saw a film on the screen and turned off all the sound," Hitchcock once said. The result was that by the time he was ready to shoot, he had memorized every take and camera angle.

In fact, the filming itself was often an anticlimax. "Because of all his planning," Leigh said, "for him, the most boring part was the actual shooting. His work and the challenge of the planning all has been done."

Some say his detailed script gave actors little chance to work out their own characterizations. But Leigh said she never found Hitchcock to be domineering or repressive as long as she worked within his frame of reference.

"When I met him before filming," she explained, "he said he would not give me a lot of direction unless I was really going off base. . . . If I wanted anything explained or needed motivation, he was there. If I needed to know anything about camera angles, or the set, or my moves on the set, he was ready to explain. The main requirement was that I fit into his pattern."

Norman Bates (Tony Perkins) outside his eerie Victorian house.

Janet Leigh as Marion Crane in the famous shower scene.

Born in London in 1899, Hitchcock was the son of a wholesale poultry dealer. There was little in his salad days to point the way to a film career. A Catholic, he went to Jesuit schools as a boy, then studied science and engineering at London University. But he became fascinated with cinema after watching American movies. When a Hollywood film company opened a London studio, the twenty-year-old Hitchcock got a job.

In early years, he apprenticed in every role from art director to script editor. Then, in 1926, he got his first directorial assignment in a movie called *The Lodger*, a story about Jack the Ripper. Critics hailed it as one of the best films of the year. More pictures followed. By the end of the 1930s, he turned out such first-rate movies as *The 39 Steps* (1935), *Sabotage* (1936), and *The Lady Vanishes* (1938). They established him as England's top director.

Eventually, Hitchcock succumbed to the lure of Hollywood. *Rebecca* (1940), his first picture there, won the Academy Award for best movie. For the next three decades, he turned out a remarkable array of movies. Of them all, many think *Psycho* was his best.[1]

Ironically, it is a film in which the most violent scene occurs closer to the start than the end. But it succeeds because the first murder is so unexpected, it creates an atmosphere of apprehension that holds up throughout the picture.

Psycho opens with a sensual scene in a sleazy hotel bedroom in Phoenix. Two lovers, Marion Crane (Leigh) and Sam Loomis (John Gavin), are dressing after a hurried lunchtime rendezvous. Sam is getting divorced. Alimony threatens to drain his meager resources and, for the time being, has blocked a permanent relationship.

The point could have been

made over coffee. However, Hitchcock, who likes to titillate audiences by inserting a bit of sex in his movies, has chosen to tell us about the couple's problem in a sensual scene. Sam is shirtless and Marion is seen lying in bed in a bra and half-slip.

When Marion goes back to the real estate office where she works, her boss (Vaughn Taylor) hands her $40,000 to deposit in the bank. On impulse, she decides to pack her bags and take the money. She drives off, heading for San Francisco, where Sam works.

As night falls, she runs into a rainstorm and pulls into the first place she finds—the Bates Motel. It is a seedy, nearly deserted establishment lying in the shadow of a hulking Victorian house.

The proprietor, Norman Bates (Tony Perkins), a giggly, shy young man who apparently lives with his cranky old mother, invites Marion to dinner. In the motel parlor decorated with Norman's stuffed birds, he tells how he has devoted himself to his invalid mother.

As he drones on, Marion begins to see her own deed in perspective. She senses the pitiful trap he has fallen into and sees a parallel situation she is creating for herself. Before she leaves him, she has decided to return the loot.

"We all go a little mad sometimes. Haven't you?"

"Yes," Marion says. "Sometimes just one time can be enough."

This meandering opening, with long stretches of silence, takes up forty minutes, about a third of the movie. But its pace is deliberately slow.

"The first part of the story was a red herring," Hitchcock explained. "...[The idea was] to distract the viewer's attention in order to heighten the murder. We purposely made that beginning on the long side...to get the audience absorbed with the question of whether she would or would not be caught....You turn the

---

[1] *Psycho* was Hitchcock's biggest money-maker. Shot with a TV crew on a budget of only $800,000, it has earned more than $20 million.

An insurance investigator (Martin Balsam) comes by to ask some questions at the motel where Marion was last reported seen.

The deed done, the phantom-like apparition flees and Marion dies slowly. She slips back against the shower stall, slides down, one arm holding the curtain, which rips from its rings one by one. With the water spraying down, we see the blood circling as it whirls down the drain. (One reason Hitchcock made the picture in black and white was that he felt it would be too gruesome to see all the blood in color.) The last shot shows a huge close-up of Marion's eye, open in death, as the camera pulls away.

It is a shattering moment. Since Leigh is the star, no one expects her to be killed one-third of the way through the picture. The director has manipulated the audience's emotions, and the movie really starts at this point.

Now, as Bates cleans up the gory scene, putting Marion's body and all her belongings into her car and pushing it into a nearby bog, the audience's sympathy temporarily shifts to him. He seems like a nervous and vulnerable young man, trying to cover up for his psychotic mother. For a harrowing instant, it appears that the car won't sink. And then it does.

A few days later, Milton Arbogast (Martin Balsam), an insurance investigator hired by Marion's boss, arrives at the motel. He sees Marion's handwriting in the register, becomes suspicious, and returns later to question Norman's mother in the dark old house. Before he does, he calls Sam and Marion's sister, Lila (Vera Miles), to report his progress.

As Arbogast walks upstairs, the screen shows his feet slowly mounting the stairs, then switches to his face. Just as he reaches the second-floor landing, a figure, who appears to be Norman's mother, darts from a bedroom wielding a long knife.

Hitchcock placed the camera high over the steps, showing a bird's-eye view of the scene. He said he did this primarily because had he shot from behind, the audience would have thought he was deliberately concealing her face and might have figured out the disguise. But he also wanted to contrast the long shot with the close-up of Arbogast's head as the knife came at him.

"It was like music, you see," Hitchcock said, "with the high shot with the violins, and suddenly, the big head with the brass instruments clashing."

The blood effect was carefully engineered. Hitchcock put a plastic tube with hemoglobin on Arbogast's face. As the knife fell, a technician pulled a string that released the blood from the tube.

There was also an unusual shot of him falling. When Arbogast fell down the stairway, he looked as if he were tiptoeing backward, lighting from step to step. "We did it by process," Hitchcock said. "First, I did a separate dolly shot down the stairway without the man. Then, we sat him in a special chair in which he was in a fixed position in front of the transparency screen showing the stairs. Then, we shot the chair and Arbogast simply threw his arms up, waving them as if he'd lost his balance."

Norman, anticipating more visitors, hides his mother in the fruit cellar. Meanwhile, after Arbogast fails to return, Lila and Sam go to the sheriff (John McIntire). He shocks them by telling them that Bates's mother has been dead for ten years.

That night, Sam and Lila drive to the motel. While Sam engages Norman in conversation, Lila slips away to search the house. Slowly, cautiously, she rummages through rooms filled with Victorian furniture.

Sam's ruse lasts only a few moments. Norman soon becomes suspicious, knocks Sam out, and dashes out. But before Norman gets to the house, Lila retreats to the cellar. There, in the film's chilling denouement, she sees what appears to be Mrs. Bates in a viewer in one direction and then in another. You keep him as far as possible from what's actually going to happen."

In the celebrated shower scene, Marion appears to be washing away her guilt until we see a shadowy figure through the plastic shower curtain. The sound of the water robs Marion of any chance of hearing her assailant. Naked and vulnerable, she is off guard when the curtains snap open and the dark shadow comes at her flashing a butcher knife. With the chilling sound of Bernard Herrmann's music in the background —a piercing cry like the scream of birds—the camera shifts frantically from a flurry of stabbing shots to Leigh's agonized face.[2]

"We had a torso specially built for that scene with the blood that was supposed to spurt away from that knife," Hitchcock said. "But I didn't use it. I used a live girl instead, a naked model who stood in for Janet Leigh. We only showed Miss Leigh's hands, shoulders, and head. All the rest was the stand-in."

Why a stand-in? In his book *Hitchcock*, John Russell Taylor says that Hitchcock was always solicitous of his leading ladies. Filming Leigh in the nude "did not sort with his idea of what was and was not proper for a star."[3]

Robert Bloch's novel, on which the picture was based, disposed of the murder quickly. "It was the knife that, a moment later, cut off her scream. And her head."

Building on these two sentences, Hitchcock created his memorable forty-five-second scene by splicing seventy-eight pieces of film. They run through the projector at great rapidity. Ironically, the audience never sees the knife cutting Marion's flesh. "You went to her face, you went to her feet, you went to the assailant in quick, rapid shots," Hitchcock said. "But the overall effect given the audience is one of an alarming, devastating murder scene."

[2]Controversy has arisen over the issue of credit for this famous scene. Saul Bass, graphic designer who did titles for *Psycho*, *Vertigo* (1958), and *North by Northwest* (1959), claims the sequence was really his work. Bass said that in addition to drawing the storyboards for the scene, he also directed it. After Bass shot a rehearsal of the sequence, Bass said Hitchcock told him: "You know how to do it. You do it." Bass added: "He sat Buddhalike, and I directed." Bass made this claim after Hitchcock's death. However, in his 1983 book *The Dark Side of Genuis*, Donald Spoto supports Bass's contention.
Wrote Spoto: "About that central sequence, which has elicited more study . . . than any other in the history of the cinema, Hitchcock always retained a cool attitude. And rightly so, for he delegated the design and the shooting to . . . Bass." Spoto went on to portray Hitchcock as a man embarrassed by his obesity and frustrated by his inability to form close personal ties. He depicted Hitchcock as a person given to cruel practical jokes, haunted by cool, idealized blondes whom he sought for his films.

[3]Leigh says she knows little about a stand-in being used in the shower scene. In her book *There Really Was a Hollywood* (Doubleday), she said Hitchcock had originally intended to use a model for some of the shower shots. "But he said he abandoned that thought because we had already accomplished what was essential," Leigh wrote. "I have observed this film many times, and I can't find any glimpse of an unfamiliar shot in that montage." However, there is no dispute over the fact that Perkins did not appear in the famous scene. He was in New York, rehearsing a play. A stand-in took over. "It's rather strange," Perkins said, "to go through life being identified with this sequence."

Marion meets Norman, a motel owner with a strangely possessive mother.

On the set, director Alfred Hitchcock and Leigh talk about the picture's opening scene.

rocking chair facing the other way. When Lila touches the figure, a mummified face seems to wheel and confront Lila.

While the basement's bare lightbulb swings wildly and Herrmann's shrill bird music shrieks, Norman rushes in wearing his mother's dress. Before he can commit his third murder, Sam grabs him from behind and subdues him.

Hitchcock has one more surprise. He has a psychiatrist (Simon Oakland) explain Norman's schizophrenic personality to Sam, Lila, and the sheriff. After Norman's father died, the psychiatrist says, Norman and his mother lived alone. That all changed when his mother found a lover.

Norman felt she had rejected him, and Norman killed them both. Then, to erase the horrible crime in his mind, he dug up her corpse, stuffed it, and tried to create the illusion of her as a living person.

Some critics felt the psychiatrist's explanation was redundant. But Hitchcock thought if he did not include it, there would be loose ends to the story, and he would run afoul of the "icebox

trade." He explained that inside phrase like this:

"The people who get home after seeing a movie go to the icebox, and take out the cold chicken. While they're chewing on it, they discuss the picture. In the morning, the wife meets the neighbor next door. She says to her, 'How was the picture?' And the wife says, 'It was all right. But we discovered a number of flaws in it.' Bang goes your word of mouth."[4]

---

[4]In 1983, Perkins and Miles appeared in *Psycho II*, a sequel directed by Australian Richard Franklin (*Road Games*). The picture opens by showing the celebrated shower scene to jog our memory, then picks up with Norman's release from a mental institution twenty-two years later. Norman returns to the creepy Victorian house and starts seeing visions and hearing the voice of his dead mother. Is he still crazy, or what? A good start. Unfortunately, without the master's touch, the plot soon becomes convoluted. It disintegrates into a gory, grisly mess with an ending that is more mystifying than satisfying. In 1986, Perkins directed and starred in the second sequel, *Psycho III*.

Chinatown
(1974)

Directed by Roman Polanski. Screenplay by Robert Towne.☆ Photography, John A. Alonzo. Music, Jerry Goldsmith. Editor, Sam O'Steen. Art director, W. Stewart Campbell. Produced by Robert Evans. Paramount. Rated R. 131 minutes.

J.J. Gittes	JACK NICHOLSON
Evelyn Cross Mulwray	FAYE DUNAWAY
Noah Cross	JOHN HUSTON
Lt. Lou Escobar	PERRY LOPEZ
Yelburton	JOHN HILLERMAN
Hollis Mulwray	DARRELL ZWERLING
Ida Sessions	DIANE LADD
Claude Mulvihill	ROY JENSON
Man with knife	ROMAN POLANSKI
Loach	DICK BAKALYAN
Walsh	JOE MANTELL
Duffy	BRUCE GLOVER
Sophie	NANDU HINDS
Lawyer	JAMES O'REARE
Evelyn's butler	JAMES HONG
Gardener	JERRY FUJIKAWA
Katherine	BELINDA PALMER
Mulwray's secretary	FRITZI BURR
Boy on horseback	CLAUDIO MARTINEZ
Barber	GEORGE JUSTIN
Customer	DOC ERICKSON

☆ Academy Award winner

"**H**old it there, kitty cat," says Roman Polanski, playing a sadistic little hood. "Hold it."

He and a hefty plug-ugly named Claude (Roy Jenson) advance on Jack Nicholson alone in a deserted street at night.

"Hello, Claude," says the flippant, insouciant Nicholson. "Where'd you get the midget?"

Nicholson is portraying a gutsy private eye in the Bogart tradition. He is the cynical but honest hero. Even when Nicholson is vulnerable, there is no letup in his bravado.

Suddenly, the plug-ugly grabs Nicholson and pins his arms. Polanski, stung by Nicholson's wisecrack, whips out a switchblade and inserts it in his left nostril. "You're a very nosy fellow, kitty cat. You know what happens to nosy fellows? They lose their noses."

Polanski flicks the razor-sharp blade upward. Blood gushes. "Next time, you lose the whole thing. Cut it off and feed it to my goldfish."[1]

This is one of the chilling scenes from *Chinatown*, an engrossing, fast-paced film that is both a parody and a revival of the old Hollywood gumshoe genre. It

---

[1]In his autobiography, *An Open Book*, John Huston points out that Nicholson's bandaged nose was not in the original screenplay. It was easily incorporated, however, because the picture was shot in continuity. It's the way Huston liked to work. "If you haven't locked yourself into a corner by shooting scenes toward the end of a picture early on," Huston said, "you are free to incorporate ideas that present themselves as you go along." Towne, in an interview with filmwriter John Brady, took credit for the idea. ". . . I just sat back and asked, 'What is the most horrible thing I can think of that would really scare you?' And I just came up with that. I thought of slitting his ears and everything else. But he's a nosy guy, and a knife up his nose seemed to work."

The way Polanski created the sequence aroused much curiosity. Logan Frazee, the special-effects man, suggested a false nostril. But Polanski wanted to base the trick on illusion, not artifice, and ordered a knife with a hinged tip. A retaining spring gave under the slightest pressure, making it look as if the blade were passing through the nostril. At the same time, Polanski squeezed a tube connected to a bulbful of blood. The audience, distracted by the blood, never noticed the deception.

Jack Nicholson plays private detective Jake Gittes, who is investigating scandals involving one of Los Angeles's leading families. As Gittes's bandages unravel, so does the mystery.

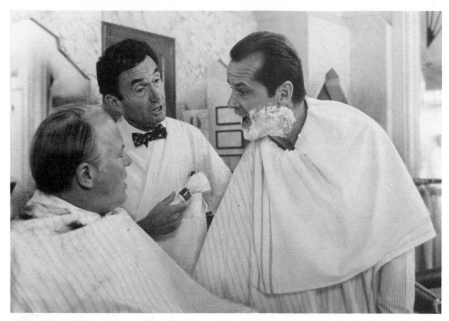

Gittes's trigger temper explodes as he hears criticism about his detective work. Doc Erickson is the customer. George Justin is the barber.

is also a complex picture. Its plot is mercurial and Byzantine. Anyone who leaves his seat, even for an instant, risks missing a new turn in the twisting story.

Like Nicholson's bandaged nose, *Chinatown* is about a cover-up. As Nicholson's bandage unravels and his wound heals, we discover more and more about what is actually happening or what is apparently happening. Nothing is what it seems, which is, as we will learn, the reason for the picture's name.

Chinatown is the district where Jake Gittes, the character Nicholson plays, started his career as a cop. It is a section of Los Angeles where bizarre things happen regularly. Cops who want to survive in this world learn that if in doubt, it is best to back off and do nothing.

Much of the film's success is due to Robert Towne's first-rate screenplay. Originally, he wrote the script like a standard detective movie that he planned to direct himself. Then he saw some photographs of Los Angeles circa 1930 and became fascinated with the old-time looks of the city. At the same time, he did some research into LA's early years and found that some municipal fathers had enriched themselves by acquiring land that was the source of the city's water supply.

So *Chinatown* became a fictionalized account of corruption and greed in the Los Angeles of pre-World War II days. Interwoven with this story are two puzzles—the water-supply mystery and family mystery.

The title itself, Towne said, came from a conversation he had with a former policeman. "He told me, 'The one place I never

The relationship between Gittes and his socialite client Evelyn Mulwray (Faye Dunaway) turns cool when he suspects she is lying to him.

worked was Chinatown. They really run their own culture.' And that struck me as a notion for a kind of detective story where you think you know the ground rules, but you don't."

The film, reminiscent of a Sam Spade movie, opens in the office of private eye J.J. Gittes (Nicholson). Gittes's client, a middle-aged woman, thinks her husband is cheating on her. It seems a routine case, except in this instance, the husband is the city water commissioner, Hollis I. Mulwray (Darrell Zwerling).

Gittes and his two assistants follow Mulwray and find that he is spending much of his time at reservoirs. "The guy's got water on the brain," one of Gittes's henchmen says. One day, Gittes spots Mulwray with a young lady and sneaks some pictures of her kissing him.

When one of the photos appears on the front page of the local newspaper, Mulwray's wife pays Gittes another call—except this wife turns out to be another woman (Faye Dunaway). Cool, haughty, dressed to the teeth in a snapbrim hat, turtleneck shirt, and tailored suit, she tells him she is the real Evelyn Mulwray.

"I see you like publicity, Mr. Gittes," she snaps. "Well, you're going to get it." Her lawyer hands Gittes court papers.

Nicholson and Dunaway evoke memories of Humphrey Bogart and Mary Astor in *The Maltese Falcon* (1941).

Nicholson, who is on camera all during the 131-minute movie, adds character and dimension to the role and, by doing so, enhances the part. He has a feisty style, a spontaneity that lends freshness to the conventional private eye figure. Nicholson shows us a veteran investigator who half falls for his beautiful client although she never seems to be telling the whole truth. Yet, he has the integrity to keep at arm's length and get the job done.

Dunaway, in her eleventh pic-

Roy Jenson holds Nicholson as director Roman Polanski plays a knife-wielding hood who tells Gittes what happens when private detectives get too nosy: "They lose their noses."

ture, is sensual and seductive, and yet neurotic and enigmatic. She is the guilt-ridden woman trying to conceal her shameful past. "Evelyn is the most complex character in the movie," Dunaway said. "The audience—and Nicholson, who represents the audience—doesn't know what she is doing until the end." Dunaway conveyed this tension in her voice, her movement, and her nervous reactions. In one scene, she lights two cigarettes for herself, one right after the other.

Determined to get to the bottom of the hoax he has been drawn into, Gittes goes to see Mulwray. He is too late. The commissioner has drowned, ironically, in the middle of a summer drought. At night, Gittes drives to the scene of the drowning and finds water from the city's nearly dry reservoir pouring out through a storm drain. It is a costly discovery. Before he can get into his car, two thugs waylay him, cut open his nose, and warn him to stop prying.

Gittes won't quit. He sees Mrs. Mulwray again. "Something be-

sides the death of your husband is bothering you," Gittes says. "I think you're hiding something." She tells him that she knew about her husband's affair. However, she says she wasn't upset, implying, Gittes thinks, that she was cheating on him as well.

So the layers of deception thicken. But Gittes makes some headway by learning that Evelyn Mulwray's maiden name is Cross. Noah Cross (John Huston), her father, turns out to have been Mulwray's partner. The two owned the water that the city tapped for its municipal supply. They quarreled when Mulwray insisted they sell it to the city.

"You may think you know what you're dealing with," Cross tells Gittes. "But believe me, you don't."

"That's what the district attorney used to tell me in Chinatown," Gittes says.

Then Cross surprises Gittes by hiring him to find Mulwray's girlfriend.

Now things start to move fast. Gittes goes to look at some of the parched valley farms that are up for sale. But he runs into an angry farmer who looks on Gittes as a snooper and has his men beat him up. At the city's Hall of Records, Gittes learns that speculators are buying up land in the valley under dummy names. Someone is forcing the farmers out by diverting their irrigating water, then buying their tracts at cut-rate prices after their crops fail.

Next, Gittes finds Hollis Mulwray's girlfriend—or the young lady who appeared to be the dead man's girlfriend—in an apartment where she seems to be held by Mrs. Mulwray.

"Who is she?" he asks.

"She's my daughter," Mrs. Mulwray says.

Gittes slaps her.

"She's my sister."

Mrs. Mulwray has revealed her shameful secret. But it is too bizarre for Gittes to understand. He slaps her again.

"My daughter."

Slap

"My sister."

He throws her down. "I said I want the truth."

Gittes is moved to violence because he thinks Mrs. Mulwray is trying to make a fool of him. And that strikes a raw nerve.

Says screenwriter Towne: "The single most important question one must ask oneself about a character is what are they really afraid of. . . . If you ask that question, it's probably, for me, the single best way of getting into a character. And that's how stories are really told—with a character that's real. Gittes was afraid of being made to appear to be a fool. And he would overreact."

Mrs. Mulwray spells it all out. "She's my sister and my daughter. My father and I—understand? Or is it too tough for you?"

"He raped you?"

"Hollis came and took care of me," Evelyn says. "I was fifteen . . . I couldn't see her then. Now I want to see her and take care of her." Cross has been trying to wrest the girl away. Evelyn, in

In the picture's gripping last sequence, Evelyn Mulwray turns her gun on her father.

turn, has been attempting to protect her from her incestuous father. Cross, bent on having the girl at all costs, killed Mulwray when he tried to interpose.

In the picture's climax, all the characters converge in Chinatown. Cross, finally catching up with Evelyn and her daughter, pleads with Evelyn. He asks her to let him raise the girl.

"How many years have I got? She's mine, too."

"She's never going to know that," Evelyn says.

Cross tries to pull the girl away. "You'll have to kill me first," he says. Even though police are on the scene, Evelyn is able to draw a small pistol and shoot Cross in the arm. Then she drives off with the girl.

Two cops open fire as the car gets smaller and smaller in the distance. It looks as if she has gotten away. Suddenly, the car stops and the horn starts blaring. Gittes

runs over. Evelyn has fallen against the wheel, shot to death.

Ironically, in Towne's original screenplay, the movie did not end in Chinatown. Nor did a single scene take place there.[2] As far as Towne was concerned, that wasn't the point. Chinatown did not exist at all, except as a state of mind.

"But one horrible day at the studio about two weeks before the shooting, everyone went crazy," Towne said. "Someone said, 'My God. There's no scene in Chinatown, and it's called *Chinatown*.' Of course, I felt that . . . to have a scene there would be pushing the metaphor.

"The meeting was insane. Somebody even said, 'Well, maybe if Gittes liked Chinese food . . .' Finally, at this meeting, where some normally very bright people lost their heads, it was collectively agreed—but not by me —that the film should end in Chinatown."

---

[2]Nor did Evelyn Mulwray die. Instead, she went to jail and her daughter ran away to Mexico. But Polanski did not like this ending. So he started shooting with the last scene open. During the final days of filming, he rewrote the sequence to have Evelyn die in a kind of operatic finale with everyone around. In his book *Roman*, Polanski justified his version. "I knew that if *Chinatown* was to be special, not just another thriller where the good guys triumph in the final reel, Evelyn had to die. Its dramatic impact would be lost unless audiences left their seats with a sense of outrage at the injustice of it all." In my opinion, Polanski's ending was the right one.

War Is Hell

THE BATTLE OF ALGIERS

THE DEER HUNTER

JUDGMENT AT NUREMBERG

SEVEN BEAUTIES

APOCALYPSE NOW

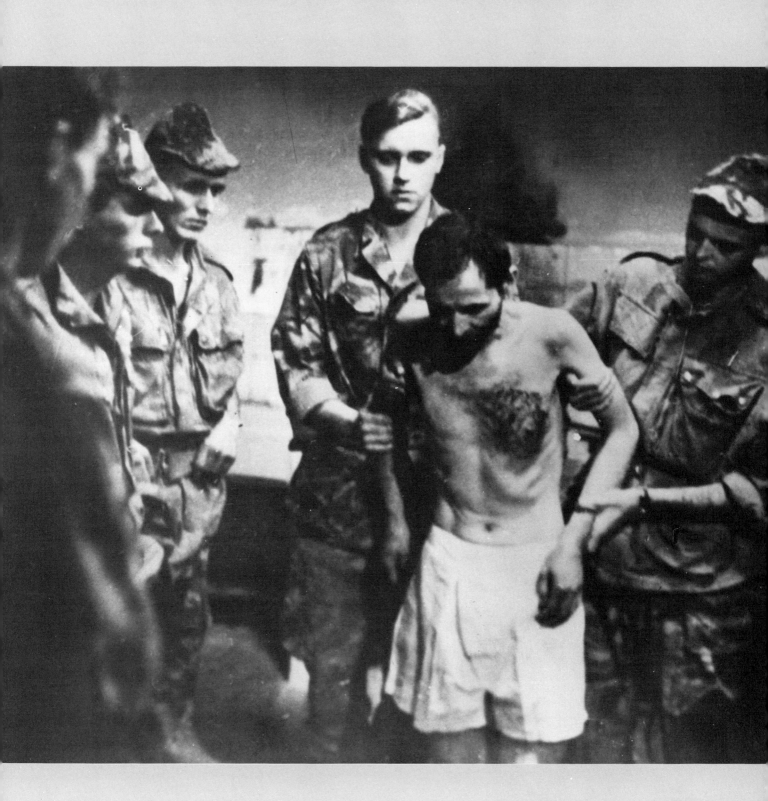

The Battle of Algiers (1966)

Directed by Gillo Pontecorvo. Screenplay by Pontecorvo and Franco Solinas. Photography, Marcello Gatti. Editors, Mario Serandrei and Mario Morra. Music, Pontecorvo and Ennio Morricone. Produced by Antonio Musu, Igor Films of Rome, and Yacef Saadi, the Casbah Film Co. Filmed in Algiers in 1965. Released by Rizzoli Film and Allied Artists. B/W. 123 minutes.

Saari Kader	YACEF SAADI
Ali la Pointe	BRAHIM HAGGIAG
Colonel Mathieu	JEAN MARTIN
Captain Dubois	TOMMASO NERI
Le Petit Omar	MOHAMED BEN KASSEN
Halima	FAWZIA EL-KADER
Fathia	MICHELE KERBASH
Captain	UGO PALETTI

In the Casbah, the native quarter of Algiers, three Arab girls dress up to look like French women.

The audience roots for them as they pass through military checkpoints into the European part of the North African city. There they collect time bombs and plant them in crowded public places. Now the audience recoils.

Although the sympathies of the filmmakers of *The Battle of Algiers* are clearly on the side of the rebels, they make no attempt to mitigate the terrorists' atrocities. They are telling us there are no unblemished victories even in a just cause. And that is the strength of this movie, a picture that realistically depicts Algeria's bitter struggle for freedom from France from 1954 to 1957.

In the bomb scare, we watch the intended victims through the eyes of the Arab women. What they see are not vulgar French colonials but people for whom the women bear no animosity. They are average-looking men, teenagers dancing the cha-cha to jukebox music, a child licking an ice-cream cone.

So when they are blown up, the audience is left without any exhilaration. Instead, there is only the sense of loss over the killing of decent human beings by their fellows.

If *Battle* tries to portray the quest for independence objectively, it is aided immensely by the "documentary" nature of the film. Italian director Gillo Pontecorvo has achieved a miracle of verisimilitude.

Not one foot of the movie is documentary film. Yet most of the picture seems absolutely real. It is as if you are watching a newsreel, as if you are looking not at actors but at the flesh-and-blood participants who lived and died in this tragic confrontation.

Pontecorvo created his authentic effects with hand-held cameras that produced jerky, off-center, slightly out-of-focus pictures. He added to the realism by pushing fast film to the limit to produce flat, grainy negatives and by using as much available light as possible. He took riot scenes with telephoto lenses, giving the audience the feeling that the scene was too explosive for the cameraman to move closer.

The movie has a cast of thousands, yet only one is a professional actor—Jean Martin, who plays the paratroopers' commander, Colonel Mathieu.

"What I want first is the face," Pontecorvo said. "If I can find an actor with the right face, that's fine. But many times that is impossible. And I will find someone—anyone—with the right look."

Pontecorvo discovered the actor who played the crucial role of the rebel leader, Ali la Pointe, in the open market in the Casbah. He was a street boy. "He looked like he was going to steal some-

Using torture tactics, the French force a captured Algerian rebel to betray his comrades.

161

thing," Pontecorvo said. "He looked like a tiger ready to spring. He didn't understand when we told him we wanted him for a film."

As important as the special effects were, it was the story that had to grip the audience to make the movie work. And here, Pontecorvo excelled. The plot was high drama. It was told in flashback but not from one viewpoint.

Colonel Mathieu's paratroopers surround the hideout of Ali la Pointe (Brahim Haggiag), sole surviving leader of the National Liberation Front. Mathieu has given la Pointe and three young followers minutes to surrender or be blown up.

As Mathieu waits, Pontecorvo flashes back to 1954, the year the Front began its war against the occupying French.

We see the sectors of Algiers—first the beautiful European quarter with its wide, tree-lined boulevards and modern buildings, then the Casbah with its squalid alleys and medieval stairways linking one street to another.

The film shows us the beginning of the rebel organization as it tries to clear out the prostitutes and drug dealers and begin its guerrilla attacks on French military personnel. The French strike back with a bomb that kills innocent women and children in the Casbah.

Top: A French youth trips an Algerian as emotions heat up in the North African country's struggle for independence.

Center: Colonel Mathieu (Jean Martin) and his crack paratroopers are called in to quell the rebellion. Martin was the only actor in the film.

Bottom: Shielded by a tank, French troops move in on a rebel position.

The Deer Hunter 🎥
(1978)

Directed by Michael Cimino. 🎥 Screenplay by Deric Washburn. Story by Cimino, Washburn, Louis Garfinkle, and Quinn K. Redeker. Photography, Vilmos Zsigmond. Art directors, Ron Hobbs and Kim Swados. Editor, Peter Zinner. 🎥 Music, Stanley Myers. Sound, Richard Portman, 🎥 William McCaughey, 🎥 Aaron Rochin, 🎥 Darin Knight. 🎥 Main title theme performed by John Williams. Special effects, Fred Cramer. Produced by Barry Spikings, Michael Deeley, John Peverall, and Cimino. An EMI Films Presentation. Universal. Rated R. 183 minutes.

Michael	ROBERT DE NIRO
Stan	JOHN CAZALE
Steven	JOHN SAVAGE
Nick	CHRISTOPHER WALKEN 🎥
Linda	MERYL STREEP
John Welch	GEORGE DZUNDZA
Axel	CHUCK ASPEGREN
Steven's mother	SHIRLEY STOLER
Angela	RUTANYA ALDA
Julien	PIERRE SEGUI
Axel's girl	MADY KAPLAN
Bridesmaid	AMY WRIGHT
Stan's girl	MARY ANN HAENEL
Bandleader	JOE GRIFASI
VC guards	DING SANTOS, KRIENG CHAIYAPUK, OT PALAPOO, CHOK CHAI MAHASOKE

🎥 Academy Award winner

Three captured American GIs held prisoner in Vietnam are forced to play against one another in a bloody game of Russian roulette. Under duress, one of them puts a gun to his head, nervously pulls the trigger, and hears only the click of an empty chamber.

This harrowing scene from *The Deer Hunter* is one of the high points of a flawed but engrossing story about war and the mystique of male friendship. It won three major Oscars, including best picture. At the same time, it triggered strong negative feelings.

Some people were repelled because twenty-eight persons, purportedly influenced by the film, killed themselves playing Russian roulette. Others who rejected the picture said it gave a distorted picture of the Vietcong, portraying them as merciless killers, much as World War II movies did the Japanese.

Many works of art—from Shakespeare's *Richard III* to Robert Altman's *Nashville* (1975)— have bent the facts to try to present a larger truth. But the Vietnam War was so fresh in the mind and the roulette scene was so central to the story that they could not be easily isolated and taken simply as metaphoric devices.

This is not to say it is a bad movie. Director Michael Cimino has filmed a moving, if loosely edited, story tracing the evolution of the relationships of three blue-collar workers and the women, families, and friends they left behind.

The movie's theme was not entirely original. It grew out of *Thunderbolt and Lightfoot* (1974), a modest but promising film Cimino had done four years earlier. It had been his first picture, and for a while it seemed it might be his last. He began a movie for 20th Century-Fox and then started another for Paramount. In both cases, the studios stopped production after a few months because of changes in management.

Robert De Niro as Michael, one of four steelworkers whose life is changed when he and two friends go off to war.

165

Undaunted, Cimino went to work on yet another film idea. In 1976, he met with executives of EMI, a British corporation set up to produce new films by Americans, and outlined the plot of *The Deer Hunter*. They were immediately receptive—if anything, too receptive. Cimino remembers it as an almost surrealistic scene.

"They said, 'Okay. Do it.'"

"I asked, 'When?'"

"They said, 'Forthwith.'"

"I asked, 'What does that mean?'"

"They said, 'Yesterday.'"

Cimino set a shooting start only five months away, an impossible date given the fact that he had neither script, cast, nor locations. He traveled over 100,000 miles—writing as he went—to find the right spots.

"It's important for me to discover the locations myself," Cimino said. "If someone else finds them, things just don't feel right."

To depict the picture's steel-mill towns, he picked places in Pennsylvania and Ohio. But by the time shooting began, it was August, and the cast had to play the winter outdoor scenes wearing woolen shirts and parkas in humid ninety-degree heat. Between takes, technicians blotted dry Meryl Streep's hair and wiped sweat off Robert De Niro's face.

To film the war scenes, Cimino went to Thailand, a move that added months to the making of the movie and millions to the budget. Such extravagance was to exceed all bounds in his next venture, *Heaven's Gate* (1980), a four-hour film withdrawn days after it received a critical blast. Originally budgeted at $12 million, the picture wound up costing $40 million.

The Deer Hunter's Southwest Asian scenery was beautiful. But there was a tradeoff. Cimino could not see daily rushes. The country's political affairs were volatile, and there were frequent reports of an impending military coup. So

Director Michael Cimino checks out an animal skin before shooting a scene of his Oscar-winning movie.

he worked in expectation that the film would be confiscated if authorities learned of its sensitive nature. Knowing this, he shot from many angles because he realized he would not have a second chance.

When Cimino got back to Los Angeles, he began the tedious job of editing. Trimming the vast footage took fourteen hours a day for three months.

Even when that was done, Cimino was not home free. A rough version came to three and a half hours. Universal Pictures, the distributor, wanted it cut drastically. Cimino resisted, and EMI at one point told him he was no longer on the picture. But he persisted, persuading executives to let him show a sneak preview. When audiences responded enthusiastically, he won his point.

"It had been a war," Cimino said. "But we all came together in

the end." The final version runs three hours and three minutes.

Cimino's film focuses on a group of second-generation Russian-Americans, boisterous, rowdy steelworkers from the small town of Clairtown, Pennsylvania. Their tight relationship is evident from the outset as we see them get off work and head for Welch's Bar to wind down, shoot pool, and swig some beers. It is a time of transition. Michael (De Niro), Nick (Christopher Walken), and Steven (John Savage) are going to Vietnam. Another pal—Stan (John Cazale)—is staying home.[1]

Michael is clearly the leader. Like Hawkeye, the frontier hero of James Fenimore Cooper's novels, Michael retains some of the qualities of man in the wilderness. When someone notices a halo around the sun, Michael is the only one to try to explain its significance. "Those are sun dogs," he says. "It means a blessing on the hunter sent by the Great Wolf to his children. It's an old Indian thing. . . ."

That evening, Steven is marrying Angela (Rutanya Alda) at a Russian Orthodox church. The night is to be both a joining together and a farewell.

The hour-long wedding scene, a romp reminiscent of the opening of *The Godfather* (1972), is a sweeping, kaleidoscopic event. Nothing is focused. Everything is in motion, and it is through the constantly panning camera that we begin to know the characters.

People sing, dance, and flirt. Stan spots a man squeezing his girlfriend's backside while they dance. Stan avenges his honor by punching, not the man, but his girl. When Linda (Streep) catches the bridal bouquet, Nick asks her to marry him. But we don't know if he really means it.

Michael and Linda exchange lingering glances. Later, they dance. But nothing comes of it. When the newlyweds drive off, Michael runs after them, shedding his clothes until he is breathless, exhausted, naked.

There are darker omens, too. During the traditional wedding toast, the bride spills two drops on her gown, portending a bloody event ahead for Steven. Nobody notices. Then a Green Beret shows up unannounced, sits alone at the bar. The men ask him what it was like over there. He remains brooding, uncommunicative. Finally, he answers them with an obscenity.

Nick, the best man, talks of the future. He tells Michael that whatever happens to him, he wants to be brought back and buried in his hometown. "I love this f——n place," Nick says.

Some critics have contended there are homosexual overtones to the story. True, there is backslapping, hugging, and shoving. However, it is basically macho camaraderie. At the wedding celebration, Michael and Stan dance together. But they are in their cups. And when they spot two women on the floor together, they each change partners.

The most overt suggestion of homosexuality comes when Stan is miffed at Michael during the deer hunt. "I don't know how many times I must have fixed him up with girls. And nothing happened. Zero," Stan yells for all the others to hear. "There are times when I think you're a f——n faggot. Last week, he could have had that new redheaded waitress. . . . He could have had it knocked. And look what he did. Nothing."

Stan is just trying to get back at Michael because Michael has refused to lend him his hunting boots. Michael is an anomaly, a romantic idealist brought back from the pages of Kipling and H. Rider Haggard. When it comes to hunting, there is a lore, a ritual that must be followed. And Stan, who usually forgets his boots or knife or jacket, has no respect for the tradition.

The next day, Michael and his pals drive to the mountains for a last hunting trip. "One shot is what it's all about," Michael says. "A deer has to be taken with one shot." And he does it. Like the deer whose life is snuffed out with a squeeze of the trigger, Michael will find his own happiness will be transitory and fragile.

In Vietnam, the film moves quickly to the much-discussed Russian roulette scene. Michael, Nick, and Steven are held in a riverside hut, forced to play the suicide game to satisfy the gambling

---

[1]Cazale, after accepting the role, told Cimino he had bone cancer. In fact, he was a terminal patient, but he still felt strong and was confident he could do the job. An EMI executive wanted him replaced. When Cimino refused, the executive insisted that Cimino do an alternate script working Cazale out of the picture, in case he could not finish. Cimino again refused. In the end, EMI backed down. "John never missed one day, one minute," Cimino said. "And he was funny and he was terrific." Cazale died nine months after the picture was finished.

Michael and Linda (Meryl Streep) share a happy moment at a friend's Russian Orthodox wedding.

lust of their captors. Two Americans are seated at a table. A Vietcong officer puts down a pistol with one bullet in its six chambers and spins it. When it stops, he orders the American it points at to put it to his head and pull the trigger. The other Vietcong gleefully bet on whether he will blow out his brains.[2]

One of the many who took exception to the scene was Sylvan Fox, editor of the editorial page of *Newsday*, the Long Island daily. Fox felt the picture lied to the public. More than that, he thought it reinforced a racist view. "No one I know who has been in Vietnam ever heard of such a grisly sport," Fox said. "But regardless of whether it is fiction or not, it has a clear and nefarious effect: it reinforces in the American mind a cliché stereotype about Asians in general and Vietnamese in particular—that in what we often call (with a certain condescension) 'that part of the world,' human life doesn't have the same value as it has in the 'civilized' world. . . ."

The brave and dogged Michael refuses to crack. Despite the agonizing pressure, he steadies his nerve and works out a daring escape plan with Nick. He goads the Vietcong to put three bullets in the pistol, thus cutting the survival odds to 50–50. His bravado impresses his captors, and they laugh while he loads. When they are distracted for a moment, Michael swiftly turns the gun on them. And he and Nick blast their way to freedom.

After freeing Steven, they plunge into the river and float downstream, hanging to a log. A helicopter tries to airlift them, but Steven falls back into the rock-strewn river, shattering his legs. Michael leaps after him, carries him to a road filled with refugees, and prevails on a tank commander to take him to a hospital.

In Saigon, Nick, who has suffered a mental breakdown from the prison-camp ordeal, leaves the psychiatric ward of the military hospital in search of Michael. Instead, he runs into a perverted Frenchman (Pierre Segui) who introduces him to a netherworld that both repels and fascinates Nick. In a noisy, smoke-filled room with people gambling on every pull of the trigger, two men play Russian roulette for high stakes. Nick will become part of this scene.

Back home. Michael returns with military honors. But he cannot face the welcome party. He waits until morning when they are gone, then walks in on Linda. She is alone, staying in an old trailer that Michael and Nick shared. Although Michael moves in with her, their relationship is ambiguous. "Why can't we comfort each other?" she asks. They share a bed, but Michael is unresponsive, concerned that Nick should be there, instead.

Trying to get back to his old routine, Michael goes hunting with Stan and two other friends. Tension stays coiled within him. Michael again spots a deer. This

Behind barbed wires, hands tied, Michael and Steven (John Savage) await their fate from the Vietcong.

Michael and Steven float down a river attempting to escape.

time, he cannot shoot it. He has seen too much killing.

Then, one day, Michael learns that Steven is in a nearby Veterans Administration hospital. He finds him legless and despairing, too defeated to return to his wife and young child.

"I'm going to take you home," Michael says.

"I don't fit," Steven answers. But Michael won't be dissuaded.

The scene shifts to Saigon, a city in chaos as the war winds down. Thousands are evacuating the falling capital. There, Michael, searching for Nick, finally finds him, hooked on drugs, a paid player in a Russian roulette game.

While screaming bettors wager on life or death, Michael tries to persuade Nick to leave. Nick keeps playing. Michael sits down at the table. He takes Nick's turn in the game, puts the gun to his head, and pulls the trigger. He draws a blank chamber.

"One shot," Nick says, echoing Michael's hunting credo as he grabs the gun and fires. It turns out to be the chamber with the bullet.

In Pennsylvania, there is a big turnout for Nick's funeral. Steve is there in a wheelchair, and so are Linda and Michael and all Nick's friends. They carry his casket to the cemetery and strew flowers on his grave in the pale autumn sun. Then they go to Welch's Bar for coffee, beer, and eggs. It is a solemn, nearly silent occasion. None of them is articulate enough to put together a eulogy.

So one of them simply starts humming "God Bless America." Then Linda starts singing. And they all join in. It's their way of saying they harbor no bitterness. They look on the tragedy as an inevitable price to pay for patriotism. Some people will always resent the U.S. presence in Vietnam and look down on anyone who had a hand in the war. But not these ethnic Americans.

"Here's to Nick," Michael says. They all raise their beer mugs.

---

[2]Because of the Russian roulette scenes and their apparent link to real-life deaths, all three television networks turned down the movie. It was sold, instead, to independent TV stations and to Home Box Office.

Judgment at Nuremberg
(1961)

Produced and directed by Stanley Kramer. Screenplay, Abby Mann. * Music, Ernest Gold. Cinematographer, Ernest Laszlo. Editor, Fred Knudtson. A Roxlom Production. United Artists. Rated PG. B/W. 178 minutes.

Judge Dan Haywood	SPENCER TRACY
Ernst Janning	BURT LANCASTER
Col. Tad Lawson	RICHARD WIDMARK
Mme. Bertholt	MARLENE DIETRICH
Hans Rolfe	MAXIMILIAN SCHELL ☆
Irene Hoffman	JUDY GARLAND
Rudolph Petersen	MONTGOMERY CLIFT
Captain Byers	WILLIAM SHATNER
Senator Burkette	EDWARD BINNS
Judge Kenneth Norris	KENNETH MACKENNA
Emil Hahn	WERNER KLEMPERER
General Merrin	ALAN BAXTER
Wetner Lammpe	TORBEN MEYER
Judge Curtiss Ives	RAY TEAL
Friedrich Hofstetter	MARTIN BRANDT
Mrs. Halbestadt	VIRGINIA CHRISTINE
Maj. Abe Radnitz	JOSEPH BERNARD
Halbestadt	BEN WRIGHT
Dr. Wieck	JOHN WENGRAF
Dr. Geuter	KARL SWENSON
Schmidt	PAUL BUSCH

☆ Academy Award winner

Spencer Tracy, playing an American judge at the Nuremberg War Crimes Trials, is in the cell of a German judge whom he has sentenced to life in prison. The German, played by Burt Lancaster, has been convicted of handing down rulings that legalized Nazi genocide policies.

He wants it known that he was personally ignorant of the effect of his ruling. "Those people [who were killed in concentration camps], those millions of people, I never knew it would come to all that," says Lancaster. "You must believe it."

Tracy knows what Lancaster wants him to say. But he cannot give him even the smallest shred of absolution. "It came to that," Tracy says, "the first time you sentenced to death a man you knew to be innocent."

And so ends *Judgment at Nuremberg,* a provocative film whose thoughtful presentation of the grim issues raised by World War II made it more than just another courtroom drama. When a nation kills six million Jews and other innocent civilians, the movie asks, where does the guilt stop?

On trial in the picture are second-rank Nazis—judges who, in the name of the Fatherland, permitted the mass killings as well as illegal acts like the sterilization of enemies of the state.

The film's ultimate answer to the question of who shares the guilt is not clear. But it is not fair to criticize a movie for failing to find an answer that has eluded philosophers and politicians.

What could have been improved, some critics said, was the picture's cast. For all his skill, Spencer Tracy is still playing himself. Marlene Dietrich and Richard Widmark are more recognizable as actors with whom we have become familiar than as the characters they are portraying.

Stanley Kramer, the picture's producer and director, disagreed. "The deal I made with United Artists was if I casted with commercial stars we would then have the chance to make the film as we wanted to make it," Kramer said in an interview for this book. "Life is full of compromises. Anybody who says he never compromises is

Montgomery Clift won critical acclaim for his moving performance as a German sterilized by the Nazis. He played the part for no salary.

not telling the truth. But you mustn't compromise in principle. I don't think principle was compromised in the film, even though I would have preferred that some of the casting be done with unknown actors.

"But," Kramer added, "saying that about Tracy, most particularly, is ridiculous. If I had my choice again, I would still cast him. Nobody could read those lines that way. And nobody could play that judge that way."

The criticism about the film's actors being more identifiable as their real selves is certainly not universally true. In my view, Montgomery Clift, as a victim of Nazi sterilization policies, Judy Garland, as a German imprisoned in an interracial sex relations case, and Lancaster,[1] as one of the judges on trial, avoid the trappings of their own fame. And Maximilian Schell, playing the defense lawyer, shows a wide range of emotions.

Perhaps director Kramer's greatest accomplishment was the way he sustained the picture's excitement and suspense over the film's nearly three-hour running time. *Judgment* differs from other trial movies in that there was no jury. The prosecutor and defense lawyer delivered their questions and speeches from a lectern instead of pacing before jurors.

So, since the actors were pinned down, Kramer made the camera mobile. He sectioned off the courtroom and put it on rollers so that the cameras could work in 360 degrees. At several points in the trial, the camera swept entirely around Schell and Widmark as they made their arguments. The visual fluidity helped keep the audience's attention during their long monologues.

Kramer made the movie after seeing Abby Mann's 1959 television drama of the same name on "Playhouse 90." Months later, Kramer bought the movie rights and revised the script for film production.

Stanley Kramer directs Marlene Dietrich and Spencer Tracy as they walk through the streets of Nuremberg.

Kramer wanted to make the picture in Germany, but the Nuremberg courtroom became unavailable at the last minute. So, reversing the usual Hollywood convention of doing location scenes first, Kramer built a replica of the courtroom and started shooting in a Hollywood studio. Only after the bulk of the film was made did Kramer take the cast overseas for the final German background parts.

More than 300 newsmen from twenty-six countries came to the premiere in Berlin, focusing global attention on the event. Questions came thick and fast at Kramer's press conference.

Didn't he think the Germans themselves could have done better with the subject? Yes, Kramer said, and he would have been delighted if they had made such a picture. As the years pass, he said, he thought they would become increasingly interested in the subject.

Had he encountered any resistance? Yes—not only in Germany but in the United States. It came from persons who thought the war was best forgotten.

Why had he made the picture? Because it was important that there should be more knowledge of what had happened and how it happened. It was a story not only of the past but of the future.

Did he understand that the German judges were only carrying out the laws of the land? With some irritation, Kramer responded that the laws of humanity transcend all others. Some newsmen applauded.

A few accused Kramer, a Jew, of reopening old wounds because of his religion. "Some felt it was a personalized kind of thing," Kramer said. "I tried to keep it objective. But it doesn't matter whether it was personalized. The question is: How true was it? I think it had truth."

He added: "Trying to estimate

Laurence Olivier was to have played the German judge. But Olivier got married just before the production started and decided not to come to the United States to appear in the picture.

somewhere beyond emotion what the historical significance of an event is when we are so close to it is difficult. What is fifteen years? A breath. What is more important to me is that the youth of Germany will now be able to see these things as translated from outside the country."

In fact, the movie failed to draw large audiences in Germany until two decades later. It was reissued there after *The Holocaust*, a television series, played on German public television, and only then did it make major impact.

Judgment takes place in the aftermath of World War II. It is 1948. We are in Nuremberg, the city where Hitler held his early party rallies. The highly publicized trials of the major Nazi war criminals are over. Now the court is cleaning up with the trials of lesser-known functionaries—four judges. One of them, Ernst Janning (Lancaster), an internationally known jurist and one of the framers of the Weimar Republic that preceded Hitler's regime, refuses to enter a plea.

A Maine judge, Dan Haywood (Tracy), defeated for reelection, is presiding. The prosecutor, Colonel Lawson (Widmark), wants to indict the whole Nazi system of justice and obtain the maximum punishment. "The defendants did not personally administer the concentration camps. They never had to beat victims or pull the levers that introduced gas into the chambers.... [But] these defendants fashioned and executed laws and rendered judgments that sent millions of victims to their destinations."

The defense lawyer, Hans Rolfe (Schell), contends that if the judges stand trial, then all of Germany must be tried. "A judge does not make the law. He carries out the laws of his country.... Should he refuse, he becomes a traitor."

Nevertheless, the prosecution's first witness, Dr. Wieck (John Wengraf), Janning's former law professor, says the Nazis changed the laws to fit their needs. "Some judges resigned," Wieck says. "Others were forced to resign. Others adapted [to the new order]."

The consequences of Nazi rule were not clear at first, he says. But later, they were. Yet, under cross-examination, Rolfe gets Wieck to admit that even he, apparently to protect his pension, swore an oath of allegiance to Hitler.

While the trial drags on, Haywood meets the woman in whose former house he is staying—Mrs. Bertholt (Dietrich), widow of a general executed during the war crimes trials.

As the weeks pass, Haywood, a widower, finds he is becoming attracted to Mrs. Bertholt. But her bitter memories strain their relationship. "My husband and I hated Hitler," she says. "What did my husband know of the crimes they convicted him for?... He was part of the revenge the victors always take on the vanquished. It was political murder."

The rejection of guilt echoes in every conversation Haywood has. Even his housekeepers deny any knowledge of concentration camp atrocities. "We were not

Burt Lancaster in an out-of-character part—portraying German judge Ernst Janning, who legalized Nazi genocide policies.

political. . . . We never attended meetings. . . . We knew nothing about it. . . . And if we did know, what could we do?"

Haywood can only shrug. "As far as I can make out, no one in this country knew [of the concentration camp killings]."

When the trial resumes, Colonel Lawson calls Rudolph Petersen (Clift) to show how the Nazis terrorized their opponents. Petersen testifies that he was sentenced to sterilization only because he was in a fight with a Nazi official and because he showed no interest in Hitler.

But in an intense cross-examination, Rolfe shows that Petersen was in a class of backward children at school and that his mother was feeble-minded. He cannot construct a simple sentence from the words "hare," "hunter," and "field," a test the Nazis routinely gave to mental defectives. Sterilization of the mentally disabled, Rolfe says, was supported in other countries and even by Oliver Wendell Holmes, the famous American jurist.

Clift played the part only for expenses, because the role intrigued him. Kramer had offered him $100,000 to do the part, which is only a single scene that could be filmed in one day. "I thought it was more practical to do it for nothing," Clift told the *New York Times*, "rather than reduce my price or refuse a role I wanted to play."

Clift was ill and nervous on the set, forgetting lines and fluffing take after take. "Finally, I got him together with Tracy and we agreed that he would ignore the lines," Kramer said. "I told him, 'Never mind the lines. You know what was done to him. Look into Tracy's eyes and explain how he feels.' So Clift ad-libbed a lot. And all that hesitation and that kind of jerky, out-of-synch motion was Clift playing the man who had been sterilized."

For his performance, Clift was

Dietrich as Mrs. Bertholt, the widow of an executed German general, removes belongings from her home. Helping is Tracy, portraying Judge Dan Haywood at the Nuremberg war crimes trials. Looking on is Virginia Christine, playing a housekeeper.

nominated for an Academy Award for best supporting actor.[2]

As the proceedings resume, Irene Hoffman (Garland)[3] testifies about her trial on charges of "racial pollution"—that is, having sexual relations with a non-Aryan. The Nazis sentenced to death a Jewish merchant accused of being intimate with her when she was seventeen. Hoffman says the charges were trumped-up.

But on cross-examination, Rolfe gets her to admit that her Nazi landlady saw her kissing the old

man and sitting on his lap. "It was nothing like you are trying to make it sound," she says hysterically.

"What else do you admit to?" he asks over and over.

"Enough," Janning shouts, interrupting the trial. "Are we going to do this again?"

Despite Rolfe's efforts to keep him quiet, Janning takes the stand and insists the Germans knew of the atrocities. "Where were we when our neighbors were dragged out in the middle of the night to

---

[2]Also nominated from *Judgment* were Garland, Tracy, Schell, Kramer, Ernest Laszlo (for photography), Abby Mann (for best screenplay), and the picture itself. Only Schell and Mann won Oscars.

[3]Kramer cast Garland even though she was overweight, taking drugs, and troubled by psychiatric problems. But Kramer gambled because he was aware of her dramatic talent. "Most people never realized how brilliant an actress she was because she was such a marvelous singer," he said. "But I had known her since the days when I was a film editor at MGM and she was just starting as Judy Gumm. When I cast this part, I went to her first. She was doubtful. But then she decided, 'Why not?' . . . She did a very substantial job."

[4]"The perfect tribute was given Lincoln's Gettysburg Address by utter silence," Kramer said. "We had utter silence. But I knew it was no perfect tribute."

Dachau? If we didn't know the details, it was because we didn't want to know. . . . If there is going to be any salvation for Germany, we who know our guilt must admit it."

Kramer, who was seventy-one when interviewed for this book in 1984, thinks the H-bomb issue is an American parallel to the concentration camp issue. "Today, we ask ourselves about the bomb. What do you do? Today, in what I prefer to call my minor dotage, I decided to be an activist. So I'm doing everything I can—joining [anti-H-bomb organizations of] physicians, women, and church groups."

As the trial draws to a close, the political winds begin shifting. Russia blockades Berlin and General Merrin (Alan Baxter), who organizes the airlift, suggests to Colonel Lawson that he go easy on the Nazi judges. The United States now needs Germany as an ally. "You don't get the help of the German people by sentencing their leaders to stiff prison sentences," Merrin says. "The thing to do is survive. . . ."

Lawson won't recommend leniency. Instead, he makes no recommendation and asks the court to fix judgment.

Haywood, shouldering the burden himself, finds the four judges responsible for their actions. "The principle of criminal law in every civilized society has this in common: Any person who is an accessory to a crime is guilty." The four German judges, Haywood rules, consciously took part in a "nationwide, government-organized system of cruelty and injustice." Haywood finds them guilty and sentences them to life in prison.

A few days later, as Haywood is leaving for America, Rolfe comes to his home to ask Haywood to visit Janning in prison. Rolfe adds that he is willing to bet that the life sentences don't last five years. Rolfe's analysis may be logical, Haywood says, but being logical doesn't make it right.

There is the moving scene in Janning's cell. Then, as Haywood walks out of the prison block, we hear in the background the voices of German soldiers singing a rousing Nazi marching song. On the screen, two sentences tell us that Rolfe's prediction was not far from wrong.

"On July 14, 1949, judgment was rendered in the last of the Nuremberg Trials. Of 99 sentenced to prison terms, not one [in the year 1961] is still serving his sentence."

In its Berlin premiere, an uneasy air permeated the audience. Throughout the movie, there was no audible reaction—no applause, no sobs, no laughter—just silence.[4] A polite smattering of applause broke the stillness when the light came on.

Maximilian Schell won an Oscar for Best Actor as the German judge's defense lawyer. Richard Widmark, the prosecutor, listens to a translation.

Seven Beauties
(1975)

Directed by Lina Wertmuller. Screenplay by Wertmuller. Photography director, Tonino delli Colli. Editor, Franco Fraticelli. Art director, Enrico Job. Original music, Enzo Iannacci. Produced by Wertmuller, Giancarlo Giannini, and Arrigo Colombo. Cinema 5 Release. Italian. Rated R. 116 minutes.

Pasqualino Frafuso	GIANCARLO GIANNINI
Pedro	FERNANDO REY
Commandant	SHIRLEY STOLER
Concettina	ELENA FIORE
Don Raffaele	ENZO VITALE
Totonno	MARIO CONTI
Francesco	PIERO DIORIO
Mother	ERMELINDA DE FELICE
Carolina	FRANCESCA MARCIANO
Lawyer	LUCIO AMELIO
Socialist	ROBERTO HERLITZKA

"I don't want to die," says a gaunt concentration camp inmate, watching his fellow prisoners being led to their death. "...I want to live, though it's been a disgusting life so far. I've been miserable with it, but I don't want it to come to an end. I'm not going to let them end it."

This is the desperate credo of Pasqualino Frafuso (Giancarlo Giannini), the hero of Lina Wertmuller's black comedy *Seven Beauties*. Unlike conventional heroes, Pasqualino is not an idealist nor a man of principles. In fact, he has no principles. His one unique quality is being a survivor.

Pasqualino will do whatever is necessary to stay alive: execute friends, collaborate with the enemy, make love to an obese camp commander, kill an unarmed man. Yet we feel no revulsion for this amoral man because Wertmuller makes no ethical judgment about his actions. And that is the strength of her highly original movie.

"It isn't the bad guys who make society what it is," she explains. "It is us. We have to keep clear that society is *us*, the result of our own choices. So it is necessary to live with your protagonist, to follow him to the end, to love him to the end. You have to live his life. Even if you were doing Hitler, in theory at least, you'd have to follow his life, understand him."

Restless and mercurial, Wertmuller writes all her scripts and frequently sleeps no more than three hours a day while working on a movie. Then she puts her all into the filming the next day. She acts all the parts herself, feeding lines to the players. (In Italian movies, the dialogue is dubbed in later.) She squats behind the camera lens, dangles from a roof to help find a better shooting angle, barks at the crew. Some have called her a slave driver.

"Ten hours of work with her," says Tonino Delli Colli, her cameraman, "is the equivalent of twenty hours with another director." Once, in *Seven Beauties*, she decided she wanted a scene shot in a driving rain. Delli Colli balked. In an instant, Wertmuller was out with the camera filming away.

Wertmuller has been accused of throwing temper tantrums. She denies this. She says she works on a tight schedule and some actors have to be aroused to heighten their performance. So she yells and cajoles.

Some would not have it any other way. "I like working with Lina," says Raffaele, her prop man. "She's the kind of person who, while she is beating you to death, manages to convince you that it's really you who are killing her."

The daughter of a successful lawyer, Wertmuller began her studies to prepare for a teaching

Slowly, carefully, Pasqualino (Giancarlo Giannini) steals out on the street with a bag holding the remains of his sister's pimp-boyfriend.

career in deference to her father's wishes. At the same time, she secretly attended Rome's Academy of Dramatic Arts with her friend Flora Carabella (who later married Marcello Mastroianni). Wertmuller went on to serve apprenticeships in the theater, where she both wrote and directed.

After she became Fellini's assistant director on 8½ (1963), she managed to borrow his crew and a few friends to make her first film, *The Lizards* (1963). The movie, a story of stultifying life in a small town, won fourteen international prizes.

Within a few short years, the gifted young director—whose flamboyant clothes and white-rimmed glasses would be her trademark—became her country's top money-making director. Her black comedies, mixing tragedy and humor, both depressed and tickled audiences. *The Seduction of Mimi* (1972), about a Sicilian who follows his macho code but forfeits his happiness, was a hit. And so was its successor, *Love and Anarchy* (1973), about an assassin's relationship with the prostitutes who give him a home.

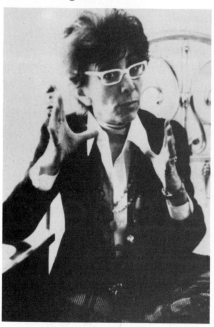

Lina Wertmuller, Italy's brilliant, hardworking filmmaker.

One year later, she scored with *All Screwed Up* (1974), about young people victimized by the system, and again with *Swept Away* (1974), the story of an upper-class woman and a lower-class seaman stranded on a deserted island. All these films were playing in the United States at the same time. Then came *Seven Beauties* (1975).

As the movie opens, we find ourselves in a murky forest with two Italian soldiers who have deserted from the front during World War II. As they flee, they wander across a grisly scene. A German firing squad is executing Jews in mass graves. Watching from a distance, one of the soldiers, Francesco (Piero DiOrio), feels guilty for having condoned fascism.

The second, Pasqualino, shrugs. To have fought, he says, would have been suicide. He is here, Pasqualino says, because he killed a man, and the camera flashes back to a seedy Naples vaudeville house where Pasqualino's fat sister is onstage, making a fool of herself as a dancer. Pasqualino is the self-appointed family protector. His nickname is Seven Beauties, after his seven less than appealing sisters.

Pasqualino is a self-centered, arrogant, swaggering dandy. He envisions himself a Don Juan. In reality he is a loser, a petty manager of a mattress-stuffing factory. His sister knows this and defies him by continuing to dance. She even adds the supreme insult by starting to work in a whorehouse.

Pasqualino draws the line here because she is trifling with his own honor. A two-bit Mafioso has told Pasqualino that the Mafia cannot support people who are not respected. So Pasqualino sneaks into the bedroom of his sister's pimp-boyfriend, Totonno (Mario Conti), and shoots him while he is asleep.

Wertmuller likes to use nonprofessional actors, and Mario Conti was one of them, although his

casting was due to a stroke of luck. Maureen Orth of *Newsweek* made the discovery. She was working in the production to do a first-person story, and Wertmuller sent her into the back streets of Naples to find some interesting faces.

"*Scusi,*" she said to an obese man seated next to his doorway. His face was perfect for the pimp. "*Le interessa fare un film?*"

"*Sì,*" he replied. Totonno's casting was that simple.

Pasqualino cuts up Totonno's body, stuffs the parts in a suitcase, and ships them around Italy. Despite his elaborate deception, he is quickly caught. His lawyer tells him there is a clearcut choice: execution or the insane asylum, death or dishonor. For Pasqualino, it is no choice at all.

While in the asylum, he is told that Mussolini is taking criminals in the army. And so begins his military career.

The camera now switches back to the war, and we see Francesco and Pasqualino captured by the Nazis and tossed into a concentration camp. Pasqualino is appalled by the conditions. However, a fellow prisoner, a Spanish anarchist named Pedro (Fernando Rey), sees there is little better on the outside. The world will soon be overpopulated, he says. People will be so desperate they will be at each other's throats for an apple.

These dark forebodings notwithstanding, the life force still runs deep in Pasqualino's veins. Remembering his popularity with the fairer sex, he decides to try to charm the camp commander (Shirley Stoler), a female Goliath with blond braids and a beefy, impassive face.

Stoler was hired after Wertmuller saw her in *The Honeymoon Killers* (1970), in which she portrayed a 200-pound murderess. For her twenty-four days in Italy to do *Seven Beauties*, she got $2,500 plus air fare. She played the commandant as one devoid of emotion, a sardonic, cold-blooded

Pasqualino's sister (Elena Fiore) pursues a dancer's life. He can tolerate that but draws the line when she becomes a whore.

woman who casually condemns prisoners to death. "Lina told me she wanted me to play the character like a Buddha," Stoler said. "But she also wanted me to be very evil. I thought about it and just somehow or other became that character inside."

Pasqualino makes love to the corpulent commandant, and she spares him. Still, she is repelled by his will to live at all costs, and orders him to pick six fellow prisoners to die. Pasqualino is a reluctant executioner. But life is a stronger urge. And, in the end, he shoots his comrades in arms.

The finale comes with his return to Naples after the war. Pasqualino marries the girl who has waited for him, though she has become a prostitute. They must bear many children, he tells her, haunted by Pedro's terrible prophecy, to help defend them from an anarchistic world and those who would kill for an apple.

Pasqualino has learned nothing from life. He is no wiser, no more compassionate; In a sense he is not far removed from the Nazis he despises.

Pasqualino's seven sisters come to court to watch his trial.

Shirley Stoler, playing the cruel, cold-blooded concentration camp commander, holds a whip while Pasqualino grovels.

Apocalypse Now
(1979)

Directed and produced by Francis Ford Coppola. Screenplay by John Milius and Coppola. Narration, Michael Herr. Photography, Vittorio Storaro.🎬 Music, Carmine Coppola and Francis Coppola. Coproducers, Fred Roos, Gray Frederickson, Tom Sternberg. Production designer, Dean Tavoularis. Supervising editor, Richard Marks. Sound montage and design, Walter Murch.🎬 Art director, Angelo Graham. A United Artists Release. Rated R. 146 minutes.

Col. Walter E. Kurtz	MARLON BRANDO
Lt. Col. Bill Kilgore	ROBERT DUVALL
Capt. Benjamin Willard, narrator	MARTIN SHEEN
Chef	FREDERIC FORREST
Chief	ALBERT HALL
Lance B. Johnson	SAM BOTTOMS
Clean	LARRY FISHBURNE
Photojournalist	DENNIS HOPPER
General	G. D. SPRADLIN
Colonel	HARRISON FORD
Civilian	JERRY ZIESMER
Colby	SCOTT GLENN
Sergeant MP No. 1	BO BYERS
Kilgore's gunner	JAMES KEANE
Mike from San Diego	KERRY ROSSALL
Injured soldier	RON McQUEEN
Supply sergeant	TOM MASON
Playmate	CYNDI WOOD
Terry, Playmate of the year	COLLEEN CAMP
Playmate	LINDA CARPENTER
Agent	BILL GRAHAM
Mrs. Kurtz	ELIZABETH OROPESA
Film director	FRANCIS FORD COPPOLA
Soldier in trench	JACK THIBEAU

🎬 Academy Award winner

An American patrol boat chugging upriver in Vietnam stops a sampan with a native family aboard. Guns at the ready, the GIs pull alongside to search the vessel.

The soldiers are weary from their long voyage and jittery from riverside skirmishes. Suddenly, a woman rushes toward a can. Without warning, the soldiers open fire, slaughtering everyone in the boat.

It turns out there are no weapons aboard. In the can is a puppy.

This is one of the insanities of war that Francis Ford Coppola shows us in *Apocalypse Now*, a powerful but flawed $32 million work that was four years in the making.

Coppola was so intent on filming this extravaganza that he invested much of his own personal fortune. However, so numerous were his production problems that it turned out to be an achievement just to complete his cinematic epic.

For one thing, Coppola had to shoot it in the Philippines because the U.S. Defense Department wouldn't cooperate. Then, no fewer than five actors turned down the leading role: Robert Redford, James Caan, Jack Nicholson, Steve McQueen, and Al Pacino. Nicholson and McQueen said they had other commitments. (McQueen later was offered the role of Colonel Kurtz, but negotiations ended abruptly after he asked for $3 million.) The others did not want to spend months in the steaming jungle.

In his remote jungle outpost, Colonel Kurtz (Marlon Brando) discusses his philosophy of war with Captain Willard (Martin Sheen).

181

Entertaining troops at a remote camp in the Mekong Delta are (*from left*) Cyndi Wood, Coleen Camp, and Linda Carpenter.

Coppola then hired Harvey Keitel, a relative unknown, but fired him after three weeks. Finally, he got Martin Sheen, a seasoned actor whose reputation came from Broadway plays and TV specials like *The Execution of Private Slovik* and *Blind Ambition*.

Sheen's signing did not end Coppola's troubles. After two months of location filming, a typhoon ripped across the island, destroying major sets. Many in the cast and crew had to go back to the United States for two months while technicians rebuilt the properties.

Even when production started anew, working in primitive areas took its toll. Some could not tolerate the Asian food. Once the Italian crew ordered $700 worth of groceries from Rome. Shipping charges came to $8,000.

There were frequent power failures, equipment breakdowns, interruptions in telephone calls to the States—not to mention the oppressive tropical heat and humidity that drained the strength of the actors and crew alike.

The worst calamity occurred when Sheen suffered a heart attack. He was hospitalized in Manila for six weeks. After the picture was finally finished, Sheen questioned the wisdom of taking the part in the first place. Sheen said he "wouldn't change the experience . . . [or] do away with that pain and all the problems in shooting." But, speaking from hindsight, he said, "I would not [accept the role]."

Editing became a monumental task. Coppola shot a record 1.5 million feet of film. About twenty-three hours of film had to be cut to hold it to manageable length. "A lot of clarification was left on the floor," Sheen said, "a lot of scenes between Marlon [Brando] and me that made both our characters a lot clearer."

In the end, the 146-minute picture took twice its projected location time to shoot. It ran to double its budget and had to have its premiere rescheduled four times. At one point, Coppola became so frustrated he gathered up his five Oscars at home and hurled them out the window.

For all the dedication and labor, the picture is uneven and sluggish and murky. It is also too long. But it is a film of unusual visual beauty, cinematic innovation, and explosive action. Coppola plunges the audience visually and viscerally into the center of Vietnam's green hell, making it feel the hallucinogenic nightmare of war.

Apocalypse Now is adapted from Joseph Conrad's nineteenth-century novella "Heart of Darkness" (for which Coppola made no reference in the credits). It tells the story of sailor Charlie Marlow's journey into central Africa to find the ivory agent of a European trading company. Kurtz, the sought-after agent, has become a corrupt jungle lord of a native tribe, reigning like a lawless butcher. In the end, Marlow learns that he, too, shares some of Kurtz's bloody primitive instincts. But, knowing this, Marlow can control them.

In Coppola's version, the army sends a captain (Sheen) on a river pilgrimage to Cambodia to seek out and kill a former Green Beret officer named Kurtz (Brando) who has apparently lost his sanity. Kurtz has become the godlike leader of a band of headhunters and has started waging war by his own rules, presumably against the Vietcong.

The plot of the movie, like the story, is sparse. Captain Willard, a trained army assassin who has been close enough to men he has killed to feel "their last breath," is moodily drinking in a hotel room in Vietnam while awaiting another mission. "Saigon," he says. "Shit . . . I'm still only in Saigon." So many expletives follow that some critics thought the dialogue sounded like a parody of a private detective movie.

The next day, Army brass assign him to "terminate" Colonel Kurtz's renegade command. "I was going to the worst place in the world," says Willard, ". . . hundreds of miles up a river that snaked through the war like a main circuit cable and plugged straight into Kurtz. I really didn't know what I'd do when I faced him."

As the journey progresses, we hear his rambling comments all through the voyage, a voice that comes through in flat, disembodied tones. To me, this is a major failing of the movie.

We need Willard to react so that we, the audience, who identify with him, can react. But he is cold, almost robotlike in his responses to the carnage we will see. In fact, Willard's voice is so passive and remote that the frightening psychedelic odyssey seems to pass benignly by like so many clouds in the sky.

On the patrol boat is a motley crew of draftees—Chef (Frederic Forrest), a gourmet cook from New Orleans; Chief (Albert Hall), a tough boat pilot; Lance (Sam Bottoms, the deaf mute in *The Last Picture Show*, 1971, and the brother of Timothy Bottoms), a surfer who practices his specialty in the midst of war; and Mr. Clean (Larry Fishburne), a seventeen-year-old jive-talking ghetto kid.

Before they find Kurtz, they encounter:
● A gung-ho air cavalry colonel (Robert Duvall) who "Loves the smell of napalm in the morning." He wears a horse soldier's hat, sunglasses, and a yellow dickey. A surfing fanatic, he attacks a Vietcong-controlled waterfront village, sacrificing some of his own troops and massacring civilians and guerrillas alike, in part to get in some surfing at a village beach that has six-foot waves. His helicopters play Wagner's "Ride of the Valkyries" on loudspeakers "to scare the hell" out of the enemy.
● Playboy bunnies (Cyndi Wood, Linda Carpenter, and Colleen Camp) flown in to entertain troops at a riverside depot. Their bumps and grinds are so tantalizing that the sex-starved GIs rush on stage.
● American patrol boats playing "chicken"—trying to get one another to swerve out of the way. One boat firebombs them.

Brando, with shaven head, playing the seemingly mad Colonel Kurtz.

Captain Willard, in camouflage paint, cuts an eerie figure in the steaming Vietnam jungle.

● A sampan with Vietnamese civilians. A routine search triggers a slaughter of innocents. Willard kills the last one alive, a wounded woman, rather than divert his boat to get medical help. "I told you not to stop," he says. "Now let's go." Without being aware of it, this wanton act of killing has changed Willard, making him, in essence, much like the man he has been sent to kill.

Finally, Willard reaches Kurtz's outpost. Operating from a decaying Angkor Wat–style temple hacked out of the jungle, Kurtz is leader of a ferocious band of Montagnard tribesmen. The decapitated heads of their enemies decorate their primitive camp.

The film has been leading to the confrontation between Willard and Kurtz. But when it finally comes, it is a letdown. No bond is established between the protagonists. Nor is any connection made to what we have previously experienced.

Brando, eighty pounds overweight, is shown only in halflight. Instead of an exchange of views that would clarify Brando's aberrant activities and illuminate his character, Brando's scenes with Willard consist mainly of monologues.

In his major speech, Brando/Kurtz pays homage to the dedication of Vietcong guerrillas who sever the arms of native children inoculated against polio by Kurtz's special forces. "Then I realized they were stronger than we.... They have the strength to do that. If I had ten divisions of those men, then our troubles here would be over very quickly. You have to have men who are moral and, at the same time, who are able to utilize their primordial instinct to kill without feeling, without compassion, without judgment. Because it's judgment that defeats us."

Kurtz lacks that detachment.

After a successful helicopter mission, Lieutenant Colonel Kilgore (Robert Duvall) plays guitar for Chief (Albert Hall) and Captain Willard.

He tells Willard that he is worried about his son "that he might not understand" and therefore judge his father's raids to be atrocities.

He also knows that Willard has been ordered to kill him. But by now, Kurtz is so lonely and depressed he views Willard's mission as an act of mercy. He allows the captain to creep into his presence at night and end his nightmare with a machete. Like Conrad's Kurtz, Coppola's Kurtz dies muttering the words, "The horror. The horror."

In her book about the making of the movie, called *Notes*, Coppola's wife disclosed that Coppola was undecided about the film's last sequence. At first, he had Kurtz's temple sanctuary firebombed by ground and air. But Coppola scrapped this volcanic spectacle— perhaps because he thought it detracted from Kurtz's death—and used it instead as a background to the credits.

A second ending shows Willard walking in the midst of Kurtz's native troops, apparently replacing Kurtz as leader. But this would have been a puzzling finale because it implies that Willard believed in Kurtz's cause, a cause that is never made clear.

The ending that Coppola eventually used has Willard leaving the jungle war behind, going back in the patrol boat to Saigon and civilization.[1]

Apocalypse Now is a picture that remains intellectually muddled and unfulfilling. But its camerawork is masterful, its evocation of war striking, and its action scenes superb.

---

[1]In the Conrad story, Marlow, Willard's counterpart, returns to civilization and sees Kurtz's sweetheart. Feeling the truth about Kurtz's death is too bleak to impart to her, he lies and tells her, "The last word he pronounced was—your name."

Death
and the
Supernatural

CARNIVAL OF SOULS

DON'T LOOK NOW

NIGHT OF THE LIVING DEAD

ROSEMARY'S BABY

Carnival of Souls
(1962)

Produced and directed by Harold "Herk" Harvey. Screenplay by John Clifford from an original story by Clifford and Harvey. Music, Gene Moore. Assistant director, Raza Badiyi. Cinematographer, Maurice Prather. Editors, Dan Palmquist and Bill DeJarnette. Sound, Ed Brown and Don Jessup. A Herts-Lion International release. B/W. 80 minutes.

Mary Henry	CANDACE HILLIGOSS
John Linden	SIDNEY BERGER
Landlady	FRANCES FEIST
"The Man"	HERK HARVEY
Doctor	STANLEY LEAVITT
Minister	ART ELLISON
Boss	TOM MCGINNIS

It was on a long drive back from a location job on the West Coast that Herk Harvey first saw the huge, crumbling amusement park pavilion that would become the key set of his only commercial film.

Harvey, a director for an educational film company, was approaching Salt Lake City when he spotted the strange silhouette in the distance. Twilight flickered off Moorish turrets. "It was weird to see with the white lake and the sunset behind it," he said. "I thought, 'What a terrific location.'"

The pavilion was a mile from the road. Harvey stopped his car and hiked over to take pictures. "The pavilion was deserted," he recalled. "Part of it had burned. It completely fascinated me."

And so began the idea for *Carnival of Souls*, a haunting low-budget movie that, after years of obscurity, is beginning to earn a niche among the best independently produced fantasy films. Spartanly made and unevenly acted, the picture nonetheless has a compelling quality that makes seeing it a memorable experience.

The heroine is a pretty Middle American girl. But there are no love scenes. No humor. One never knows where the plot is going or what is really happening until the final chilling scene. Then the whole story suddenly jumps into place, turning everything that came before into a nightmare.

Some may wonder why I include this little-known film in a book that includes modern classics. I do it to show what imagination and enterprise can accomplish with meager financ-

ing. The picture has stood the test of time, and, as a psychological fantasy, it has added to the art of filmmaking.

When Harvey got back home to Lawrence, Kansas, he showed his photographs to John Clifford. Harvey had by then directed over a hundred documentary shorts for Centron Films, a nationally known educational film company, and Clifford had written about the same number of scripts.

Clifford was eager to collaborate. First, they thought of doing a spy picture with a chase scene in the amusement park. But that had been done before. They wanted to do something original.

Clifford said: "I thought of the Reuter Organ Factory in town that manufactures church organs. I liked the weirdness of the atmosphere. I decided to make the girl an organist. That was the key for me, the catalyst. Everything flowed from that on my mental screen. It was one of those things where you write by instinct rather than anything else. The script took only two weeks."

Then came the hard part—financing the movie. But that, too, went more easily than expected. They raised $17,500 by selling shares in the production—though the final cost would turn out to be $30,000. Most shareholders were local people who invested up to $2,000.

As it turned out, they got nothing back. Harvey signed with Herts-Lion International, a new distribution company that was looking for films. "A man came out and talked to me," Harvey

Mary Henry (Candace Hilligoss) emerges from the river depths, only to find her life suspended between the world of reality and the unknown.

An auto plunges from a suspension bridge, taking Mary Henry and two other young girls into the swirling waters of a Kansas river.

said. "It all sounded good. But they went out of business before we got any money."

Nevertheless, Harvey started with high hopes. With the $17,500 he raised, he had enough to shoot the picture both in Lawrence[1] and in Utah. The Utah Board of Tourism gave permission to use the old amusement park, called the Saltair Resort, as a set. The site had a long and colorful history. Built by Mormon pioneers in 1893, its huge dance hall held 1,000 couples. It was said to be the biggest such structure between Salt Lake City and New York City.

Fire destroyed the pavilion twice, but it was rebuilt each time. Today the restored resort has become a popular attraction, complete with swimming facilities that enable bathers to test the lake's famous buoyant waters.

As important as Saltair was for its atmosphere, so was the choice of the actress for the demanding role of Mary Henry, who lives in a gray world between life and death.

Harvey had enough money to hire a professional actress for the role. He knew that a colleague, Sidney Berger, a member of the Theater Department at the University of Kansas, was going on vacation to New York City. So Harvey asked him to scout the agents' offices.

Berger did and found Candace Hilligoss, a slight, blond actress with wide, soulful eyes and high cheekbones. Weeks later, Harvey remembers his first sight of her. At the airport, she appeared so di-

[1]Two decades later, in 1983, the city would be the site of the controversial nuclear war movie *The Day After*.

[2]Hilligoss made only one other film, *Curse of the Living Corpse* (1964), whose sole distinction was that it marked Roy Scheider's film debut. But she had an active career on the stage, working for two years with actors like Scheider in the Arena Stage repertory company in Washington, D.C. Later she appeared as Stella with John Ericson and Vivian Blaine in a touring production of *A Streetcar Named Desire* and she costarred with Sam Wanamaker in a Maryland production of *Rhinoceros*. However, her career faded after she married actor Nicolas Coster and had two daughters. When this book was written, she was divorced, lived in Los Angeles, and had occasional small television parts in "Quincy" and "The Waltons." She spent most of her time writing. She was working on a novel about families who stayed behind after the dustbowl Depression of the 1930s in her home state of South Dakota.

sheveled and plain-looking that he spent a sleepless night thinking how he would tell her to go home. "But," he said, "the next morning, there was an amazing transformation. She showed up with makeup. It changed her whole appearance. She looked like a butterfly emerging from a cocoon."

Born in Huron, South Dakota, Hilligoss had studied at the University of Iowa and the American Theater Wing. She appeared with Burgess Meredith and Nina Foch in summer stock, then played in live television productions on the "U.S. Steel Hour" and the "DuPont Theater." "All I need is one big chance," she told a reporter for the *New York Daily News*.[2]

Hilligoss had never acted in a movie. But she had an air that Harvey thought was essential for the role. "I wanted a girl who had an ethereal quality and yet was pretty," Harvey said.

One problem was that Hilligoss was a method actress. She insisted on understanding the character's motivation, probing her reactions. "That was difficult to do, because Mary was a passive figure," Harvey said. "Things are always happening to her. So she never understands what is really going on as far as interacting with other people is concerned." They worked this out in evening discussions, and Hilligoss's performance added immensely to the movie's unsettling quality.

If Harvey was concerned about how Hilligoss would play the leading role, he had every right to be. She is in every scene. Even as the story opens, the camera focuses on her as she rides with two other girls across a bridge. Some boys in a passing car try to drag-race with them.

Suddenly, the girls' car loses control and crashes through a railing. Searchers find no trace of the auto. Hours later, as police drag the river, Mary wades ashore, wet and disoriented but miraculously alive.

Hilligoss, in an interview for this book, said she vividly remembers the river scene. "When I read the script in New York, I saw it had a lot to do with water," she said. "But they told me, 'Don't worry. It will be Indian summer in Kansas.' It turned out to be thirty-five degrees. Everybody was in down jackets, mufflers, and gloves. And I was in an ice-cold river and in wet clothes for eight hours."

Mary has been on her way to a small town to work as a church organist. Strange things start happening as soon as she rents an apartment in a rooming house. A middle-aged man (Harvey), leering and white-faced, stares through a window with dark, piercing eyes. The next day when she goes out, it is as if she is in a dream. She hears no sounds. People stop talking to her. They no longer seem to see her. Then everything returns to normal.

The pastor (Art Ellison) welcomes Mary at the church. But she is cold and distant. She won't go to a reception. "My dear," the pastor says, "you can't live in isolation from the human race, you know." That is exactly what her fate will be.

One day, the pastor takes her for a drive and they go out to a deserted old pavilion that used to be an amusement park. "What attraction does that have for you?" he asks. She doesn't know but she knows she will be back. All the while, an organ throbs in the background with cheerless music.

At the rooming house, John

A close-up of Hilligoss, who was making her film debut.

Linden (Berger), a brash young man who lives next door, tries to be friendly. He invites her to dinner, but she finds him too crude and turns him down. Instead, she eats alone in her room.

I think this scene is the film's major weakness. Harvey has made the young man so obnoxious, the audience roots for Mary to brush him off. His loss as a human contact is not missed.

On the other hand, if he had been more sensitive, someone who genuinely cared for Mary, he would have added poignancy to Mary's demise because her death would have ended a loving relationship. As it is, she makes no connection to anyone. No one misses her. Nobody mourns her departure.

At a doctor's office, Mary tells about her strange experiences. "It was as though for a time I didn't exist, as though I had no place in the world. . . . I've no desire for the close contact of other people. . . . I don't seem capable of being close to people."

The doctor (Stanley Leavitt) attributes her feelings to the emotional shock of the accident. But the nightmarish face comes back, and it preys on Mary's mind. When she practices the organ, her dark thoughts transform the music, and it becomes disjointed, wild, and frightening. One night the pastor hears her and accuses her of playing oddly profane and sacrilegious music, music that sounds as if it came from hell. He fires her.

Things now start falling apart for Mary. She goes out with the man at the rooming house, but he looks on her only as a conquest. She again rejects him. And the evening ends on an unsettling note when the leering, chalk-faced man shows up again.

"Something separates me from other people," she tells the doctor the next day. ". . . I don't know what is real anymore. . . . He is trying to take me back somewhere. Doctor, you've got to tell me what to do." The doctor has been sitting with his back toward Mary. When he turns around, he has the face of the man who has been haunting her.

Now Mary is irresistibly drawn to the amusement park pavilion. There a host of ghoulish creatures await her. They emerge from everywhere, dancing wildly across the ballroom floor. Then they chase her around the carousel, across the dance floor, and out onto the beach. As she falls to the sand, the white-faced specter closes in and snatches her back to the world of the dead.

"It was spooky being at the pavilion even for the cast," said Hilligoss. "It would get dark and the

A boarder (Sidney Berger) in Mary's rooming house introduces himself. But he is a boor and she repulses him.

Mary stares at the carnival of souls waltzing to eerie music in a deserted pavilion.

sun would go down and Harvey would be in this awful makeup. One time he walked out on a balcony and two little boys who had parked their bikes were coming down the walk. They saw this lone figure and he looked at them in his black suit and white face. They let out a terrible scream, turned, and ran as fast as they could."

The camera cuts back to the river, where police have pulled out the auto, and we see Mary's waterlogged corpse inside, her face immobile and frozen in death.

The ending is a gripping one. I have always thought the action between the first and last scene has taken place in a matter of seconds—the last moments of Mary's life. As she drowns, she has run over in her mind what life would have been like if she could have lived on.

But Harvey says he and Clifford conceived the time span as several weeks. Mary, in their mind, had become a spirit. Says Harvey: "She has been a girl who never 'lived,' never let herself be loved, never engaged in interpersonal relationships. So now, her terrific desire to live causes her to try to return to the real world. And yet death is always calling her back. Death is represented by water, the river, the salt lake, and, finally, the man. He calls her back. He says, 'You have no right to life.'"

Carnival did not have a New York City opening, and because of its unconventional plot, it failed to get many theater bookings. But *Variety* gave it a favorable review, and television syndication enabled it to have a sizable national audience. Over the years, it became a cult favorite, particularly on col-

lege campuses. In New York City, it ran at the famous Thalia revival house in 1981 in a Halloween twin bill with *Night of the Living Dead* (1968).

"*Carnival of Souls* deals out terror in the manner of Val Lewton rather than George Romero," said Jeffrey Frentzen, writing in the sci-fi, horror, and fantasy magazine *Cinefantastique*, "staying close to implied psychological horror rather than graphic violence."

Why does the movie hold interest for the young? Scriptwriter Clifford thinks it relates to their underlying concern about what lies ahead. "The future has many unknowns for them. Sometimes they are acutely aware of the voids within. They know what it is to fear that if one looks too deeply inside there may be nothing there."

Don't Look Now (1973)

Directed by Nicolas Roeg. Screenplay by Alan Scott and Chris Bryant adapted from a short story by Daphne du Maurier. Photography, Anthony Richmond. Editor, Graeme Clifford. Music, Pino Donnagio. Produced by Peter Katz. Executive producer, Anthony B. Unger. A British-Lion presentation, an Anglo-Italian coproduction, distributed by Paramount. Rated R. 110 minutes.

John Baxter	DONALD SUTHERLAND
Laura Baxter	JULIE CHRISTIE
Heather	HILARY MASON
Wendy	CLELIA MATANIA
Bishop Barbarrigo	MASSIMO SERATO
Christine Baxter	SHARON WILLIAMS
Inspector Longhi	RENATO SCARPA
Johnny Baxter	NICHOLAS SALTER
Dwarf	ADELINA POERIO

From the very start, we know something horrible is going to happen.

The opening scene is a cameo of domestic tranquillity in the English countryside. John Baxter (Donald Sutherland) is quietly working at his collection of slides: old Italian churches with brightly colored stained-glass windows. An archaeologist, Baxter is an expert at restoring the past. Across the room, his wife, Laura (Julie Christie), reads by the fire, contented, a bit dreamy. On a chilly fall day, their five-year-old daughter, Christine (Sharon Williams), and her older brother, Johnny (Nicholas Salter), play outside.

In the den, the conversation is incidental. One of the children, Laura says, has posed a curious question: "If the world is round, why is a frozen pond flat?"

"Nothing is what it seems," John replies offhandedly.

Just perceptibly, the pace quickens. The camera cuts more sharply from image to image. Christine, dressed in a red slicker with a pointed hood, plays near the pond. Nearby, her brother runs his bike over some glass. It snaps. Christine tosses a ball near the edge of the pond. Inside, John examines a slide of an old church, and in a closeup, we catch a startling image—a small figure in bright red, seated in one of the pews.

Who is it? We do not know. But by now, bombarded by images, we are on the alert: Look for details.

At that moment, John Baxter overturns his drink. Slides crash to the floor. Again we hear the breaking of glass. Outside, there is catastrophe. Christine slips beneath the surface of the pond, drowning. We cut back to the den. A sinister red substance—is it dye?—spreads across one of the slides, the one with the strange figure in the foreground.

John leaps up. Something is wrong. He rushes from the house, but is too late. His daughter is dead. He attempts to breathe life into her, then raises his head in a howl of anguish.

So Don't Look Now begins. During the next hour and a half, inexplicable terror follows. It is lonely and isolating terror. Not scary in the campy horror-film sense. No mummies fall out of closets here. Nicolas Roeg's terror is quiet, painted in red, often caught only in a glance. It flashes back and forth in time—and it upends our deepest sense of how the world really works.

The plot is drawn from a short story by Daphne du Maurier, whose work Roeg had admired for many years. "I was looking for a story that was a yarn," he said in a 1973 interview for *Sight and Sound*. No matter what cinematic variations evolved, Roeg was committed "to stick to the yarn."

Earlier, as a cinematographer, Roeg filmed *The Masque of the Red Death* (1964), Truffaut's *Fahrenheit 451* (1966), and Richard Lester's *Petulia* (1968). His first films were *Performance* in 1970 cordirected with Donald Cammell, and *Walkabout* in 1971. Later came *The Man Who Fell to Earth* in 1976, a fantasy in which we encounter again Roeg's view that surfaces do not always reveal the truth.

Commenting about *Don't Look Now*, Roeg pointed out that Donald Sutherland's line "Nothing's what it seems" was not in the original du Maurier story. "But," he

Laura (Julie Christie) on a funeral boat with the two psychics (Hilary Mason, *center*, and Clelia Matania).

said, "it is the key to the whole premise—and is exactly the feeling I have about life anyway."

Roeg's yarn takes us to Venice, where John Baxter is at work on an old church, matching brightly colored mosaics along the crumbling walls. It is winter and the Baxters are seeking to repair their lives after their daughter's death.

This is not picture-postcard Venice. The portrait is somber gray with curious splashes of red, a sinister canvas: a city sinking into the sea, a maze of canals, alleys, and dead-end courtyards. Roeg's story seems simple enough: The Baxters hope to recapture the comfortable intimacy of their married life. They dine out. They wander through the city. They make love. One day, at lunch, they meet a blind psychic (Hilary Mason) who claims that she has spoken with Christine. Their daughter is happy, she says. But John is enraged. "My daughter is dead," he insists.

That day, the Baxters learn that a mad killer is roaming the alleys of Venice. And, the blind psychic warns, John's life is in grave danger in Venice. But how? We do not know. Then another mystery complicates John Baxter's life: he believes his wife has vanished. Has she been kidnapped? Has she been murdered? The questions move us swiftly toward a terrifying resolution.

Along the way, we travel through a series of plot twists as baffling as the city's maze of canals and alleyways. The Baxters—and we—are caught in a patchwork of colors and shapes, foreboding images we cannot understand until it is too late.

The sense of uncertainty comes at the most mundane moments. A bishop crushes a piece of red mosiac underfoot. A voice on a telephone is strangely garbled. A broken doll is washed up from a canal. We see a figure in red disappearing around a corner. Is it Christine, who drowned in her red rain slicker? We are not sure. But we know we must weigh every clue as we slip more deeply into the puzzle, aware that something horrible is going to happen.

Yet, the surface is promising. The Baxters are an appealing couple, and their relationship —gentle, devoted, passionate at times—is rare in films of terror. And the film's best-known scene is an erotic sequence played with virtuosity by camera and actors. The love scene, running about four minutes, is a synthesis of their marriage, a blend of passion, intimacy, and mutual dependency. Seldom is a married couple etched in such convincing detail on the screen.

But the scene also intensifies our sense of foreboding, as Roeg repeatedly cuts backward and forward in time—heightening our uncertainty about the way time works. At one moment, we watch the naked lovers at play. Then we are propelled into the future, watching them dress for a dinner party. Then back again, as their lovemaking grows more passionate, and again into the future: They embrace tenderly. They sip wine. They leave arm in arm for their dinner party.

Donald Sutherland playing John Baxter, an architect who tries to make sense out of a series of psychic experiences.

In its time shifts, the scene is unsettling, but it is also pivotal in portraying the couple's love and mutual dependency. Later, when their lives are threatened, our concern for their well-being is a crucial emotion in the film. Recalling the love scene, Roeg has said: "I desperately wanted the feeling that at that moment of making love, Laura might become pregnant again. I wanted to make it clear that it's not just billing and cooing. It isn't a sexual scene. I wanted to get a reality to it of two human beings."

For Roeg, small details serve as building blocks of terror. In a bleak restaurant, where Laura encounters Heather, the blind psychic, there is an undercurrent of danger. The room is too cold. The waiter does not take their order. Later, after Laura speaks with the psychic, she faints. Dishes crash to the floor. Again, the sounds of breaking glass, recalling the clatter of glass in the opening scene of the film.

Roeg observes: "Glass sets up a sensation of fear, of something dangerous. Almost everyone has a fear of shattered glass. So firm at one moment and so dangerous the next."

After her meeting with Heather, the blind psychic, and her sister (Clelia Matania), we are

Laura and John try to unravel a mysterious prophecy from women with psychic powers.

Julie Christie is Laura Baxter, whose serene life is disturbed by sudden death and terror.

sure that Laura is in danger. Heather is reassuring, of course. But soon after, Roeg stages a brief and curious scene: The psychic and her sister are alone, in their room, and they are laughing maniacally. Why? We are never sure. Nor are we sure who is in danger. Laura Baxter? Her husband, John? False clues lead us astray. So we are afraid of these laughing sisters. Are they charlatans or co-conspirators? Roeg tantalizes us with doubt.

The scene was not in Roeg's original script. But, he said later, he felt the two characters were becoming too obvious to the audience, "being too definitely and certainly clairvoyant." So the shot of the laughing sisters was inserted. "I wanted it to appear bizarre," Roeg said.

And the sense of the bizarre intensifies. When a body is pulled out of a canal, an image of the drowning Christine flashes across John Baxter's mind—and ours. Later, in an alley, John sees a small figure in red, darting out of sight. Who was that? We do not know, not as yet.

There is another mystery. When Laura leaves for England, to visit their son, John encounters a strange sight: Across a canal, he sees three women in a boat, dressed in black, in a funereal pose. It is Laura and the strange sisters. John calls out but he is

unheard. The women stare ahead, in another world.

Has Laura been kidnapped? Is she dead? Is his daughter alive? Who is the mad killer? John Baxter—and we too—are engulfed with questions. Then, abruptly, we learn Laura is safe, still in England. When she returns to Venice, Laura finds Heather in a nerve-jangling trance.

The psychic tells Laura that her husband is in great danger. "Warn him," she pleads. Laura dashes into the night.

In the darkness, John is following someone through the alleyways. He comes to a familiar church. There, in a pew, is the figure in red, wearing a hooded coat which resembles Christine's slicker. It also recalls the image on the slide in the film's opening scene. Slowly, the figure turns.

It is terrifying: the face of a wizened dwarf (Adelina Poerio). The figure draws out a long knife and, in repeated motions, slowed in time, the arm rises and falls, as the knife cuts into the side of John Baxter's neck.

He falls, his face contorted in disbelief. We too are stunned. Red blood seeps slowly from John's neck, as slowly as the blob of red dye oozed across the mysterious church slide in the opening scene—a signal, perhaps, of his own death.

In a closing scene, we see

Laura and the two sisters, dressed in black, on their way to a funeral—a replay of John Baxter's vision. On that morning, he had feared his wife was in danger, not understanding that he was seeing his own future. Could John Baxter have seen the warning signals? Perhaps not.

In the du Maurier story, John Baxter dies with a final line: "What a bloody silly way to die." In a film, Roeg decided, "it would be crazy to have him say it." But, he says, du Maurier's line was "superb."

Death, he admits, is a subject which obsesses him. "At the end, John looks back...he knows Laura's there and yet he has to go on. It's a crazy thing.... People do things that will them to their death. There's some extraordinary force that is waving them on and they can't help going."

Here, death evokes feelings of sadness and loss, mixed in with Gothic horror. As a couple, the Baxters had grown more endearing. "I wanted them to be almost golden people," Roeg has said. They seemed destined to endure. We were wrong, of course. Suddenly, we were told: "Don't look now. It's over."

—David Behrens

John struggles for his life after the scaffolding in a Venetian church mysteriously collapses.

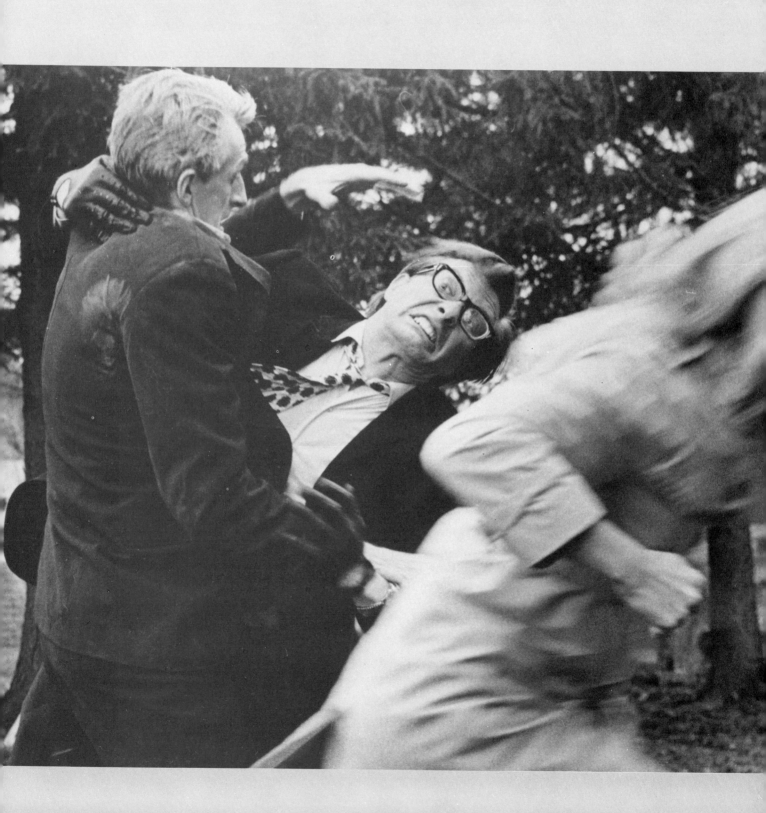

Night of the Living Dead (1968)

They are coming, rising rotten from their graves, filling the night with a furious howl, and staining the earth bloody red.... They are growing, their powers are swelling, from feasting on flesh and gnawing on bone, now they are drunk on the sweet taste of blood....Now they are here, and they march to the rhythm of death....

—Back-cover blurb of the novel *Night of the Living Dead* based on the screenplay by John A. Russo.

Directed by George A. Romero. Screenplay by John A. Russo. Produced by Russell Streiner and Karl Hardman. Photography, Romero. Makeup, Hardman and Marilyn Eastman. Special effects, Regis Survinski, Tony Pantanello. Editor, Romero. Released by the Walter Reade Organization through Continental Distributing of an Image 10 Production. B/W. 90 minutes.

Barbara	JUDITH O'DEA
Johnny	RUSSELL STREINER
Ben	DUANE JONES
Harry Cooper	KARL HARDMAN
Tom	KEITH WAYNE
Judy	JUDITH RIDLEY
Helen Cooper	MARILYN EASTMAN
Karen Cooper	KYRA SCHON

[1]The figure that has been used over the years is $70,000. But Romero said the correct total was $114,000 when all the bills, including actors' salaries, were paid.

[2]Estimates are wide-ranging on *Night*'s ultimate gross. They range from $15 million to $60 million. Complicating the matter is that many prints were pirated and there was a payment dispute with the Walter Reade Organization. Image 10, Romero's investor corporation, sued Reade and won a $3 million judgment, Romero said. But Reade went into bankruptcy before the money was paid. "We settled for getting the rights to the picture back," Romero said. He calculates that it has earned about $1 million for him and the corporation's twenty-seven other investors.

One of the "living dead" attacks Johnny (Russell Streiner) as his sister, Barbara (Judith O'Dea), flees.

Night of the Living Dead is that rare example of a low-budget independent film that transcends its origins and soars to cinematic heights to become a classic with a worldwide cult following.

Since 1968, the year twenty-eight-year-old George A. Romero directed it, the movie has played before packed houses in midnight shows across the country. Made for $114,000[1] with local talent from Pittsburgh, the picture became so popular its sound track was dubbed into seventeen languages. It appeared on the *Variety* charts of top-grossing films in 1969 and 1970. By 1972, it had grossed $3 million, making it the most profitable horror movie made outside a Hollywood studio.[2]

Yet, like all independent filmmakers, Romero had to struggle to get his picture shown. No distributor was willing to handle it. For one thing, it was Romero's first commercial effort. For another, it was made in black and white and it looked like what it was—a shoestring production.

Because he shot it around a commercial film schedule, which was his regular income source, Romero financed *Night* as he went along. The acting was occasionally amateurish, the film was grainy, and the movie had a downbeat ending. Yet, all these shortcomings became strengths, blending to make a realistic nightmare few Hollywood-made films ever created.

197

Rising from their graves, the silent, zombielike ghouls march in search of the living.

"We showed it to distributors in New York and Los Angeles before going to the Walter Reade Organization [which eventually took it on]," Romero said in an interview for this book. "They all expressed interest. Columbia held it for three months before telling us the main reason for turning it down was that it was in black and white. American-International liked it, but they said it was too unmitigating. They said, 'How'd you like to change the ending?' They wanted an up-ending. They wanted the black guy to survive."

Even when Reade agreed to distribute the film, Romero had to give up final cut approval. After the picture was finally released, Romero felt the publicity campaign lacked imagination. "They gave it a good promotion," Romero said. "But it was a flat, drive-in, blood-and-guts promotion."

Despite the low-budget campaign, the film gradually attracted attention through the best of all advertising mediums—word of mouth. One movie house owner, Richard Westley, who runs the Hampton Arts Theatre in Westhampton Beach on Long Island, remembers his first experience with the movie.

"I got it for fifty dollars to show at midnight for a weekend," said Westley. "I wanted to show it to a few friends. But I decided to open it to the public. I was amazed at the turnout. And it grew from week to week. People started telling other people. We played it at midnight for a whole summer. We made thousands."

Why did it catch on? "It was done in stark black and white and dealt with real people," said Westley. "It had incredible suspense, and it was really scary."

There are other reasons. The plot, which tells what would happen if the dead come alive, seems even more chilling because its use of TV newscasts gives it a realistic documentary style. The picture was also an oddity because Romero took a chance and pushed the genre by showing grisly flesh-eating scenes.

That ploy had a two-edged effect. A number of critics were so revolted they reacted negatively to the whole picture. "There have been numerous movies in the course of film history that might be said to have turned your stomach," said Leo Mishkin in the *New York Morning Telegraph*. "But *Night of the Living Dead* is one that pursues this aim with greater effect than ever before." Said one magazine: "Wait until you're dead to see it."

Jibes like that actually stimulated curiosity in the film. Then there were also favorable reviews. Harry Pearson of *Newsday*, the Long Island daily, called *Living Dead* "the most gruesome and frightening film ever made." *Newsweek* labeled it "a true horror classic." And Rex Reed said it worked "in the way the old Val Lewton epics worked, by pulling the viewer into the film itself." The picture is now part of the permanent film collection of New York's Museum of Modern Art.

The project started when Romero and a friend decided to shoot a movie around an idea derived from a short story Romero had written. A graduate of the theater school of Pittsburgh's Carnegie-Mellon Institute, Romero had an apprenticeship in movie work. He spent summers as a grip on major films shot in the East, including scenes from *Peyton Place* (1957) and *North by Northwest* (1959). Later he and school associates started a film company in Pittsburgh, where production costs were half what they were in New York City. At first they concentrated on commercials and industrial and promotional films.

Then Romero and his crew took a fling on a full-length feature movie. Their approach was unorthodox to say the least. Even before they finished the script, they started casting. One of the first picked was Duane Jones, a black actor who played the hero, Ben.

He was an unusual choice in the late 1960s, and some critics have attempted to draw conclusions about a black trying to lead whites out of a crisis, and, in the end, being killed by whites. But the selection of Jones was purely circumstantial. "Duane was just the best actor we knew among our friends," Romero said.

The ghouls, the most memorable characters, were mostly clients who had invested in the picture and friends in the advertising community. "I can't take credit for their performance," Romero said, "because when I tried to direct them, they all did the same thing. So I found it was best to let each one do what he wanted to do.... It's just the ham coming out in the people playing the zombies, although there was some selection in the editing."

Filmed over a seven-month period (which actually included only thirty production days), the picture has a riveting opening. Barbara (Judith O'Dea) and her brother, Johnny (Russell Streiner), drive to a cemetery to put a wreath on their father's grave. When Barbara takes a long time at the gravesite, Johnny becomes bored and kids her about paying her respects. Then he pretends to be a monster and tries to scare her.

His acting foreshadows a nightmare that will follow. As they are leaving, a macabre-looking man approaches with a stiff-legged gait. Suddenly, he lunges at Barbara and starts strangling her. Johnny pulls the man off. But the man turns on Johnny. His strength is enormous. To our astonishment, we watch as he kills Johnny. The movie isn't five minutes old, and one of the heroes is dead.

Now the zombielike creature starts after Barbara. She dashes to

Hiding in the basement of a farmhouse are Harry (Karl Hardman), his wife, Helen (Marilyn Eastman), and their sick daughter, Karen (Kyra Schon).

her car only to find she does not have the ignition key. The man lunges for the door, but Barbara just manages to lock him out. With a hand-held camera inside the auto, we, like Barbara, see her attacker pound on the window, then bash it in with a rock.

Fighting off hysteria, Barbara releases the emergency brake. The car starts downhill. Frightened and out of control, she can't hold the car on a straight track and she crashes into a tree.

Before her stalker reaches her, she is out again, running and stumbling through the countryside, until at last she comes on an old abandoned farmhouse. When she slams the door behind her, it is the first time the audience has had a chance to catch its breath.

Barbara's fright is just starting. Inside, she finds a half-eaten head. Then, almost in a state of shock, she sees the door open. A black stranger, Ben, enters the house. Like Barbara, he has been chased by silent zombielike creatures.

"What's happening?" Ben asks. Barbara isn't answering. She is slowly losing her grip on reality, and a transition in the audience's rooting interest begins to occur. Ben takes her place as the hero and we start to identify with him.

As the creatures gather outside, Ben boards up the windows. When he turns around, he finds he is not alone. He sees Judy (Judith Ridley) and Tom (Keith Wayne), a teenage couple who have been hiding in the basement. With them are Helen (Marilyn Eastman), Harry (Karl Hardman), and their sick daughter Karen (Kyra Schon), who has been bitten by one of the ghouls in her flight to the house.

All the players were unknowns and nonprofessionals. Judith O'Dea, a Pittsburgh native, had just returned from the West Coast, where she had gone seeking an acting career. Judith Ridley was a social secretary, and Keith Wayne, a singer, was doing nightclub work. Karl Hardman and his wife, Marilyn Eastman, were two investors, and their ailing little girl was their daughter in real life.

The group in the house find a TV and listen to a newscaster explain the bizzare events. An orbiting satellite has returned from the planet Venus, scattering radioactive rays that somehow have caused the newly buried dead to return to life. Corpses are rising and devouring the living. Anyone bitten by a ghoul becomes prey to the flesh-eating disease.

In the farmhouse, the group try to map out a survival plan. They can't agree, and the meeting ends in a bitter argument. Ben wants to stay upstairs where they can defend themselves. Harry thinks their only chance is to stay barricaded in the cellar. Finally, they split up, with Harry and his family retreating into the basement.

In fact, Ben has made the wrong move. He, Tom, and Judy rush outside to a pickup truck—using torches to fend off the ghouls. When they try to fuel it, the truck catches fire. Tom and Judy are burned and become a feast for the ghouls.

This was the most controversial scene. Some felt it went too far. Romero said it would have been his personal preference to suggest the cannibalism. But he defended the explicit action because he

In a tense moment in the farmhouse, Ben (Duane Jones) and Harry fight over what strategy to use against the ghouls.

wanted to go further than any other moviemaker in terms of graphic violence.

"It was done intentionally with the idea of not cutting away when everyone else does," Romero said. "It was done for shock value. It does go over the line into bad taste. But that in itself is a statement. In some people's mind, that was something to recommend the film. Part of the audience sits there and celebrates that [the gore]. They say, 'Yeah. That's what we're talking about.' It's like Grand Guignol. And now it's a trademark, and it's hard to think of one of my films in this series without doing that."

Ben barely makes it back into the farmhouse—no thanks to Harry, who has come up from the cellar and all but barred the door.

That sets the stage for a showdown between the two, a fight that ends when Ben shoots Harry with a shotgun. Now the TV newscast is blaring again, telling of sheriffs' posses roaming the countryside to subdue the wandering corpses. (The zombies can be stopped by a bullet in the head.) But can the gallant bunch hold out in their fragile retreat?

The ghouls start storming the farmhouse, pouring through every crack and crevice. The living open fire. But the dead keep coming like a never-ending colony of ants.

One by one, the embattled living succumb. Family ties make no difference. Barbara's face turns from elation to terror when she sees Johnny, her lost brother, and rushes to him—only to realize he has become one of "them." The little girl, who has finally died from the bite she received, begins eating her dying father, then turns on her mother.

By dawn, the crisis has passed. Police have all but wiped out the zombie army. Only Ben, who has locked himself in the basement, has survived.

A posse comes on the scene, shooting anything that moves.

Johnny returns from the dead and confronts his sister.

The ending is ironic. Ben slowly emerges from his hiding place. Far away, one of the posse's sharpshooters spots someone inside the house. Mistaking Ben for a ghoul, the deputy gets a bead on him, opens fire, and cuts him down. Like the zombies he has been battling, he ends up on a common pyre.

Some feel the zombies represent the silent majority and the movie is making a statement about the end of individuality. For his part, Romero says he and his coworkers talked about the metaphor of a new society devouring the old. But these concepts are vague and not developed in any tangible way. The movie's real point of departure is its creation of an unrelenting mood of terror, and in that respect, few films have surpassed it.[3]

[3]A little-known fact is that Romero's original title was *Night of the Flesh Eaters*. He later changed it to *Night of the Nubist* (a mythological god of the dead who revived corpses and enticed them to follow). Neither appealed to the Walter Reade Organization, which gave the film its present title. I like it the best.

Rosemary's Baby
(1968)

Directed by Roman Polanski. Screenplay by Polanski based on Ira Levin's novel. Editors, Sam O'Steen and Bob Wyman. Photography, William Fraker. Music, Christopher Komeda (incorporating "Für Elise" by Beethoven). Art director, Joel Schiller. Producer, William Castle. Paramount. Rated R. 136 minutes.

Rosemary Woodhouse	MIA FARROW
Guy Woodhouse	JOHN CASSAVETES
Minnie Castevet	RUTH GORDON ☆
Roman Castevet	SIDNEY BLACKMER
Hutch	MAURICE EVANS
Dr. Sapirstein	RALPH BELLAMY
Terry	ANGELA DORIAN
Laura-Louise	PATSY KELLY
Mr. Nicklas	ELISHA COOK, JR.
Elise Dunstan	EMMALINE HENRY
Joan Jellico	MARIANNE GORDON
Dr. Shand	PHIL LEEDS
Dr. Hill	CHARLES GRODIN
Mrs. Gillmore	HOPE SUMMERS
Tiger	WENDY WAGNER

☆ Academy Award winner

The titles float across the screen as the camera skims along Manhattan's skyline and descends on a massive Victorian apartment house fashioned after the famous Dakota overlooking Central Park.

Here, where the notorious Adrian Marcato once practiced witchcraft and the horrid Trench sisters cooked and ate several children, a young couple, Guy (John Cassavetes) and Rosemary Woodhouse (Mia Farrow), find a vacant flat. Hutch (Maurice Evans), an old friend, warns them about the building's dark past.

But that happened half a century ago. Since then, the once eccentric house has become a respectable, if not fashionable, West Side residence. The two, charmed by its spacious rooms and high ceilings, decide to move in.

So begins Rosemary's Baby, a thriller that Polish director Roman Polanski fashioned after Ira Levin's best-selling novel. So familiar was the story that it became a popular diversion to try to guess the cast. In the New York Times, book reviewer Eliot Fremont-Smith picked Eva Marie Saint for Rosemary, Laurence Harvey for Guy, and Spring Byington for the distaff side of the odd couple down the hall. Another popular choice was Richard Chamberlain as Guy.

Few actresses, in my opinion, could have improved on the performance of Farrow,[1] who came into her own with this part, or, for that matter, of Ruth Gordon, who, to my mind, stole the movie. In fact, Gordon won the picture's only Academy Award. Cassavetes, despite a sardonic smile, did not appear to be egocentric enough to betray his wife. And Sidney Blackmer failed to be sinister enough for my taste as the coven leader.

But Polanski, who was making his American film debut, was the perfect foil for Levin. The latter

Convinced that she is in the clutches of a Satan-worshiping coven, Rosemary (Mia Farrow) rushes from her apartment.

[1]Farrow got the part because she was the choice of Robert Evans, the Paramount studio boss. Cassavetes was picked by Polanski. He had seen him in Shadows (1960), which Cassavetes directed. "The studio was opposed to signing him," Polanski said, "and I put up a big fight." In the end, Polanski found him difficult to work with. "He's one of those method actors who constantly scratch their ear or groin. . . . It caused problems in working. I had to do a big deal of editing."

was a storyteller without abundant style and polish. Polanski was just the reverse. The result was a horror movie with subtlety and pace.

Rosemary spends her days brightening the gloomy apartment while Guy, an actor, tries unsuccessfully to land a big part. They are not there for long before they meet Roman and Minnie Castevet (Blackmer and Gordon), who live in the adjoining apartment.

Invited to dinner, Rosemary and Guy find their neighbors to be warm and congenial. There is a hint of darker things to come when the conversation turns to the Pope's impending visit, an event that will get only moderate press coverage because of a newspaper strike.

"No Pope ever visits a city where the newspapers are on strike," says Roman.

"I heard he's going to postpone it and wait till it's over," says Minnie.

"Well," says Guy, "that's show biz."

"That's exactly what it is," says Roman, "all the costume and rituals, all religions."

Later, Roman takes an interest in Guy's floundering career. The next evening, Guy visits the Cas-

---

Guy (John Cassavetes) and Rosemary admiring a crib for their baby.

tevets by himself. A few days later, an actor who has been chosen over Guy for a key role suddenly goes blind. The part goes to Guy.

Now he becomes distant and self-absorbed and spends more and more time with the Castevets. Then one day he comes home early with flowers and proposes that he and Rosemary have a baby. While they are eating dinner, Minnie brings over two dishes of chocolate mousse. Rosemary detects a "chalky undertaste" and dumps most of it in her napkin. But she soon becomes drowsy and then disoriented, and Guy puts her to bed.

There she drops off into a misty nightmare in which she finds herself on a huge bed surrounded by naked men and women—including Minnie, Roman, and Guy. There are also figures resembling the Pope, and John and Jacqueline Kennedy. Guy starts making love to her, then gradually undergoes a transformation. His eyes yellow, his hands become scaly and clawed, and he sprouts horns. A devilish hand strokes Rosemary while the group ties her legs to the bed. "This isn't a dream," she cries. "This is really happening."

Because of this scene and some others, the National Catholic Office for Motion Pictures (the Legion of Decency) gave the film a C (for condemned) rating. "Much more serious, however," the office said, "is the perverted use which the film makes of fundamental Christian beliefs, especially the events surrounding the birth of Christ, and its mockery of religious persons and practices. The very technical excellence of the film serves to intensify its defamatory nature."

In England, the British Board of Film Censors ordered fifteen seconds cut from the dream sequence because of "elements of kinky sex associated with black magic." Polanski replied: "The censors' attitude belongs to the Inquisition." Nonetheless, the scene was cut in England as well as in the United States, at least for television viewing.

The next morning, Rosemary finds scratches on her body and Guy tells her apologetically that he wasn't too sober and was a little rough when they had intercourse.

Weeks later, when the Castevets hear that Rosemary is pregnant, they insist that she change her obstetrician to their friend Dr. Sapirstein (Ralph Bellamy), a noted specialist. Sapirstein recommends a herbal mixture that Minnie prepares, a drink that he says will be fresher, safer, and more vitamin-rich than any pills on the market. Rosemary also starts wearing a tannis-root brooch, a gift from Minnie.

As the days pass, Rosemary begins suffering severe pains. Instead of gaining weight, she gets thinner, until dark blotches frame her eyes. One day, when Hutch pays a call, he is horrified by her appearance. When he sees her tannis-root charm and meets her strange neighbor Roman, he rushes off to do some research into witchcraft. That research is short-lived. The next day, he falls into a deep coma from which he will never recover.

Days pass into weeks and weeks into months. New Year's Eve comes, and Rosemary and Guy spend the night with the Castevets and their friends. At midnight, Roman toasts the new year, 1966, which he calls "the Year One."

Then Hutch dies. At his funeral, a friend gives Rosemary a book Hutch had left for her. In it, he had written, "The name is an anagram." The book, called *All of Them Witches*, tells, among other things, about the strange practices of Adrian Marcato and his son, Steven. Using Scrabble letters, Rosemary figures out that Steven Marcato is Roman Castevet.

Now she believes that the Castevets and their friends are witches who want her baby for their strange rituals. Guy poohpoohs the idea, but more clues pile up to reinforce Rosemary's fears. When she finds that Dr. Sapirstein wears a tannis-root charm too, she rushes to a phone booth to call her original obstetrician, Dr. Hill (Charles Grodin). William Castle, the picture's producer, has a walk-on role in this sequence as a tall man waiting patiently for the phone outside the booth.

Rosemary persuades Hill to see her right away and pours out the whole fantastic story in his office. He asks her to lie down while he arranges to admit her to a hospital. Instead, he calls Sapirstein and Guy, who spirit her away to her apartment. There she goes into labor almost immediately.

When she comes to, Guy tells her she has had a boy. Later, Sapirstein tells her there were complications and the baby died. She calls them witches and accuses them of stealing her child. Sapirstein quiets her with a sedative. A few days later, she hears a baby crying next door. That night, she takes a kitchen knife and slips into the Castevets' adjoining flat.

Until this point, the story exists on two levels. The first, the obvious one, is that of a woman fighting against real witches who are after her unborn child. But another possible version is that of a neurotic, hysterical woman, driven off balance by her pregnancy, fantasizing all this. In the last scene, Polanski makes clear which point of view is the real one.

Top: Minnie (Ruth Gordon) offers Rosemary a herbal mixture supposed to be more vitamin-rich than any pills on the market.

Bottom: Roman (Sidney Blackmer) toasts the devil's new child.

Rosemary listens to her obstetrician, Dr. Sapirstein (Ralph Bellamy).

In the Castevets' apartment, Rosemary finds a group assembled, including Guy, near a black-draped cradle under an inverted crucifix. It is clear that the people are members of a coven come to pay their respect to the baby.

"Satan is his father, not Guy," says Roman. "He came up from hell and begat a son of mortal woman. And his name is Adrian. He shall overthrow the mighty and lay waste their temples. He shall redeem the despised and reap vengeance in the name of the burned and the tortured. . . . God is dead. Satan lives. The heir is one."

Rosemary stares at the child with Satan's eyes—whom the audience never sees. Though she drops the knife, she rejects the group and spits in Guy's face.

But as one coven member rocks the cradle and the baby cries, Rosemary instinctively moves toward it and takes over her motherly role, gently rocking the child to sleep.

The camera moves outside, and shows the same view of the brooding apartment house it filmed at the outset, panning slowly across the sprawling city skyline.[2]

---

[2]I thought this muted ending, in which the camera pulls back and comes full circle, worked well. But some, like science fiction writer Ray Bradbury, thought it was too low-key. "The truth is," Bradbury said in an article in the magazine *Films and Filming*, "I simply do not believe or accept the ending." In Bradbury's version, which he wrote for a magazine, Rosemary snatches the baby and flees into the rainy night. The coven members run after her, but she finds refuge in a cathedral. As the group watch from every door, she dashes to the altar, holds the baby out, and asks God to "take back [his] son." That is how Bradbury feels the picture should end. After all, Bradbury says, didn't the angel Lucifer stand by the Throne of God before the Lord cast him out of heaven for trying to use his power against God? Hasn't this fallen angel suffered enough? Does not God forgive? "Would not the Lord take back his ancient enemy and make of him once more a son upon the right hand of the Throne?"

In 1976, Paramount released to TV a sequel, starring Stephen McHattie as Adrian, called *Look What's Happened to Rosemary's Baby.* Unfortunately, it was a second-rate production. In it, Rosemary is killed and Adrian is raised by a coven member in a Western community. At twenty-one, he is prepared for a satanic ceremony to become the devil incarnate. But the cult finds he lacks a certain coldness—he develops a close relationship with someone outside the witches' society—and therefore is an "imperfect vessel." Instead, they use his body to impregnate yet another female who, as the picture ends, now carries the heir to the throne of the underworld. Ray Milland replaced Sidney Blackmer (who died in 1973) as Roman, but Ruth Gordon again played Minnie.

Crime
and
Punishment

BONNIE AND CLYDE

A CLOCKWORK ORANGE

THE FRENCH CONNECTION

Bonnie and Clyde
(1967)

Directed by Arthur Penn. Screenplay by David Newman and Robert Benton. Camera, Burnett Guffey.☆ Art director, Dean Tavoularis. Editor, Dede Allen. Music, Charles Strouse. Produced by Warren Beatty. Warner Bros. 111 minutes.

Clyde Barrow	WARREN BEATTY
Bonnie Parker	FAYE DUNAWAY
C. W. Moss	MICHAEL J. POLLARD
Buck Barrow	GENE HACKMAN
Blanche Barrow	ESTELLE PARSONS*
Capt. Frank Hamer	DENVER PYLE
Malcolm Moss	DUB TAYLOR
Velma Davis	EVANS EVANS
Eugene Grizzard	GENE WILDER
Bonnie's mother	MABEL CAVITT

☆ Academy Award winner

"They're young...they're in love...and they kill people." So read the advertisements. And, in fact, their slow-motion death dance and the violence erupting all through the movie fulfilled the promise of its advance billing.

But *Bonnie and Clyde* is more than a mindless display of holdups and bloodbaths. And that is the reason it has held up through the years. It is a film that combines a realistic evocation of rural society with a skillful portrait of the senseless drift of American life toward gunplay.

What disturbed many was the fact that the picture romanticized crime. It twisted facts to make Bonnie and Clyde sympathetic and likable as they would want to have been, instead of stupid and dull-witted as they really were. The movies made them naive, thrill-seeking kids who didn't know what they were plunging into until they were in too deep.

Also unsettling was the fact that the film had a jazzy touch and a light tone that added a discordant note to all the killings. It made their life of perpetual flight seem more like a slapstick comedy than a nightmare.

Bonnie and Clyde, then, were not the stereotypes of the Hollywood gangster. And the picture's shift of focus from levity to horror was not what the film capital had conditioned audiences to expect in this genre.

So it was not unexpected for director Arthur Penn to be on the defensive when he met the press. In interview after interview, he tried to make the point that neither death nor violence was at the core of what he had in mind.

"The question of violence in itself never really occurs to me," Penn told Vincent Canby, critic for the *New York Times*. "...The important question is whether the work itself is good or bad art.

"The trouble with the violence in most films is it is not violent enough. A war film that doesn't show the real horror of war—bodies being torn apart—really glorifies war."

Penn bristled at suggestions that *Bonnie and Clyde* glorifies crime. "God, no," he said. "I think it shows the squalor, the isolation, the terrible boredom of these people. Bonnie and Clyde and the others were in constant flight. And they got none of the rewards usually associated with crime."

The truth is that audiences came away with an ambivalent feeling. No matter how many

"Okay, folks. Don't anyone move." Bonnie (Faye Dunaway) and Clyde (Warren Beatty) doing their thing.

209

banks Bonnie and Clyde robbed and people they killed, they remain attractive characters. Certainly more attractive than the insensitive bankers who foreclosed homes of Depression-poor farmers and the bumbling lawmen who finally tracked them down.

The story, of course, was based on the exploits of Bonnie Parker and Clyde Barrow, two backwoods hicks who cut a wide swath through the Southwest in the 1930s, sticking up banks and gunning down anyone who got in their way. They were part of a colorful era of outlaw folk heroes like John Dillinger, Pretty Boy Floyd, Baby Face Nelson, and Machine Gun Kelly. These outlaws were just as vicious as modern hoodlum killers. But in that faded era, their hair-raising exploits seemed fascinating to a frustrated society beaten down by a sick economy.

From the start, the movie gets right to the business at hand. Bonnie (Faye Dunaway), a bored waitress, meets Clyde (Warren Beatty), a footloose ex-convict, as he tries to steal her mother's car. Yearning for excitement, she joins him, and is thrilled when he holds up a grocery and they drive off with some cash. There is no killing on this first job. So it all takes on a fun-and-games aura until they go to bed and Clyde confesses, "I'm not much of a lover boy." However, it is not clear whether his impotence is fact or fiction.

Top: Before their first robbery, Clyde shows Bonnie his pistol, which becomes a symbol of his manhood.

Center: On the run after a bank robbery. *From left:* C. W. Moss (Michael Pollard), Buck Barrow (Gene Hackman), Clyde, and Bonnie.

Bottom: The gang. *From left:* Buck and his wife, Blanche (Estelle Parsons), Clyde, Bonnie, and C. W. Moss, their driver.

Wounded during a chase, Bonnie struggles to keep her balance in a stream. Moss and Clyde go to help her.

"We made conjectures about their intimate life," Penn said, "because we didn't know that much about it. There were stories that he was homosexual in prison and another that she was pregnant by him at the time of the ambush. But we do know that he was deeply devoted to her."

Clyde's pistol becomes a symbol of his manhood. At one point, Bonnie touches it while he jerks a wooden match up and down in his mouth. But if Bonnie cannot be satisfied sexually, she finds their criminal exploits a substitute.

Later, their ranks swell. Clyde's brother, Buck (Gene Hackman), and sister-in-law (Estelle Parsons) join the team. So does C. W. Moss (Michael J. Pollard), a grease monkey who becomes a mechanic for their stolen cars. There are more robberies, and their notoriety grows. Rollicking banjo music strums during hectic chase scenes, giving them a frolicsome flavor. But the merry-go-round eventually winds down. As the holdups and killings increase, their life becomes more frenzied. They are constantly on the run. One day, police kill Buck in a shootout at a tourist camp and wound his wife.

In the midst of the turmoil, Bonnie and Clyde share a rare moment. She writes a poem about them which so moves Clyde that he shouts, "Hot damn," and makes love to her for the first time.

In the end, there is no place for them to go. Police ambush the doomed lovers on a backwoods road. Dressed in white in a stolen white car, the two die under a hail of bullets, their bodies writhing in slow-motion agony.[1]

[1] In real life, the two were killed near Arcadia, Louisiana, in 1934. For years, their bullet-ridden Ford Deluxe toured auto showrooms, drawing thousands of curious viewers. One of them was my wife, Sara, who as a child saw the car when it came on tour to her hometown of Conway, South Carolina. She remembers it as cream to yellow in color and filled with rusty bullet holes.

A Clockwork Orange
(1971)

Directed and produced by Stanley Kubrick. Screenplay by Kubrick from the novel by Anthony Burgess. Editor, Bill Butler. Photography, John Alcott. Music, Walter Carlos. Production design, John Barry. Warner Bros. Rated X, later re-edited and rerated R. 137 minutes.

Alex	MALCOLM MCDOWELL
Mr. Alexander	PATRICK MAGEE
Mrs. Alexander	ADRIENNE CORRI
Minister of the Interior	ANTHONY SHARP
Prison chaplain	GODFREY QUIGLEY
Dim	WARREN CLARKE
Georgie	JAMES MARCUS
Pete	MICHAEL TARN
Deltoid	AUBREY MORRIS
Cat lady	MIRIAM KARLIN
Mum	SHEILA RAYNOR
Dad	PHILIP STONE
Dr. Brodsky	CARL DUERING
Tramp	PAUL FARRELL
Prison governor	MICHAEL GOVER
Lodger	CLIVE FRANCIS
Dr. Branom	MADGE RYAN
Psychiatrist	PAULINE TAYLOR
Stage actor	JOHN CLIVE
Chief guard	MICHAEL BATES
Julian	DAVID PROWSE

"There was me, that is, Alex, and my three droogs. That is, Pete, Georgie, and Dim. And we sat in the Korova Milkbar trying to make our rasudox as to what to do for the evening. The Korova Milkbar sold milk-plus.... This would sharpen you up and make you ready for a lot of old ultra violence."

The speaker is Alex, a mean young punk who, with his gang of London hoodlums, or "droogs" as they are called in the teenage lingo of the future, enhance their life of boredom and frustration with nights of robbery, mugging, and what Alex calls the quick "in-out, in-out."

They symbolize a society out of control. Moral and spiritual life has gone awry. After-dark crime abounds.

Yet, this frightening world is not that far removed from contemporary life. In major urban centers, it is not unusual for police to patrol the subways, for stores to hire their own security men, and for apartment owners to hook up burglar alarms to their homes and cars. Many, seeking refuge, have fled to the suburbs —leaving the central cities even more vulnerable.

In *Clockwork Orange*, Alex is one of the bullies who thrives on this vulnerability. He gets himself high on drugged milk for nights of prowling and combat. Still, curiously, with all his vices, he remains a not totally repulsive subject.

"Alex is a character who, by every logical and rational consideration, should be completely unsympathetic, and possibly even abhorrent, to the audience," said Stanley Kubrick, the director. "And yet, in the same way that Richard III gradually undermines your disapproval of his evil ways, Alex does the same thing and draws the audience into his own vision of life."

This happens because the government, pressed to put an end to the mounting crime rate, uses Alex in an experimental brainwashing program. The idea is to turn him into a docile, law-abiding citizen. It does. But it also deprives him of free will—in a sense dehumanizing him—and makes him prey to the very evils he himself perpetuates.

Alex (Malcolm McDowell), a young punk of the future, out for a night of ultra violence.

The Korova Milkbar, where plastic nudes serve as tables. Alex and his "droogs" (gang mates) sharpen up on legally dispensed drugs before their evening romp.

The droogs come upon a tramp—their first victim.

Wearing a codpiece and mask, Alex cuts the gown of a rape victim as director Stanley Kubrick films.

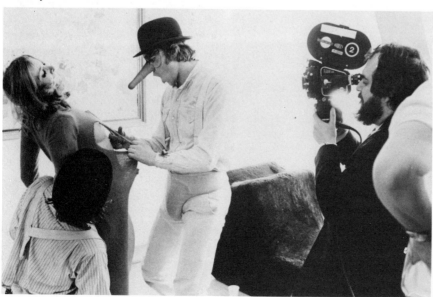

Kubrick seems to be cautioning against the temptation to turn toward a totalitarian regime that could put into effect instant solutions. "I could see very serious social unrest in the U.S. that would probably be resolved by a very authoritative government," said Kubrick. "And then you could only hope you would have a benevolent despot rather than an evil one. A Tito rather than Stalin —though of the Right."

Because of the film's violence and some brief scenes of full nudity (in a rape sequence and one fast-motion orgy), the film drew an X rating, which made it controversial from the day it opened. The Detroit News banned ads of the picture. About thirty other newspapers did the same thing or reduced the ad size.

Kubrick fired back. He compared the censorship action to a speech by Hitler in which the Nazi dictator outlawed "degenerate" art. In a letter to the Detroit paper, Kubrick said that "high standards of moral behavior can only be achieved by the exercise of right-thinking people and society as a whole and cannot be maintained by the coercive effect of the law. Or that of certain newspapers."

The idea for the film came from a 1960 novel by Anthony Burgess, whose wife was the victim of violence when three GI deserters raped her during a bomb blackout. The meaning of the title, which came from an expression Burgess heard listening to an old cockney, is not clearly defined in the movie. But in the novel, it was interpreted as something mechanical that appears human on the outside.

Burgess thought Kubrick's film was not just another interpretation but a "radical remaking" of his book. Yet, its spirit remained intact. Said Burgess: "The feeling that it was no impertinence to blazon it as 'Stanley Kubrick's Clockwork Orange' is the best tribute I

The French Connection 🎥
(1971)

Directed by William Friedkin. 🎥 Based on the book by Robin Moore. Screenplay by Ernest Tidyman. 🎥 Music composed and conducted by Don Ellis. "Everyone's Gone to the Moon" by Jim Webb, sung by the Three Degrees. Photography, Owen Roizman. Editor, Jerry Greenberg. 🎥 Stunt Coordinator, Bill Hickman. Produced by Philip D'Antoni. Filmed in New York, Marseilles, and Washington, D.C. 20th Century–Fox. Sequel was *French Connection II* (1975), also with Hackman and Rey. Rated R. 104 minutes.

Jimmy "Popeye" Doyle	GENE HACKMAN 🎥
Alain Charnier	FERNANDO REY
Buddy Russo	ROY SCHEIDER
Sal Boca	TONY LoBIANCO
Pierre Nicoli	MARCEL BOZZUFFI
Henri Devereaux	FREDERIC DE PASQUALE
Mulderig	BILL HICKMAN
Marie Charnier	ANN REBOTT
Joel Weinstock	HAROLD GARY
Angie Boca	ARLENE FARBER
Lt. Walt Simonson	EDDIE EGAN
Officer Klein	SONNY GROSSO
Maurice La Valle	ANDRÉ ERNOTTE
Themselves	THE THREE DEGREES
Reporter	MELBA TOLLIVER
Dope pusher	ALAN WEEKS

🎥 Academy Award winner

Director William Friedkin and producer Philip D'Antoni worked on the script of *The French Connection* for a full year. But one scene eluded them. They couldn't quite bring off the picture's high-action chase sequence.

Though it was a pivotal segment, they had gone through two scenarios without figuring out how to fit it in. Or, for that matter, how to compose it. Without this critical scene, the script wouldn't jell.

Then one day Friedkin and D'Antoni took a long walk up Lexington Avenue in New York City, bouncing ideas off each other. As Friedkin remembers it, the conversation suddenly took this turn:

"What about a chase where a guy is in a car, running after a subway train—"

"Fantastic," D'Antoni said. "Who's in the car?"

"Well, it would have to be [Popeye] Doyle."

"Who's he chasing?"

"That would have to be Nicoli."

"Listen, what would happen if Doyle is coming home after having been taken off the case and Nicoli is on top of Doyle's building and tries to kill him?"

"And in running away, Nicoli can't get to his car."

"Doyle can't get to his."

"Nicoli jumps on board an elevated train, and the only way Doyle can follow is by commandeering a car."

"Terrific."

It was like one bulb flashing on after another to light up a darkened tunnel. And so began the first successful draft of *The French Connection*.

It was a movie that would turn many people off. They would react negatively to its raw violence and sadism. But many others saw it as a realistic depiction of undercover police work in New York City. This was, by far, the majority view.

From the start, Friedkin and D'Antoni had no interest in doing a film focusing on the social problems that created the narcotics market. They wanted to produce a thriller pure and simple. That's precisely why their movie works.

The famous picture of fleeing French assassin Nicoli (Marcel Bozzuffi) shot by detective Jimmy "Popeye" Doyle (Gene Hackman).

There is never a letdown in the action.

"Everything we did was calculated to entertain," Friedkin said. "Before we had a script, we laid down a format that had a violent killing in the first two minutes, followed by an attempt to kill a cop, followed by another fifteen minutes of plot, followed by a surprise and an ambiguous twist [ending]."

Added to the fast-moving plot were first-rate camerawork and Gene Hackman's superlative performance as Popeye Doyle. He is a sardonic, hard-driving cop, a police character audiences had seldom seen before. Given to excesses, he stops at nothing to get the job done. He pistol-whips a drug pusher, works around the clock on his own time, recklessly puts his life on the line. Finally and tragically, he accidentally shoots a fellow cop while smashing a drug ring.

In fact, Popeye, pressured by a self-imposed mission in life, is almost an antihero. He is driven, obscene, brutal. And he is a racist. He cracks jokes about blacks who "pick their toes," has a kinky interest in girls who wear boots, and lives in a chaotic apartment. His redeeming feature is his incorruptibility.

Popeye is not entirely fiction. He and his sidekick Buddy Russo (Roy Scheider) are based on two New York City detectives who got a reputation for being the terror of the narcotics underworld. Eddie Egan and Sonny Grosso started with roundups of street junkies. They were nicknamed the Seven-Up Kids because those they arrested usually wound up with seven-year sentences.

In 1962, they climaxed their career with a major drug bust—the smashing of a international dope ring and the seizure of 120 pounds of pure heroin. The record loot was estimated to have a street value of $32 million. Producer D'Antoni hired Egan and Grosso as consultants, but they ended up with minor roles in the film.

Egan had his troubles in real life. Some of his colleagues disputed his role in the case, saying he took too much credit. They said, for example, that the lead that led to the heroin seizure came not from Egan's police work but from an FBI source. Egan said his appearance in the movie triggered jealousy and ill will.

However controversial Egan's career, there is no disputing the fact that *The French Connection* is a superior crime movie.

Filmed almost entirely on location in New York City, the movie is full of cross-cutting. At the outset, a man in Marseilles trudges into the entranceway of his walk-up apartment, carrying a loaf of bread. He fails to notice a shadowy figure holding a .45-caliber automatic—until it is too late. A shot slams into his body, the force of the impact toppling him backward into the apartment entranceway. His assailant (Marcel Bozzuffi) pockets the gun, callously breaks off a piece of bread, and walks away.[1]

Meanwhile, in New York, a hot dog vendor and a street Santa Claus set off after a dope pusher, shedding their costumes as they run. Cornered, the dope pusher slashes one cop with a knife before he is overpowered and beaten. Santa and the hot dog vendor turn out to be detectives Jimmy "Popeye" Doyle (Hackman) and Russo (Scheider), two undercover men.

After booking their prisoner, they are through for the night. But Doyle persuades Russo to go to an East Side nightclub for a drink. There Doyle sniffs the first clue of what will turn out to be a major dope-smuggling operation.

He spots a small-time dealer flashing big money at his table. On a hunch, Doyle and Grosso follow the dealer and his girlfriend, who lead them to a seedy candy store that they run. The man is Sal Boca (Tony LoBianco), who will become the middleman in the heroin deal.

The camera cuts to France, where businessman Alain Charnier (Fernando Rey) persuades

Doyle and his partner Buddy Russo (Roy Scheider) tapping a dope smuggler's line.

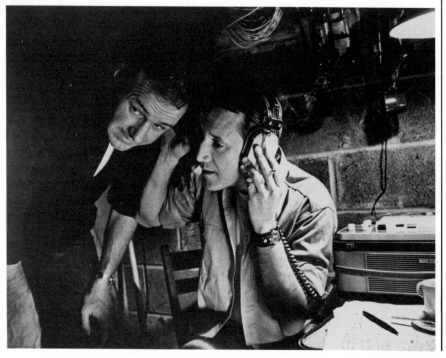

Doyle, disguised as Santa Claus, and Russo, dressed as a hot dog vendor, subdue a knife-wielding dope pusher (Alan Weeks).

TV star Henri Devereaux (Frederic de Pasquale) to join the operation. Devereaux, who is going to the United States to film a special on America, agrees to let Charnier plant a heroin cache in his custom-made car. It is being shipped on the same ocean liner that Devereaux is taking to America. Boca's job will be to bring Charnier together with a buyer, Joel Weinstock (Harold Gary), one of the chief backers of illicit narcotics traffic.

Doyle and Grosso stay on Boca's trail. They gradually learn more about the impend-ing heroin deal and persuade their boss, Lieutenant Walter Simonson (Egan), to detach them from their regular duties and allow them to wire-tap the candy store.

Two FBI men join the surveillance. One day they overhear arrangements for a meeting. But just as they think they are close to an arrest, things start to fall apart. Charnier, an old hand at underworld operations, discovers he is being watched and eludes Doyle on the subway.

Then Charnier's hired gun, Pierre Nicoli (Bozzuffi), tries to assassinate Doyle from an apart-ment rooftop. Instead, his wild shot hits a bystander, and Doyle goes after him. The gunman sprints to an elevated train. Doyle misses the train but commandeers a car and takes off in hot pursuit. Below the tracks, he weaves in and out of traffic, struggling to keep the train in sight.

Cars swerve as Doyle recklessly drives on, one eye on the train overhead. At one point he seems headed for a woman pushing a baby carriage. Somehow, he avoids her.

The brilliant car-train chase, which improved on one in *Bullitt* (1968), previously produced by D'Antoni, took five weeks to film. With the camera cutting between Doyle in the car and the gunman in the train, the scene became the standard of car-chase sequences.

---

[1]The opening scene, though a grabber, failed to have any relationship to the rest of the movie. It was one of two flawed sequences. The other: the scene where the French narcotics operator Alain Charnier is in the posh, warm French restaurant while outside in the bitter cold, Popeye and his partner munch pizza, shuffling their feet to keep from freezing—in full view of Charnier's window table.

Says Carlos Clarens in *Crime Movies*: "Cops pictures can be indexed from here on by the number of junked cars and cubic mass of demolished hardware."

Yet, Friedkin was disappointed when he first saw it on the screen. "When I looked at the first rough cut of the chase, it was terrible," Friedkin said. "It didn't play. It was formless, in spite of the fact that I had a careful shooting plan I followed in detail." There began a long, slow editing process.

"It became a matter of removing a shot here or adding a shot there. Or changing the sequence of the shots. Or dropping one frame or adding one or two frames. And here is when I had enormous help from Jerry Greenberg [the editor]."

At the end of the sequence, the train crashes into the rear of another train and Doyle guns down his would-be assailant.

Now the trail leads to Devereaux and his car. After a painstaking search, police find the massive heroin cache hidden in the auto's splash panels. They replace the heroin, allow the exchange to be made on a nearly deserted island in the East River, then close in on Charnier, Weinstock, Boca, and the others.

Some of the smugglers elect to shoot it out. Others surrender. Charnier flees into a derelict building with Doyle after him. A shadowy figure steps out of a corner and Doyle blasts away—only to find he has shot and killed an FBI man (Bill Hickman) who was on his own surveillance team.

There is still another irony. Titles at the end tell us that Charnier was never caught and Weinstock's case was dismissed for lack of proper evidence. Most of the other smugglers got off with suspended or reduced sentences. Doyle's and Grosso's reward was to be transferred out of the narcotics bureau and reassigned.

Alain Charnier (Fernando Rey), the French heroin dealer, and his hired gunman.

The man pointing is former New York detective Eddie Egan playing a police lieutenant. With him is an FBI man played by Bill Hickman, a stunt man.

We the People

DAVID AND LISA

HARRY AND TONTO

MIDNIGHT COWBOY

ONE FLEW OVER THE
CUCKOO'S NEST

THE SHOP ON MAIN STREET

David and Lisa (1962)

Directed by Frank Perry. Screenplay by Eleanor Perry based on a book of case histories by Dr. Theodore I. Rubin. Music composed by Mark Lawrence, arranged and conducted by Norman Paris. Photography, Leonard Hirschfield. Editor, Irving Oshman. Sets, Gene Callahan. Produced by Paul M. Heller. Continental Distributing Inc. Filmed in Philadelphia. B/W. 94 minutes.

David	KEIR DULLEA
Lisa	JANET MARGOLIN
Dr. Swinford	HOWARD DA SILVA
Mrs. Clemens	NEVA PATTERSON
John	CLIFTON JAMES
Mr. Clemens	RICHARD MACMURRAY
Maureen	NANCY NUTTER
Simon	MATTHEW ANDEN
Kate	CONI HUDAK
Carlos	JAIME SANCHEZ
Sandra	JANET LEE PARKER
Josette	KAREN GORNEY

It was made on the flimsiest of shoestring budgets and shot in less than a month.

Its writer had never done a film script. Its director had never directed a movie. The cameraman's only experience had been TV commercials, and of its three leading players, two were relative unknowns and the third was returning to the movies after being blacklisted for a dozen years.

Despite this laundry list of liabilities, *David and Lisa* turned out to be a unique and memorable film, a picture that stands as one of the outstanding movies of the 1960s. A tender, moving work, it was acted and filmed with sensitivity and grace. In a word, it was that rarely seen creation—a genuine sleeper.

The idea for the picture traces back to a day in the early 1960s. Director Frank Perry's nineteen-year-old daughter, then a student at Sarah Lawrence, brought home a book by Dr. Theodore Isaac Rubin about an autistic boy. Perry read it and liked it.

A few days later, he was in a bookstore, saw another Rubin book titled *Lisa and David*, and bought it. The short novel, a fictionalized case history, was a testament to the healing power of love. It centered around two emotionally troubled adolescents who, through a developing affection and trust, find their own way out of their mental maze of troubles.

Perry thought the story was not only engrossing but ideal as the plot for a movie. In fact, he decided he wanted to make it himself. The timing was just right. Perry, then an associate producuer at the New York Theater Guild, was ready to make the plunge into the world of cinema. He had just sold a script to Universal Studios, and the sale gave him enough money to be independent for a while.

"I thought the theater in New York then was becoming moribund," said Perry in an interview for this book. "On the other hand, films were coming alive. Small films from Europe were starting to happen. It was the time of *Lysistrata*, *The 400 Blows*, and early Bergman. I said, 'Jesus, this is the art form of the future.'

"I also saw there was no American equivalent to those European art films—what we would now call 'personal films.' *David and Lisa* really was a watershed in that it was the first independent American film to achieve a major success."

Perry's next job was to find a film writer. He did not have to go far. His wife, Eleanor, had written *The Third Best Sport*, a play that had had a respectable run on Broadway. Mrs. Perry, who had a master's degree in psychiatric casework, was enthusiastic, too. "It was a great love story," she said in a television interview before her death in 1982. "They clasp hands at the end and all that stuff. I knew [it would work]. I saw the movie immediately." Months later, she put in the final revision for the movie script and the Perrys tried the studios.

The answer was always the same. It wasn't commercial. It was too small a picture. It wouldn't make enough money. "We can't afford to make small

David (Keir Dullea), an alienated, emotionally disturbed teenager, finds himself drawn to the quiet, dark-haired Lisa (Janet Margolin).

pictures," one studio executive said. "We have too much overhead."

Undaunted, the Perrys took another route. They were both familiar with the tried and tested practice of getting plays on the boards by raising money from small investors. So they offered to sell shares in their movie at $312.50 apiece. Scripts poured out in the mail to 500 potential backers. Money trickled back from only one.

"We're awfully sorry we can't see our way to investing," one lady wrote. "But my husband wants you to know, darlings, he thinks you did a beautiful job of mimeographing." Another offered $100,000 if a rape and seduction scene was added.

A textile manufacturer finally came through with $70,000. "My wife read the script and loathed it," he said. "I'll back anything she hates." His contribution paved the way for more sales. With $150,000 in hand—the picture would eventually cost $210,000—they had enough to go on location.

"It was absolutely necessary to limit the shooting to twenty-five days," Perry said. "We couldn't go over an hour. We were in hock to the hilt. And there was no one else to turn to."

Over the years, Perry estimates the film has grossed well over $5

million, including earnings from TV, cable, and other subsidiary rights. But because of the complexity of distribution deals, he says little of it has come back to him.

With producer Paul M. Heller, also in his first film venture, they picked a shooting location outside Philadelphia, where they found an old vacated mansion. It had served as a small private school for girls. For a $2,000 donation, the new owners, an Armenian church group, let them take over the quarters.

Casting became an adventure. They wound up using no stars. Instead, they chose two promising performers: Janet Margolin, an eighteen-year-old actress whose only experience had been television and Broadway, and Keir Dullea (duh-LAY), still six years away from his starring role in *2001: A Space Odyssey* (1968).

Dullea was a second choice. He was picked only after the leading actor quit for a more lucrative production. The incident became a source of worry. Even after settling on Dullea, Perry agonized over whether he would look too old for the part. "He was playing a high schoool junior, and he was twenty-five," said Perry. As it turned out Dullea was actually one year older, but Perry's concern proved unnecessary.

Dullea had a small-featured face that belied its years, and he had just gotten a short haircut that made him look even younger. As Dullea recalled events in an interview for this book, when the leading actor left, Dullea was hurriedly summoned to the Perrys' apartment. "When I came into the apartment," Dullea said, "the foyer was a little dark and Eleanor said, 'Oh, Keir, if you were only ten years younger—' It was as if her voice stopped in its tracks. I stepped into the light. It was just the haircut. But hair can change your whole looks."

The veteran in the cast was Howard Da Silva. He was making

his first picture since the House Un-American Activities Committee had blacklisted him for failing to answer questions. Perry was advised not to court trouble. But Perry felt Da Silva was right for the role. "He had a wonderful *haemisha* [homey] quality," Perry said.

Despite the time pressure of the location filming, Dullea remembers it as an extraordinary experience. Perry had a way of putting actors at ease, and he, Margolin, and Da Silva were a natural team. "It was like falling off a log," Dullea said. "It was effortless and full of joy. The three of us could hardly wait to work."

The story of the film is simplicity itself. David (Dullea), a tormented young man, is brought to a school for troubled adolescents by his doting mother (Neva Patterson). He is bright and sophisticated. But he has one obsession. He cannot bear to be touched. He believes "touch can kill" and is plagued by a fear of death. He has an insane desire to stop time and so live forever. He keeps aloof from the other residents and rejects his psychiatrist, Dr. Swinford (Da Silva).

Also at the home is Lisa (Margolin), a lonely schizophrenic girl lost in a dark world of her own. She believes she is two persons. As Lisa, she talks only in childish

Lisa, a lonely schizophrenic girl, spends part of her day drawing pictures.

Lisa shows David a paper on which she has written the words "Play with me."

rhymes. "A big fat sow—and how and how." As Muriel, she communicates only in writing because she can't talk. Her condition, too, is not responsive to therapy. But Dr. Swinford persists.

One day, a remarkable thing happens. Lisa goes over to David and says, "Me, the same. Lisa's the name." Instead of ignoring her, he responds in rhyme: "Me, the same. David's the name." Thereafter, they chat but only if David answers in rhyme.

David's paranoia keeps him from making friends. He relates only to clocks, because although he cannot control people, he can start and stop clocks at will.

One day, David tells Lisa, "I see a girl who looks like a pearl. A pearl of a girl." She brightens and allows him to speak without rhyming. Then she draws a picture that shows her two personalities merging into one.

As the months go by, David begins to feel more at ease with Dr. Swinford. Gradually, the barriers go down. Their relationship takes on a different character.

David's personality, too, changes. No longer is he sullen and withdrawn. Instead, he shows a healthy anger at his mother's domination. Hurt, she takes him out of school. But David finds life at home intolerable and returns to school.

There, his affection for Lisa deepens. But inevitably, they quarrel, and Lisa runs away. Dr. Swinford and school officials search for the terrified girl all night. When at last they find her huddled on the steps of a museum, it is David who goes to her—a lost child reaching out toward a kindred soul.

For the first time, Lisa talks without rhyming. "You were mean to me," she says. He apologizes and Lisa offers her friendship again. "Let's go back to school," she says. To show his faith and love, David tentatively, painfully, extends his fingers. "Lisa, take my hand," he says.

Dr. Swinford (Howard Da Silva) talks to David's mother (Neva Patterson).

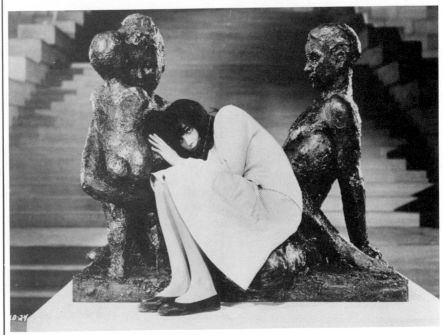

Outside a museum, Lisa huddles on a statue of a family.

Gently, Lisa closes her hand around his. As the music swells, the final shot is a high camera angle. Through the museum's tall columns, we see the two holding hands as they start back toward Dr. Swinford and school.

The movie fared well on the festival scene. It won the Venice Film Festival prize for best film by a new director. At the San Francisco International Film Festival, Dullea and Margolin were named best actor and actress.

The picture also got outstanding reviews. *Time* called it a "minor masterpiece... easily the best U.S. movie released in 1962."

Some critics felt the music somewhat schmaltzy and the last scene a little heavyhanded. Perry remains satisfied. If he could shoot the movie again, Perry said, he would have a less throbbing score. But he would not change the final sequence. "It was fundamental," he said. "It was inherent in the film. It has to do with hope and the picture's underlying philosophy."

Harry and Tonto (1974)

Produced and Directed by Paul Mazursky. Screenplay by Mazursky and Josh Greenfield. Music, Bill Conti. Photography, Michael Butler. Editor, Richard Halsey. 20th Century–Fox. Rated R. 115 minutes.

Harry	ART CARNEY ☆
Shirley	ELLEN BURSTYN
Jacob	HERBERT BERGHOF
Burt	PHIL BRUNS
Jessie	GERALDINE FITZGERALD
Norman	JOSHUA MOSTEL
Eddie	LARRY HAGMAN
Ginger	MELANIE MAYRON
Elaine	DOLLY JONAH
Leroy	AVON LONG
Cat woman	SALLY MARR
Hooker	BARBARA RHOADES
Medicine man	CHIEF DAN GEORGE
Junior	CLIFF DeYOUNG
Wade	ARTHUR HUNNICUTT
Tonto	WALTER PLINGE
Grocery man	RENE ENRIQUEZ

☆ Academy Award winner

There was a *New Yorker* cartoon by Stevenson that ran early in 1985 which seems all the more memorable as time passes. It shows an older couple approaching a movie booth apprehensively. The man says, "How old are the people in this movie?"

As the people in films seem to get younger and younger, and come from more far-off planets, and more and more assault each other and us, the movie *Harry and Tonto* assumes a warmer place in the heart. It is a picture about an old man and a cat and their adventures traveling from New York across America. It is low-keyed, rich in texture, warm and loving, funny and sad. It is a gem.

Harry and Tonto was made in 1974. Paul Mazursky, the director, wrote it with Josh Greenfield, then labored mightily to get backing for it. "I found that nobody wanted to make it because it was a movie about an old man. As one producer told me, 'I don't want to see a movie about my father.'"

He, and all of us, should only have been so lucky as to have a father like Harry. He is Harry Combs, played wonderfully by Art Carney, who won the Academy Award for best actor for his performance. He is a crusty guy, old in years, but young in spirit. He is a former teacher who quotes from Shakespeare. He is skeptical and embittered, yet he is also open-minded and tolerant. Carney makes of him a memorable character who stays with you just as Paul Muni did of the embattled Dr. Samuel Abelman in *The Last Angry Man* (1959).

Harry is a widower, in his late sixties or early seventies, living on the West Side of Manhattan with his cat, Tonto, evicted from his apartment because his building is to be demolished for a parking lot. He goes to live with his son (Phil Bruns) and his family in the suburbs. That doesn't work, so he takes to the road with the cat, visiting his oft-married and oft-divorced daughter (Ellen Burstyn) in Chicago, then moves on to see his dead-broke four-flusher son (Larry Hagman) in Los Angeles. Along the way, from New York to Los Angeles, we meet a succession of characters, some of them improbable, but believable enough in the context of this picaresque fantasy of the American road.

There is the Puerto Rican grocery man (Rene Enriquez). Harry walks Tonto on a leash on upper Broadway into a grocery store, where he buys better food for Tonto than he does for himself. "Eating is the most important thing in the life of a cat," he tells the grocery man. The grocery man says, "My grandfather is eighty-two and he never stops screwing." Harry asks, "What's the secret?" The grocery man says, "Maybe it's because he eats bananas, maybe because he doesn't know he's eighty-two." Later, we see Harry eating a banana. And the joke is extended just enough when he hears about

Art Carney is Harry, a septuagenarian who takes a cross-country trip with his cat, Tonto, a friend and confidante as well as a pet.

227

a man who became a father at ninety-two. "He must have eaten lots of bananas," says Harry.

Jacob (Herbert Berghof), the bitter old socialist, is the most pungent of all the characters, lashing out at the capitalistic ("kehpitalistic" is the way he spouts it) bastards who are ruining the world. Berghof is brilliant, conjuring up an image of the old radicals who sit on the benches of the big cities, bemoaning broken dreams, pining for the days when immigrants built the unions, joined the Socialist and Communist parties, supported Roosevelt and the New Deal, worked together with the "capitalistic bastards" to defeat Hitler.

When Harry tells him he is being evicted from his apartment and he will get a lawyer to stop them, Jacob says, "You can't fight in the court. You got to go to the streets, man the barricades, man the dynamite, blow up the cesspool." He says, "We are in for a depression that will make the thirties look like paradise. Maybe it's a good thing. The hard hats and the phony liberals will kill each other."

In a quieter moment, Harry asks Jacob, "When did you last sleep with a woman?" Jacob answers quickly, "Saturday night"— and after a long pause—"March, 1951." He tells about his first conquest in Poland, a milkmaid "who had tits bigger than the cow." His

father almost killed him, but he then "started slipping into her regularly—he was a capitalistic bastard." Berghof also tells us in that blustery, rough voice about the cold winters in Poland. "Your piss would freeze before it hit the ground."

In an interview for this book, Mazursky said, "There's a wonderful group of actors in New York; there always will be. Berghof, who taught acting classes there, was one of them. Instead of rehearsing them in the studio, I would have them do it on a bench on the street. The Upper West Side scenes were shot on Broadway at 116th Street, near the Columbia University campus. I would start them and then walk away, and I could see them continuing to rehearse. They were both a little deaf and talked loud, and that helped the scene."

Harry's nephew, Norman (Joshua Mostel), is a hippie at odds with his family because he is into a vow of silence and a strange diet. Harry is tolerant of this "as long as it is growth-promoting." He meets an old native American medicine man (Chief Dan George) who cures Harry's ailing back ("I practice good medicine on good people, bad medicine on bad people") and takes in payment a blender Harry bought from a vitamin salesman. He sizes it up as "a demonstration model."

There is a high-priced hooker

(Barbara Rhoades) who picks Harry up and gets so horny she drives up into the hills with him for a matinee (the most unlikely scene of all); a black janitor (Avon Long) who plays piano for Harry and the family at their apartment; Harry's old girlfriend (Geraldine Fitzgerald), now dotty, whom he finds in a rest home in Indiana and dances with. He continues his journey with a fifteen-year-old hitchhiker (Melanie Mayron) who eventually hooks up with nephew Norman to live in a commune in Boulder, Colorado. The part of the lady with the cats at the beach in Santa Monica who propositions Harry to live with her is played by Sally Marr, Lenny Bruce's mother.

Some of the lasting images from the film are the opening shots of old men and women around Broadway, walking, shopping, sitting on street benches; Harry being carried out of his apartment building by the police while sitting in his living-room chair, kicking and screaming, quoting from Shakespeare's Lear; the wrecking ball slamming into the red brick wall of his apartment house; Harry hitching on the side of the road with Tonto; and Harry and his daughter fighting old wars framed by Lake Michigan on Chicago's Lake Shore Drive.

The movement of the old man and the cat across the country is as charming as it is improbable. That improbability is what makes *Harry and Tonto* stand out among movies. With it all, the scenes in New York glow. They represent the best aspect of the writing partnership between Mazursky and Josh Greenfield, which earned an Academy Award nomination for best screenplay. They both grew up in Brooklyn during the Depression, and the film came out of their common experience and sensitivities about their parents and New York and old people. It no doubt pleased many people like the couple in *The New*

Harry on a shopping outing with Tonto.

Midnight Cowboy 🎥

(1969)

Directed by John Schlesinger. 🎥 Screenplay by Waldo Salt 🎥 based on the novel by James Leo Herlihy. Photography, Adam Hollender. Editor, Hugh A. Robertson. "Everybody's Talkin'" by Fred Neil sung by Nilsson. Harmonica accompaniment, Toots Thielemans. Produced by Jerome Hellman. United Artists. Rated X, later rerated R. 113 minutes.

Enrico (Ratso) Rizzo	DUSTIN HOFFMAN
Joe Buck	JON VOIGHT
Cass	SYLVIA MILES
Mr. O'Daniel	JOHN MCGIVER
Shirley	BRENDA VACCARO
Towny	BARNARD HUGHES
Sally Buck	RUTH WHITE
Annie	JENNIFER SALT
Woodsy Niles	GIL RANKIN
Little Joe	GARY OWENS, T. TOM MARLOW
Ralph	GEORGE EPPERSEN
Cafeteria manager	AL SCOTT
Mother on bus	LINDA DAVIS
Old cowhand	J. T. MASTERS
Old lady	ARLENE REEDER
Rich lady	GEORGANN JOHNSON
Gretel McAlbertson	VIVA
Party guest	ULTRA VIOLET
Young student	BOB BALABAN

🎥 Academy Award winner

Joe Buck, "one helluva stud" from Texas, comes to the Big Apple convinced he'll be the answer to the prayers of legions of love-starved women.

It doesn't take him long to find out how badly he has miscalculated. In his first encounter—with a garish, aging call girl—he gets enmeshed with her remote channel selector in their frenzied carnal act. As they go at it, the TV set changes channels in time to their love tempo. Then, to Joe Buck's chagrin, the floozie becomes outraged when he asks her for money. In the end, it is he who pays—coughing up cab fare as she rushes away to her next date.

This is a scene from *Midnight Cowboy*, the first X-rated film to win an Oscar, a picture that focuses on the seedy crowd drawn to Manhattan's garish 42nd Street. Once the center of New York City's fabulous white way, the street has long since lost its luster. Its west half has become the haven for pimps and prostitutes, hawkers and hustlers, and legions of young men and women with haunted looks in their eyes and needle holes in their arms.

In this cheerless world, Joe meets Ratso Rizzo, a gimpy, consumptive petty thief. He cons Joe Buck out of some money. Then, to make amends, he takes Joe Buck to his filthy hole in a building marked for demolition. "Not bad, huh?" says Ratso in a deadpan voice.

The two lost, lonely souls find little joy in their life, and they wallow in reveries. Joe Buck remembers his boyhood in Texas—his fast and loose grandmother and the girl he left behind. Ratso fantasizes about rejuvenating his crippled body, dreams of running gracefully along the sun-dappled sand and rippling surf of a Florida beach.

These poignant sequences—all with a touch of humor to give them a biting edge—are expertly put together by British director John Schlesinger, who shows the same attention to detail as he did in *Darling* (1965).

For example, in casting for the film's coltish hero, Schlesinger and producer Jerome Hellman first went through 500 photos of

Ratso Rizzo (Dustin Hoffman) and Joe Buck (Jon Voight), two lonely drifters in New York City.

Joe, a young Texas stud, meets his match in a blond New York City floozie played by Sylvia Miles.

Down on his luck and money, Joe beats up a conventioneer (Barnard Hughes) and steals his money.

Ratso dreams of playing craps and winning the pot in Florida.

young actors. Then they scoured Off-Broadway shows, picking several actors, among them Jon Voight. At first, Voight was overlooked. However, Marion Dougherty, the casting director, insisted he get another reading.

Needless to say, Schlesinger and Hellman were not sorry she persisted—though Voight was far from a midnight cowboy in real life. The son of a Yonkers, New York, golf pro, he caddied as a youth and played well enough to score in the low 70s. But golf did not suit him as a career. Nor did law, a profession his family urged him toward. "I played an eighty-year-old man in a school play," said Voight. "After that, acting was all I wanted to do."

If Schlesinger and Hellman were surprised by Voight's sensitive performance, so was author James Leo Herlihy by the movie fashioned from his novel. "I never dreamed anyone would dare make a film of it, particularly the film that was made," Herlihy said. "Even while it was being made, I had no interest in it because the word around Hollywood was that it was going to be a flop. When I went to the premiere in New York, I got interested." After the movie was released, he said he "absolutely loved it—most of it."

Schlesinger's craftsmanship is there from the beginning, when, to the soft strains of country singer Nilsson crooning "Everybody's Talkin' (at Me)," Joe Buck quits his dishwashing job in a small Texas town. He dons his best drugstore cowboy finery and says he's off to the big city to save those rich New York women from all those "tutti frutti" men.

On the bus, we get a portrait of the Bible belt from Joe Buck's transistor. A radio faith healer solicits contributors: "I got a letter here with ten dollars and two tumors a sister coughed up while listening to our show last week." Joe Buck daydreams about his home, and in a flashback we see him as an orphan raised by his good-time grandmother and her men friends.

In New York, Joe wanders from his sleazy hotel room and meets a brassy bleached blonde (Sylvia Miles), who takes him to her penthouse apartment. When Joe asks for payment, she gives him a piece of her mind:

"You were going to ask *me* for money. . . . Who the hell do you think you're dealing with? In case you didn't bother to notice it, you big Texas longhorn bull, I'm one helluva gorgeous chick. I'm twenty-eight."

The book put great emphasis on homosexual aspects of the city's downtrodden. But the film plays down these scenes. Instead, it presents an unflattering picture of women, who come across as cheap, tawdry, and aggressive.

Miles, who got a supporting Oscar nomination, had read Herlihy's book and asked producer Hellman for the part. She met Hellman outside an Off-Broadway theater in which she was appearing. "Oh, I'm sure we'll have stars for all those cameos," he told her offhandedly. But Hellman was wrong. A few days later, Schlesinger happened to see Miles in a B thriller called *Psychomania* (1963). He was impressed and called her to read with Voight.

Unquestionably, it was Voight's performance that made the picture. He acted with great sensitivity, in part because the film was shot on location and he got to meet some of the flotsam and jetsam of the sordid world of drifters. "The thing I learned rubbing elbows with these people is compassion. . . . We all hurt in the same place. I want people to go away from it [the movie] realizing that people like these have a kind of stature, you know. I don't want people to merely be glad they are better off. I want them to have compassion for the ones who aren't."

Joe is hustled again when he bumps into Ratso Rizzo (Dustin Hoffman), a creepy, unshaven flimflam artist who offers to be his manager. Instead, he cheats Joe out of $20 and fixes him up with a client who turns out to be a religious fanatic with an altar in his bathroom.

When Joe sees Ratso again, Joe is so tired and lonely he forgets his rage over being hoodwinked. Winter is coming, and Joe accepts Ratso's offer to share quarters in a bleak building slated for the wrecker's ball. In this dreary rat's nest, Ratso dreams of going south to Miami and basking at a pool alongside a bevy of beautiful girls. In reality, he is coughing away his life as the mercury drops and pneumonia settles into his lungs.

At the same time, Joe is becoming more and more disillusioned with the city. He meets some women at a Warholian psychedelic party peopled by such underground film favorites as Viva and Ultra Violet. But except for a brief coupling with a swinger (Brenda Vaccaro), he strikes out.

Unable to make a go at it as a gigolo, Joe starts selling himself to homosexuals. It is a sordid life. He services a nervous young man in the balcony of a 42nd Street movie house, only to find the kid is broke. He lets an out-of-town conventioneer persuade him to come up to his hotel room. Then, to his own disgust, Joe beats him up, shoves the phone in the frightened man's mouth, and steals his money.

Joe's only solace is that he and Ratso have held together in their mutual despair. They have developed a bond.

In the end, Joe scrapes up enough money to take his sickly crony to a warmer climate. But it is too late. The pathetic little hustler is beyond help. Even as their bus lumbers into the Promised Land, he dies in Joe's arms.

Joe drags Ratso to the bus that will take them to Florida.

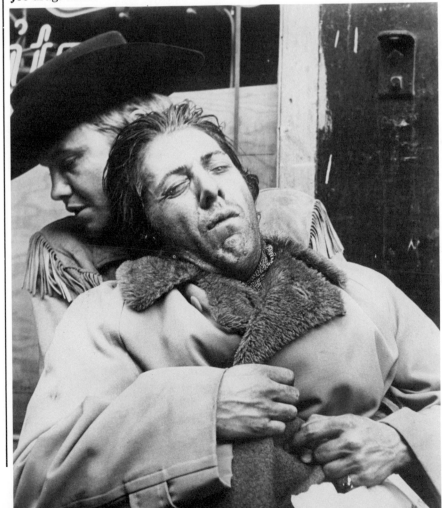

One Flew Over the Cuckoo's Nest ☀ (1975)

Directed by Milos Forman.☀ Screenplay by Lawrence Hauben☀ and Bo Goldman ☀ based on the novel by Ken Kesey and the 1963 play by Dale Wasserman. Photography, Haskell Wexler. Music, Jack Nitzsche. Editors, Lynzee Klingman and Sheldon Kahn. Produced by Saul Zaentz and Michael Douglas. Released by United Artists. Rated R. 129 minutes.

R. P. McMurphy	JACK NICHOLSON ☀
Nurse Mildred Ratched	LOUISE FLETCHER ☀
Harding	WILLIAM REDFIELD
Chief Bromden	WILL SAMPSON
Billy Bibbit	BRAD DOURIF
Ellis	MICHAEL BERRYMAN
General Matterson	PETER BROCCO
Dr. Spivey	DR. DEAN R. BROOKS
Miller	ALONZO BROWN
Turkle	SCATMAN CROTHERS
Warren	MWAKO CUMBUKA
Martini	DANNY DE VITO
Hap Arlich	TED MARKLAND
Sefelt	WILLIAM DUELL
Bancini	JOSIP ELIC
Nurse Itsu	LAN FENDORS
Washington	NATHAN GEORGE
Beans Garfield	KEN KENNY
Harbor master	MEL LAMBERT
Nurse Pilbow	MIMI SARKISIAN
Candy	MARYA SMALL
Charlie Cheswick	SYDNEY LASSICK

☀ Academy Award winner

R.P. McMurphy (Jack Nicholson), a prisoner who feigns madness, and Miss Ratched (Louise Fletcher), the authoritarian head nurse.

Sometimes the behind-the-scenes activities that go on before and during the making of a movie are, in their own way, as fascinating as the film itself.

Take, as an example, *One Flew Over the Cuckoo's Nest*, a picture that won five major Oscars in 1975.

For starters, there was the thirteen-year delay between the time Kirk Douglas bought the rights to Ken Kesey's best-selling book and the year the movie was made.

The delay, as it turned out, was a fortuitous one. It enabled Jack Nicholson to play the leading role. During that thirteen-year interim, he matured from a naturally gifted but unknown actor in low-budget films into a full-blown superstar doing major productions.

Few actors would have brought so much to the central part of R. P. McMurphy, the swaggering, free-spirited rogue who feigns insanity to get himself transferred from prison.

Perhaps the most interesting tale about *Cuckoo's Nest* is the story about how the director was found. The search started in 1962, the year Douglas bought the rights to Kesey's book. Douglas later starred in the Broadway production and wanted to play the lead in a movie version. Before he could get started on the project, he went on a State Department-sponsored tour of Eastern Europe.

There he got to know filmmaker Milos Forman (*Loves of a Blonde*). It turned out to be an important meeting. Douglas came to believe that the Czech director's sensitivities made him the right man to direct *Cuckoo's Nest* and promised to send Forman the book. He did. But he never heard from Forman again.

Ten years passed. Legal and financial problems had stalled efforts to produce the film. By 1971, Douglas felt he was too old to play McMurphy and turned over the rights to his eldest son, Michael.

Suddenly, things began moving. Michael interested Saul Zaentz, chairman of Fantasy Records, and they became partners. Looking for a director, the two, acting without knowledge of the elder Douglas's previous activities, approached Forman, now living in New York City. They were stunned to learn of Kirk Douglas's prior interest.

It turned out that Kesey's book had never reached Forman. It had either been lost in the mail or confiscated by an overzealous customs agent. Said Forman: "It's like there is some kind of destiny."

It was one of Kirk Douglas's great regrets that he never did the McMurphy part on the screen. In an interview for this book, Douglas said: "I made millions on that movie. I once said to my son, Michael, 'I'd give up every nickel I made on that picture to have played that part.' Nicholson was terrific. But he played it wrong. Michael gets mad at me. But I had a whole different concept." More about that later.

Because casting was critical to the movie, Forman auditioned over a hundred actors on both coasts to select seventeen to play the ward patients.

The company's original discovery was Will Sampson, a six-foot-five Creek Indian who played the role of the supposedly deaf and dumb Chief Bromden. In real life, he was a noted Western artist whose work has been exhibited in the Smithsonian Institution and elsewhere.

Another surprise choice was Louise Fletcher. She ended up winning an Oscar for playing the key role of Nurse Ratched, who competes with McMurphy for the minds and souls of the ward patients. Five actresses—Anne Ban-

A guard escorts McMurphy into a state mental hospital where he has decided to feign madness.

croft, Geraldine Page, Ellen Burstyn, Angela Lansbury, and Colleen Dewhurst—all turned down the role. The women's movement made them reluctant to take the role of such a cruel taskmaster.

Fletcher, cast barely a week before filming started, had had only a short acting career until then. The daughter of deaf parents, she had appeared on television briefly after coming to Hollywood at twenty-one. She gave up acting to raise her children, then returned to films a decade later to play a Southern housewife in Robert Altman's *Thieves Like Us* (1974).

By chance, Forman saw the film because someone had suggested he consider Shelley Duvall, its star, for one of the whores in *Cuckoo's Nest*. "I was caught by surprise when Louise came on the screen," Forman said. "I couldn't take my eyes off her. She had a certain mystery which I thought was very important for Nurse Ratched."

That mystery might have stemmed from Fletcher's lonely childhood. "Most children with handicapped parents will tell you it's not easy," she said. "You want your parents to be like other parents. Mine were not. Every kid in our family had to have psychiatric treatment."

The entire movie was shot on location in Oregon, with most of the scenes filmed in the Oregon State Hospital. The hospital did not have to make many changes to accommodate director Forman. With the advent in the 1960s of deinstitutionalization—the humanitarian movement to send patients stabilized by drugs back into the community—mental institutions had discharged thousands. At Oregon State, the patient population had dropped from 3,000 to 600. Many wards were empty.

Dr. Dean Brooks, the superintendent, took the part of Dr. Spivey, and several patients and hospital staff members played minor roles. Some wondered why Brooks would cooperate in a pic-

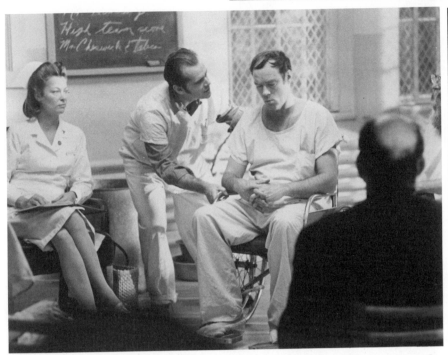

McMurphy trying to get Hap Arlich (Ted Markland) to vote for watching the World Series on television.

ture that dealt with insensitive treatment. The picture, in addition to depicting a sterile life in the wards, showed Nicholson undergoing electroshock therapy, a controversial treatment, and eventually getting a lobotomy, a brain operation now abandoned.

But Brooks felt the therapeutic benefit of having patients in the picture outweighed the harsh theme. Moreover, he made the filmmakers agree to set the scene a decade earlier and include a disclaimer saying the movie was not a factual representation of life in a mental institution.

"I just hope," Brooks said, "people realize this is an allegory about a man who can be caught up in the system."

Forman brought some of the cast to the hospital in advance of filming. "When we first started rehearsing, everything they did was exaggerated," Forman said. "So I sent them upstairs to observe the real lunatics. And many of them selected the most subtle behavioral tics to incorporate into the characterizations."

When the decision was made to do the movie, the plan was to have Kesey write the script. Because his novel anticipated the social revolt of the 1960s, it had captured the imagination of millions of young people. They recognized the metaphor of the mental hospital as the world with the patients as the people battling against authority, the medical staff.

However, Michael Douglas and Forman rejected Kesey's script because it used first-person narrative. Kesey, as in the book, told the story through the eyes of Chief Bromden, the "one" of the title who eventually escapes. "I didn't want that for my movie," Forman said. "I hate that voice-over. I hate that whole psychedelic sixties drug, free-association thing—going with the camera through somebody's head."

Kesey refused to do another version. "It's the Indian's story—not McMurphy's or Jack Nicholson's," he protested. "The emphasis should not be on the battle between McMurphy and Nurse Ratched but on the battle going on in the Indian."

Despite the change in focus, the film was generally faithful to the Kesey novel. The picture's pivotal character, of course, is McMurphy, who, as in the novel, feigns insanity to get himself out of a prison work farm.

His crime was statutory rape, and this is the breezy way the likable conman explains his troubles to the asylum doctor:

"She was fifteen years old, going on thirty-five, Doc, and she told me she was eighteen, and she was very willing, you know what I mean. Matter of fact, it would have had to take sewing my pants shut. But between you and me, I don't think it's crazy at all now.... No man alive could resist that, and that's why I got into jail to begin with. And now they tell me I'm crazy over here because I don't sit there like a damn vegetable. Don't make a bit of sense to me. If that's what's being crazy is, then I'm senseless, out of it, gone-down-the-road, wacko."

In the mental institution, he finds himself in a ward presided over by Nurse Ratched. He sees that her harsh rules narrowly restrict the lives of the inmates. They are serving her ego needs, which are anything but therapeutic for the patients.

On the screen, Fletcher brings out Ratched's steel-willed authoritarianism. Yet, her portrayal is more subtle than that of the character in the book. As conceived by Kesey, Ratched is a fire-breathing dragon. Fletcher plays her not as a sadist but as a self-righteous zealot, someone devoted to the system because she is convinced it is helping her charges.

It wasn't easy to do the more muted performance. "I envied the other actors tremendously," Fletcher said. "They were so free. I had to be so controlled."

McMurphy decides to take on

Nurse Ratched. He becomes the inmates' leader, liberating them from the ward's regulations and inspiring them to try to reclaim the sense of self-respect and joy of life they have long ago surrendered. In time, he begins to break through the personality defenses some have erected. He discovers that the Indian, who was thought to be deaf and dumb, has been pretending.

But McMurphy cannot defeat the system. Eventually, he makes a fatal mistake by losing control. When Ratched commits a vicious act of cruelty that leads a patient (Brad Dourif) to commit suicide, McMurphy tries to strangle her before the other inmates. He pays for it with shock treatment and a lobotomy.

Kirk Douglas felt that McMurphy's assault on Nurse Ratched was the wrong device because it did not bring out the underlying conflict between them. "I would have ripped her dress off and screwed her right in front of all those guys," Douglas said. "He [McMurphy] would have showed them that's all she wanted. Then, when they looked at her after that, they would have seen what she is. This way, if you just choke her, what the hell, a man choking a woman. Of course, you could beat her physically. . . . [My approach] probably wouldn't have been successful, but it would have been right."[1]

One night, Chief Bromden puts the now catatonic McMurphy out of his misery. The Indian creeps over to his bed and suffocates him, saving McMurphy from a passive life in captivity. Then the Indian flees the cuckoo's nest.

It is Nicholson's powerful performance that makes this the memorable movie it is. He has perfected the part of the nonurban, earthy Middle American, and he imparts an appealing spontaneity and humor to McMurphy that make him a three-dimensional character.

McMurphy breaks loose as Washington (Nathan George) tries to control him.

McMurphy with Candy (Marya Small), a prostitute whom he has smuggled into the hospital.

[1]The sexual tension comes through in the book because Nurse Ratched is described as a big, large-breasted woman. Louise Fletcher is a tall, slender, somewhat flat-chested actress, and so the movie does not try to play up a physical attraction between McMurphy and her.

McMurphy re-creates the play-by-play excitement of the game the inmates can't watch.

Cast as inmates are (*clockwise from upper left*): Sydney Lassick, Will Sampson, Brad Dourif, and William Redfield.

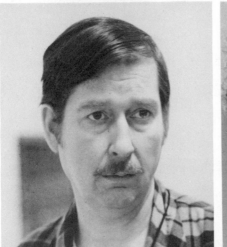

The Shop on Main Street ☗
(1965)

> Directed by Jan Kadar and Elmar Klos. Screenplay by Ladislav Grossman based on his novel *The Trap*. Photography, Vladimir Novotny. Art director, Karel Skvor. Music, Zdenek Liska. Produced by Czechoslovak State Film and Barranov Film Studios. U.S. release by Prominent Films. English subtitles by Lindsay Anderson. B/W. 128 minutes.
>
> | | |
> |---|---|
> | Tono Brtko | JOSEF KRONER |
> | Rozalie Lautmannova | IDA KAMINSKA |
> | Evelina Brtko | HANA SLIVKOVA |
> | Markus Kolkotsky | FRANTISEK ZVARIK |
> | Rose Kolkotska | HELENA ZVARIKOVA |
> | Imro Kuchar | MARTIN HOLLY |
> | Katz, the barber | MARTIN GREGOR |
>
> ☗ Academy Award winner (best foreign-language film)

How do you make a film about genocide? Or, more to the point, why do you make such a movie?

Nobody wants to be reminded of the concentration camps in all their stark and chilling terror. And so it is small wonder that American and European filmmakers have generally avoided this painful subject from the darkest days of World War II.

Nevertheless, it is a chapter in the war that still haunts us. Many feel there is a lesson here for all humanity, one that must be learned lest it be repeated.

Despite all the problems, two Czechoslovakian filmmakers decided to do the story in the 1960s —but in a markedly different way. They omitted the barbed wire, the ovens, the emaciated corpses, the tearful survivors.

Instead, they presented the story of the extermination in terms of two people—a shiftless carpenter and an elderly Jewish shopkeeper. Codirector Jan Kadar believed that nobody can comprehend the meaning of the slaughter of millions. It just amounts to so many bodies.

But people can understand, and, more important, they can be moved by, the life and death of two characters they have come to know.

"[In doing the film] I am not thinking of the fate of all the six million tortured Jews," said Kadar, who directed the picture along with Elmar Klos.

Quite the contrary, Kadar said, he was attracted by Ladislav Grossman's short novel *The Trap*, the basis for the film, because it "created a tragedy around one couple.... And, in so doing, it has seen fascism from within.... While told through two characters, it touches wider issues so that they can be applied to any type of fascism.... Nothing can outdo a picture of fascism concentrated in the tragedy of a single human being."

Kadar received Grossman's book in manuscript form. After reading only the first two pages, he knew that he must film it. "'All the big tragedy was in one drop of water.... I was fascinated by the subtlety of it. Everything was told from the inside."

Kadar picked for the locale Savinov, a small Czech town near the northeastern border that had not changed its appearance in years. He recruited local people as extras, and they added to the authenticity of the drama.

For the carpenter, Kadar cast Josef Kroner, a well-known Czech actor whose rich, Chaplinesque performance created a memorable character. There was no actress in the country with the experience to do the complex role of the old lady. So Kadar went to Poland for Ida Kaminska, the manager, producer, and leading actress of the Jewish Theater of Warsaw.

It was her first film in twenty

Ida Kaminska got an Oscar nomination for her poignant performance as the elderly Jewish shopkeeper. Here she says a Sabbath prayer.

Josef Kroner is Tono, the simple-minded carpenter who becomes the Aryan manager of the old woman's store.

Jews awaiting deportation to a concentration camp.

years. "No Jewish actors were used in Polish films except in mass scenes or in minor episodes when Jewish people were needed," said Kaminska in her autobiography, *My Life in the Theatre* (Macmillan, 1973). However, before accepting the role, she insisted they revise the character she was to play. "They wanted the woman to have a frequently comic aspect," she said. "I felt that she could elicit occasional cheerfulness. But, in essence, her character is a tragic one. . . . They agreed."

"Audiences," Kadar said, "will find it difficult to forget the white-haired, hard-of-hearing and bewildered old lady with the innocent face." The film won the Oscar for best foreign movie. Kaminska was nominated as best actress, the first from an iron curtain country.

The story is about a lazy, simple-minded carpenter who is made the "Aryan manager" of a Jewish widow during the Nazi occupation of a Czech town. The carpenter has been a failure in life —much to the chagrin of his shrewish wife (Hana Slivkova). But one day, his brother-in-law (Frantisek Zvarik), commander of the newly organized fascist guard, gives the carpenter an opportunity. He makes him the controller of an eighty-year-old widow who runs a small button store.

All he has to do is supervise the place and share the profits. The carpenter's wife can hardly control her joy, because she is convinced the old Jewish woman has treasure hidden on the premises.

As it turns out, the partly deaf and partly senile old lady can't comprehend what the carpenter tells her. Headstrong but engaging, she believes he has been appointed her assistant. Try as he may, the carpenter can't convince her otherwise.

What is even more ironic is that she is virtually bankrupt. Other Jews in the community subsidize her. Now they start paying the carpenter to be her protector. As the weeks pass, he is drawn to her in friendship, and a warm relationship grows between this strikingly mismatched couple.

It ends abruptly when the town gets word of a deportation order for all Jews. The poor carpenter faces a harrowing choice—he must turn her in or face a firing squad himself. That's the penalty for those who harbor Jews.

In the end, like those who betrayed their ideals and turned away when Nazis slaughtered their Jewish neighbors, the carpenter gives in to his fear for his own skin. "It is you or me," he screams.

It is here that the picture rises to its emotional peak. The carpenter gets drunk, then tries to force the old woman to join the deportation group. She cannot understand what he is doing. Railing and shouting at her, he accidentally throws her to the floor. She does not move. To his horror, he discovers she has suffered a heart attack and died. Full of remorse and utterly destroyed inside, he hangs himself in her shop.

The movie does not leave the audience at this juncture. It distances itself from the tragedy, adding one more scene that gives the film an ethereal ending. In a dream sequence, a band plays a waltz on the square outside the shop. We see the carpenter in a dress suit and the widow in a full-length billowy gown emerge from the shop dancing, laughing, whirling in ever-widening circles in a world full of sunshine.[1]

---

[1]*The Shop on Main Street* appeared as a Broadway musical in January 1986. But it failed to match the standards of the Oscar-winning movie. "The material cries out for more height, depth, and weight," said Allan Wallach of *Newsday*, the Long Island daily. Said the *New York Times* critic Walter Goodman: "To say an unkind word about *The Shop on Main Street* is like being rude to somebody's grandmother. But, then, not everybody's grandmother has to be on the stage."

Tono, fearful he will be punished for harboring a Jew, implores the old woman to join the deportation.

The gay and carefree fantasy sequence that ends the movie.

Index